FINANCIAL PERFORMANCE OF STEEL SECTORS

FINANCIAL PERFORMANCE OF STEEL SECTORS

By

Dr. Ashok Kumar Panda

&

Dr. Anil Kumar Sahu

DISCOVERY PUBLISHING HOUSE PVT. LTD.
NEW DELHI-110 002

First Published-2010

ISBN 978-81-8356-592-9

Published by:

DISCOVERY PUBLISHING HOUSE PVT. LTD.
4831/24, Ansari Road, Prahlad Street
Darya Ganj, New Delhi-110002 (India)
Phone: 23279245, 43764432 • Fax: 91-11-23253475
E-mail: parul.wasan@gmail.com
info@discoverypublishinggroup.com
Website: www.discoverypublishinggroup.com

Printed at:

Arora Offset Press, Delhi – 92

Acknowledgements

We are deeply indebted to my Teachers, Librarian as guide and other staffs of Department of Business Administration, Berhampur University who has assisted us inspiring, encouraging by moral and reference materials for preparation of this book.

We are grateful to the officials in M/s Steel Authority of India Ltd. (SAIL), Rourkela, who helped us in every respect for completion of this book.

We also gratefully acknowledge help received from the Company Secretary of M/s TISCO Ltd., who provided me with the useful annual accounts data of the past years required for analysis.

ANIL KUMAR SAHU
ASHOK KUMAR PANDA

Acknowledgements

Contents

1

Steel Industries of India
A Study

INTRODUCTION

Steel industry plays a vital role in the economy of the country. Steel products are used in the infrastructure projects, real estate, manufacturing sector, automobile sector, railways etc. The business in this sector has undergone a radical change during Nineties and the pace of change is still "ON".

Process of liberalization has started in the Steel Sector during this time in our country. Prior to that, only a few known companies were catering to the total Steel demand in the country. In the process of liberalization, many new steel companies came into existence adding additional capacities.

The process of globalization resulted in lifting of trade barriers with other countries. This gave rise to a drastic cut in import tariff on the steel products coming from other countries. All these have given rise to a free market situation for a large number of Steel manufacturers in the country and outside. Dumping of Steel from other countries becomes a general phenomenon whenever there is a slump in the international steel demand to take advantage of arbitrage opportunity in India.

The above changes in the market place in the steel industry have brought about major reforms in the business activities of the companies. More customer-orientation, focus on operational and financial parameters, faster implementation of IT are some of the fall-outs of this.

Since Indian steel industry is completely opened up to the world market, changes in the global steel market created ripples in the country's steel economics. However, globalization of steel sector will bring about efficiency among the existing players in the long run and create a conducive atmosphere for increasing steel capacities in the country. India has the potential to grow by leaps and bounds to come within top three steel producing nations in the world because of its rich iron ore deposits and expected high growth rate of economy in future.

The analysis of Indian Steel industry is incomplete in the absence of the analysis of Global steel scenario.

OBJECTIVE OF THE RESEARCH

The Objective of this research is to carry out an in depth analysis of the financial performance of the major steel plants in India with a specific reference to Rourkela steel plant especially in the changing steel scenario. The steel market has witnessed a lot of change in the last decade. The business activities have undergone a radical change. Monopoly situation is gradually changing to a free market situation. This is affecting the financial performance and business decisions of all the steel plants in the country. Major changes in the steel business are still to come in the coming years. India will become a major concentration area for new steel production facilities due to its rich iron ore reserves, cheaper manpower and expected growth in the per capita consumption of steel. This will call for a tough competition among the steel producers, which will affect the financial performance of the steel producers. They have to take quick and innovative steps to reorient their business activities towards customer satisfaction to survive in the market place.

A special study has been made on Rourkela Steel Plant, the first integrated steel plant in the state of Orissa and so far the biggest capacity in the state. It has got a production capacity of 2 million tons of hot metal from Blast Furnace. Its crude steel capacity is 1.9 million tons and its saleable steel capacity is 1.67 million tons.

With the change in the business scenario, this plant has witnessed major fluctuations in the financial parameters in the recent past. It started making losses from the financial year 1995-96 till 2003-04. However with a boom in the international steel market, RSP could register a huge profit in the financial year 2004-05. The profit trend still continues in the financial year 2005-06. A comparative study covering various aspects of financial performance has been undertaken *vis-à-vis* M/s Tata Iron and Steel Co. Ltd. and M/S Steel Authority of India Ltd., to formulate a strategy and to set benchmarks for future operations.

The current performance of the plant can be related to the business and investment decisions taken in the past. There was a capital investment of around Rs. 4500 crores for modernization of the plant which was completed during 1998-99. The burden of high depreciation and interest started affecting the bottom line of the company there after. Through this modernization, the plant could see a major shift in its steel making process from age old open hearth technology to the latest continuous casting technology. This could improve the quality of the steel products produced by the plant. The hotmetal capacity before modernization was 1.6 million tons, which increased to 2.00 million tons after modernization. At the same time delays in the project execution, stabilization and steel market recession affected the profit and loss account of the plant in a big way. Survival of the plant was at stake. RSP has to take proactive strategy in future for its survival against the onslaught of competition.

A critical analysis has been done in this research work regarding the survival of Rourkela Steel Plant taking into account the present constraints and the future steel policies of the country. While doing the analysis, entire gamut of business activities and financial performances have been touched upon. The advantages of raw material linkages with the captive mines of SAIL, the issues of marketing, steel production capacities, new steel policies, HR aspects have been dealt with to arrive at the future plan.

METHODOLOGY

Analysis is based on the secondary data collected from various sources and interaction with select groups. Data relating to the financial accounts have been collected from the annual accounts reports of Rourkela steel plant, Tata Iron and Steel Co. Ltd. and Steel Authority of India Ltd. for last ten years. Financial Analysis is done with the help of charts and graphs. An in depth analysis of the steel market place (current and future), steel processes in India and outside, steel economics has been done in this research work. Inputs have been gathered from various steel journals like Iron and Steel review, Steel Metals and Minerals, JPC journals and reports, Annual Accounts reports, segment reports of the major steel producers etc. the vision statements of these firms have also been considered. The study also covers analysis of the industrial policy and new national steel policy of the country, which will be instrumental in shaping the future changes in the steel sector in the country as a part of the globalization process already in vogue in this sector.

SWOT analysis has been done for positioning of the plant in the current market place. This is done through collection of secondary data and interviewing officers in the key positions of the company.

Analyses of input price and product price reveal the fluctuations in the business of the company. A detailed financial analysis is prepared involving analysis of working capital and its various components, cash flow, break-even point, financial ratios etc. The break-even model devised in the process of analysis gives the behaviour of break-even point with respect to two most critical components of the business segment, i.e., input price and product price.

With the rapid changes taking place in the steel sector in the country and outside, which had never happened in the history of steel business earlier, this study covers entire gamut of business activities, steel making processes and financial performance, which is unique of its kind. It gives a detailed guideline for future endeavours and preparedness required to be taken by the steel plants in the country, especially Rourkela Steel plant for its survival in future.

REVIEW OF RESEARCH AND LITERATURE

Steel sector plays an important role in the economic development of a nation. This sector in India is still in the growth stage. The concept of growth started after liberalization in the sector. In view of this, it is essential to review the research and literature on Liberalisation in India and its impact on the steel industry. In this context, some of the important studies in the area are reviewed in the following pages in order to pin point the importance of the present study. As a part of liberalization, new industrial policy has evolved, which gives a direction for participation of new entrants in the existing business. In this context, some of the studies in this area are reviewed in the following pages. Keeping in view the growth requirement in the steel sector in India, a revised National Steel Policy has been formulated by Government of India. This envisages a substantial increase in per capita consumption of steel in the country in the next twenty years. A study on this is also reviewed in the following pages.

In the changed scenario, quite a few studies have been made on the steel sector. Study on the present and future of RSP in the twenty first century is still to be done by any one. This piece of research work is unique with regard to the in depth analysis on the overall financial performance of Rourkela Steel Plant and its future shape. Rourkela Steel Plant is the first integrated steel plant in the state of Orissa and one of first integrated steel plants to have come in India. It has a lot of contribution towards the infrastructure developments in the country in the past and the present. In this context, some of the important studies in the areas of changing Steel

Technology, steel sector dynamics are reviewed in the following pages in order to pin point the importance of the present study. Studies on Rourkela Steel Plant undertaken by some of the scholars in the past are also reviewed. These cover aspects like working capital management, Incentive structure etc. The present piece of research work goes beyond this. The author makes an effort to prepare a thorough study on RSP using various financial models along with an in depth anlaysis of the fast changing steel scenario and a comparative analysis with other major steel plants in the country.

Anthony P D'Costa[1] in his book *The Global Restructuring of Steel Industry: Innovations, Institutions and Industrial changes* discusses about restructuring of steel industry in the context of industrial restructuring. He describes about crisis compounded restructuring due to the technological changes in the sector. The book also focuses on challenges of the technological changes in the countries like Japan, Korea, Brazil, India. The aspects of technological change and internationalization of steel industry, industrial restructuring have also been discussed at length in the book.

"Asia: Global steel's engine of growth"[2] is an article published in the Iron and Steel review periodical. This gives a lot of information regarding the production capacities in the Asian region and its comparison with rest of the world.

Chakraborty, S., Ray, A.K., Ray, S.K.[3] have discussed about the steel technologies in details in their article "Concepts of Emerging Steel Technologies".

Cochran, E.B.[4] in their book *Planning Production Costs: Using the improvement curve*, have discussed by strategies for bringing about cost improvements in on Organisation.

Das, Debendra Kumar[5] has edited the book *Economic Development Opportunities Through Liberalisation*, focuses on the perceived impact of liberalisation on different sectors. It also touches upon the new industrial policy as an off shoot of liberalization.

Dutta, S., Zamindar, D, Kumar, P. and Banerjee, U.K[6] in their article "R and D efforts in improving the product quality of an old mill for its survival" have touched upon various methods for survival of an old plant, which include technological up gradation, continuous research efforts, debottle-necking in the inefficient processes etc.

Erich, A Helfert[7] in his book *Financial anlaysis tools and techniques: A guide for Managers*, describes about important financial tools which can be used for financial planning in an Organisation.

Garth, L Magnum, Sae, Young Kim, Stephen, B Tallman[8] in their book *Transnational Marriages in Steel Industry: Experience and lesson for global business*, describe about steel industry joint ventures, Foreign Direct Investment flows in steel, role of steel in the economic development of a nation, World steel makers, challenges before the steel industry. The authors have also given their observation in the book that Mexico and India are the nations having the possibility of addition of significant steel capacities in the future.

Garth, L. Magnum, R.., Scott, McNabb[9] in their book *The rise, fall and replacement of Industry wide bargaining the basic steel industry*, have dealt with steel product and labour markets, labour productivity, HR policies in steel industry.

Gupta, S.K. in his article[10] "The relevance of different technologies adopted by flat product producers in the country-balance between investment and cost of production" discusses about the choice of technology by the steel producers.

James, O'Gill, Moira, Chetton[11] in their book *Financial analysis - the next steps*, describe about various financial analysis tools like cash flow statement, ratios etc useful for proper planning in the Organisations. The book also deals with Financial planning in an Organisation using Break even analysis tool, cost benefit analysis etc.

Krishna Gopal, M., Santra, A.K., Khan, S.C. and Karan, B.M.[12] in their article "Steel demand forecasts: India 1999-2000" have discussed about steel demand in India and the steel market in India vis-à-vis the global steel market.

Moorthy, K. Krishna[13] in his book *Engineering Change - India's Iron and Steel*, describes about historic changes in steel industry in India. He has traced the history of development of Steel Industry in independent India. As per the author, Steel has played a predominant role in the economy. He has described about the correlation between Steel industry and the economy of a developing nation. Considering the level of production of steel so far reached in India, one could easily agree with the author that the steel age has just begun in India. the author also focuses on Technological choices, Management policies, Role of parliament etc.

Muthuraman, B. and Sen, Anand[14] in their article "The future of Flat products in India" focuses on the technological changes in the area of flat products and the future additional capacities in this segment.

Sudhir, Naib[15] in his book *Disinvestment in India: Policies, Procedures, Practices*, discusses about public sectors in India, strategy of privatization, performance of the sectors after privatization, disinvestments policy in India and performance of the disinvested central PSUs.

Parida[16] has prepared his research thesis on working capital management in RSP.

Patnaik, N.K., Patnaik R.N., Mishra B.K.[17] have made a critical analysis of Sponge Iron route in the steel making in their article "Steel making through sponge iron route - Problems and Prospects". Sponge Iron technology is still in its infancy. India is the major producer of sponge iron in the world.

Prasad K.K., and Mediratta, S.R.[18] in their article "forecasting demand for Steel" have discussed about the future of steel in the world.

Samantaray, B.[19] in his PhD. thesis on RSP has discussed about the incentive structure prevailing in the organization.

SAIL - A successful Turn around story among Indian PSUs[20] is an article appeared in the magazine *Kaleidoscope - Standing conference of Public Enterprises*, which describes the success story of SAIL turnaround.

"Sailing in the Future - An Overview of Corporate Plan 2021"[21] is an article published in the in house magazine of SAIL, *SAIL News*. This gives an overview of the future plans of SAIL, the largest producer of steel in the country.

Sharon, M. Oster[22] in his book *Modern Competitive Anlaysis*, deals with Financial anlaysis tools and their utility in the steel industry.

Sinha, S.N., Kundu, A.L., Muthuswamy, C.[23] in their article "Iron and Steel Industry in India: Past, Present and Future" have discussed about the existing technology in the sector and the technological changes expected in the future. The authors have also dwelled upon the future shape of steel industry in the country on the face of technological changes and the liberalization in the sector.

Roy, T.K.[24] in his article "Steel - Die-hard Material: Yesterday, Today and Tomorrow" focuses on the influence of steel on the economy and the advancements in the technologies used in steel manufacturing.

Stovell, Sam[25] in his article "The Spring in Steel" is of the view that the steel sector is quite active now and it has a positive outlook in the near future.

Surma, John P.[26] in his article "Is Steel Back on the Financial Committees' radar screen" has discussed about the importance of steel in the economy, the steel prices etc.

Usman M.[27] has edited the book *Statistics for Iron and Steel Industry In India*, which contains information on various aspects of the steel and related industries. It contains data up to the year 2003-2004. The book touches upon areas like Availability, Demand and Supply/Consumption, Production, Dispatches, Sales, Exports/Imports Facilities etc.

Varshney, R.P.[28] in his article "Cost Economics of Sponge Iron Plants and EAFs" deals with Electric steel making technology in twenty first century and its cost economics.

Shaji, Vikraman[29] in his article "Steel sector Bail out" taking a leaf out of Uncle Sam's book describes about the ordeal that the steel sector has passed during the time of recession and the subsequent good news for the sector at the end of the tunnel.

Gupta, Vipin[30] in his book *Transformative Organisation A Global Perspective* describes about the strategic management needs in an Organisation.

Vijay, Vergis R.K. and Bhattacharya, S.K.[31] in their article "Technology Management in Steel Sector" describe the technological changes in the steel sector and its impact on the future steel growth.

Wang, Yi Tian[32] in his article "Riding China's growth curve" focuses on china; the emerging behemoth in the steel industry in the world and its growth plans ahead.

REFERENCES

1. Anthony P D'Costa, *The global restructuring of Steel Industry: Innovations, Institutions and Industrial Changes*, Routledge (UK), Taylor and Francis group, 11 New Fetterlane, London, 1999.
2. "Asia: Global steel's engine of growth", *Iron and Steel Review*, May, 2004
3. Chakraborty S., Ray A.K., Ray S.K., "Concepts of Emerging Steel Technologies", *Steel Scenario – A journal on Steel and economy*, Vol-13, Jan-Mar 2004.
4. Cochran E.B., *Planning Production Costs: Using the improvement curve*, Chandler Publishing Coy, Sanfransisco, California, 1968.
5. Das Debendra Kumar, *Economic Development Opportunities Through Liberalisation*, UGC, 1998
6. Dutta S., Zamindar D., Kumar P. and Banerjee U.K., "R and D efforts in improving the product quality of an old mill for its survival", *Iron and Steel Review*, 45(6), 2001, Page-45.
7. Erich A. Helfert, *Financial Analysis Tools and Techniques: A Guide for Managers*, McGraw-Hill publications, Sep, 2001.
8. Garth L. Magnum, Sae Young Kim, Stephen B. Tallman, *Transactional Marriages in Steel Industry: Experience and Lesson for Global Business*, Quorum Books, 88 Post Road west, West Port, CT 06881, 1996.

9. Garth L. Magnum, R. Scott McNabb, *The rise, fall and replacement of Industry wide bargaining in the basic steel Industry*", M.E. Sharpe Inc., 80, Business Park Drive, Armonk, New York-10504.

10. Gupta S.K., "The relevance of different technologies adopted by flat product producers in the country-balance between investment and cost of production", *Iron and Steel Review*, December, 2003.

11. James, O Gill, Moira Chetton, "Financial analysis-the next steps", Thomson Crisp learning, Crisp Publications Inc., 2001

12. Krishna Gopal M, Santra A.K, Khan S.C. and Karan B.M, "Steel demand forecasts: India 1999-2000", *Steel Times International*, 23(4), 1999, Page-14.

13. K. Krishnamoorthy, *Engineering Change—India's Iron and Steel*, Tech Books, India, 1985.

14. Muthuraman, B. and Sen, Anand, "The future of Flat products in India", *Iron and Steel Review*, Vol-37, Sep, 1993.

15. Naib Sudhir, *Disinvestment in India: Policies, Procedures, Practices*, Sage Publications India Ltd., New Delhi-11017.

16. Parida[26], Ph. D thesis on Working Capital Management in RSP, 1992.

17. Patnaik, N.K., Patnaik, R.N., Mishra, B.K., "Steel making through Sponge iron route-Problems and Prospects", *Steel Scenario - A journal on steel and economy*, Vol-13, Jan-Mar'04.

18. Prasad, K.K., Mediratta, S.R., "Forecasting demand for Steel", *Steel Technical report*, 1997, p. 16.

19. Samantaray, B.[27], Ph.D. thesis on Incentive structure in RSP, 1990.

20. "SAIL - A successful Turn around story among Indian PSUs", *Kalcidoscope - Standing conference of Public Enterprises*, Mar 2004, Vol-23.

21. "Sailing into the future - An Overview of Corporate Plan 2012", *SAIL News*, Vol-31, Apr-May, 2003.

22. Sharon, M. Oster, *Modern competitive analysis*, Oxford University Press USA, 1999.

23. Sinha, S.N., Kundu, A.L., Muthuswamy, C., "Iron and Steel Industry in India: Past, Present and future", *Iron and Steel Review*, Vol-37, Sep, 1993.

24. Roy, T.K., "Steel – a die-hard material: Yesterday, today and tomorrow", *JPC Bulletin*, December, 2003.

25. Stovell, Sam, "The spring in Steel", *Business Week Magazine*, Aug 2005.
26. Surma, John P., "Is Steel back on the Financial committees' radar screen", *World Steel Journal - Steel at the cross roads*, IISI-Vol. 38.
27. Usman, M., "Statistics for Iron and Steel Industry in India", *SAIL*, 14th Edition, 2004.
28. Varshney, R.P., "Cost economics of Sponge Iron Plants and EAFs", *Steel Scenario – A journal on Steel and Economy*, Vol-13, Jan-Mar 2004.
29. Shaji, Vikraman, "Steel sector Bail out: taking a leaf out of Uncle Sam's book", *Business Line*, 25th Feb, 2002.
30. Gupta, Vipin, *Transformative Organisation – a global perspective*, Grand Valley State University and University of Pennsylvania
31. Vijay Vergis, R.K. and Bhattacharya S.K, "Technology Management in Steel Sector", *The Management Accountant*, 1996, 31(5), Page-335.
32. Wang, Yi Tian, "Riding China's growth curve", *Iron and Steel Review*, April, 2004.

2

Indian Steel Industry *An Appraisal*

GLOBAL STEEL SCENARIO

Steel Economy has a direct correlation with GDP growth rate of the Economy of a country. The global economy witnessed a gradual recovery from late 2003 onwards. GDP is expected to grow at the rate of 3.8% during 2005 as compared to 1.4% during 2001, 1.9% during 2002, during 2003 and 3% during 2004.

While, the economies of USA, Japan and Europe continue on course towards economic recovery, the growth in China has become one of the major factors currently driving the world economy (Table 2.1).

Table 2.1: GDP Growth (%)

Country	2000	2001	2002	2003	2004
China	8	7.3	8	7.2	7.5
Japan	2.4	0.4	-0.4	2.7	3.1
Korea	9.3	3.1	6.3	5.0	5.0
India	4.2	5.4	5.0	5.5	6.5
World	7.0	1.4	2.6	2.6	3.0

Table 2.2: Global Finished Steel Outlook

Country	2001	2002	2003	2004	(% Change)			
					2002	2003	2004	2005(E)
China	174.2	211.2	232	255	21	10	10	10
India	27.1	29.5	31	33	9	5	6	7
Japan	73.2	72	74	72	-2	3	-3	-1.4
Korea	38.3	43.7	45	45	14	3	0	0
Taiwan	17.7	20.4	21	20	15	3	-5	
Others	48	52	53	55	8	2	4	
Asia	378	428	456	480	13	6.5	5.3	5
CIS	30	31	32	33	3	3	3	2
World	780	831	868	906	7	4.5	4.4	4.5

With a projected GDP growth of more than double of the other world economies, China has by far become the fastest growing global economy. Indian GDP is also expected to grow at 7 to 8% in the coming years.

Steel industry is growing at a rapid pace from 780 MT of finished steel consumption in 2004. If it goes like this, within 2 years this will touch 1 billion mark. To sustain the growth of steel, Research and development needs to be strengthened to find out alternative use of it. Recent demand of steel backed by research in the automotive sector is a boon for the industry.

Steel is still in relative infancy. Growth in the sector is on the cards. Steel industry must confirm to use new technologies, techno economically attractive to remain a sustainable and competitive industry. Part of the growth will be met by improving upon the unutilized capacity and partly through creation of new capacities to meet the demand supply gap. This will be done through improved technologies, which will bring about better quality of product and cost competitiveness.

Table 2.3: World crude steel production: 1950 to 2004

(million metric tons)

Year	Production (MMT)	Year	Production (MMT)
2004	1,057	1990	770
2003	969	1985	719
2002	903	1980	717
2001	850	1975	643
2000	948	1970	595
1999	789	1965	456
1998	777	1960	347
1997	799	1955	270
1996	750	1950	189
1995	752		
1994	725		

Average Growth Rates (% per annum)

Years	Growth
2000-2004	5.7%
1995-2000	2.4%
1990-1995	-0.5%
1985-1990	1.4%
1980-1985	0.1%
1975-1980	2.2%
1970-1975	1.6%

It is evident from the tables above that the steel sector passed through a recession between the years 2001 and 2002. Since mid 2002-03, steel prices have seen serial hikes almost on a monthly basis to cross peak after peaks. This has given a big relief to the steel producers, which were reeling under deep trouble for quite few years. Although positive signs for the steel producers came to their rescue after a long time, this sudden and unprecedented series of price hikes have created great concerns for the small-scale industries. The steel prices need to stabilize at a level.

Production of crude steel by major Asian nations are tabulated in Table 2.4.

Asia's total production of crude steel during 2003 is estimated at 436.8 million tons, out of a global production of 969.3 million tons with a percentage share of 45%. This percentage has further increased to 46.5% in 2004.

China recorded an annual growth of 21.2% in 2003 and 22.5% in 2004 reaching 272.5 million ton crude steel production. India recorded a growth of 10.3% in 2003 and 2.5% in 2004. Overall growth in the Asian region during 2003 and 2004 were 11.6% and 12.3% respectively against world growth of 7.6% and 9% respectively. Growth in the Asian region has been the highest in the world. It can be further seen that among Asian countries China recorded the highest growth during this time.

Table 2.4: Crude Steel Production: Asian Countries and Share of World Production

(Million Tons)

Country	1999	2000	2001	2002	2003	2004
China	123.954	127.236	150.56	181.552	222.4	272.5
Japan	94.192	106.444	102.866	107.748	110.51	112.7
Korea	41.042	43.107	43.852	48.390	46.3	47.5
India	24.296	26.924	27.291	28.814	31.78	32.6
Taiwan	15.438	16.840	17.214	18.214	18.8	19.5
Indonesia	2.891	2.848	2.78	2.8	3	3
Malaysia	2.26	3.65	4.1	2.6	4	4
Total Asia	308.289	331.840	353.184	392.4	436.8	491.8
World	788.484	847.396	849.617	900.542	969.3	1056.7
% Share	39	39	42	44	45	46.5

It shows that majority of the production increase is taking place in the Asian region. The reasons could be attributed to:

1) Cheaper availability of raw material.
2) Cheaper manpower.
3) Availability of steel making technology.
4) Open market conditions.
5) Growing Economy.

The consumption of steel products has also increased during this time, which is evident from the Table 2.5.

Table 2.5: Apparent consumption of Finished Steel

(Million tons)

Country	1999	2000	2001	2002	2003	2004
China	130.8	141.2	174.2	211.2	232	255
India	25.1	26.3	27.1	29.5	31	33
Japan	68.9	76.1	73.2	72	74	72
Korea	33.8	38.5	38.3	43.7	45	45
Taiwan	20.4	21.2	17.7	20.4	21	20
Others	31.5	35.2	48	52	53	55
Asia	**310.5**	**338.5**	**378**	**428**	**456**	**480**
World	**705.7**	**758.7**	**780**	**831**	**868**	**906**
% Share	**43.99**	**44.61**	**48.46**	**51.5**	**52.5**	**52.9**

It may be observed from the above table that between 1999 and 2004, Asia's share in global finished steel demand has increased from 43.99% to 52.9%. The highest growth rate is in China. Country-wise production of crude steel during 2003 and 2004 is shown in Table 2.6.

This clearly shows that steel producing giants are in Asian region and growth rate especially in China and India are more than world average.

Table 2.6: Country-wise production of crude steel during 2003 and 2004

	2004		2003	
Country	Rank	mmt	Rank	mmt
1	2	3	4	
China	1	272.5	1	222.4
Japan	2	112.7	2	110.5
United States	3	98.9	3	93.7
Russia	4	65.6	4	61.5
South Korea	5	47.5	5	46.3
FR Germany	6	46.4	6	44.8
Ukraine	7	38.7	7	36.9
Brazil	8	32.9	9	31.1
India	**9**	**32.6**	**8**	**31.8**
Italy	10	28.4	10	26.8
France	11	20.8	11	19.8
Turkey	12	20.5	13	18.3
Taiwan, China	13	19.5	12	18.8
Spain	14	17.7	14	16.5
Mexico	15	16.7	16	15.2
Canada	16	16.3	15	15.9
United Kingdom	17	13.8	17	13.3
Belgium	18	11.7	18	11.1
Poland	19	10.6	20	9.1
South Africa	20	9.5	19	9.5
Iran	21	8.7	21	7.9
Australia	22	7.4	22	7.5
Czech Republic	23	7.0	23	6.8
Netherlands	24	6.8	24	6.6
Austria	25	6.5	25	6.3

(contd.)

1	2	3	4	
Romania	26	6.0	26	5.7
Sweden	27	6.0	26	5.7
Kazakhstan	28	5.4	29	4.9
Argentina	29	5.1	28	5.0
Finland	30	4.8	30	4.8
Egypt	31	4.8	32	4.4
Venezuela	32	4.6	35	3.9
Thailand (e)	33	4.5	36	3.6
Slovakia	34	4.5	31	4.6
Malaysia (e)	35	4.0	33	4.0
Saudi Arabia	36	3.9	34	3.9
Indonesia (e)	37	2.8	39	2.0
Luxembourg	38	2.7	37	2.7
Bulgaria	39	2.4	38	2.3
Greece	40	2.0	41	1.7
Hungary	41	2.0	40	2.0
Others		21.4		19.7
Total World		1056.7		969.3

China's crude steel production is 272.5 MT during 2004, which has increased from a level of 130 MT during 2001 (Table 2.8). Its imports will continue till 2007, owing to demand and supply gap may be at smaller rate.

Table 2.7: Asia's top Steel producing countries are

Country	Production (MT)	World Rank 2004	World Rank 2003
China	272.5	Ist	Ist
Japan	112.7	2nd	2nd
Korea	47.5	5th	5th
India	32.6	9th	8th

Table 2.8: Major importers and exporters of steel 2003

(million metric tons)

Net Exports 2003			*Net Imports 2003*		
	Country	MMT		Country	MMT
1	Japan	30.5	1	China	34.7
2	Russia	28.9	2	United States	13.8
3	Ukraine	25.7	3	Taiwan, China	11.1
4	Brazil	12.4	4	Thailand	7.6
5	Belgium-Luxembourg	7.6	5	Iran	6.8
6	Germany	6.6	6	Italy	6.1
7	EU (15)	5.4	7	Spain	5.7
8	South Africa	4.8	8	Viet Nam	4.5
9	India	4.1	9	Hong Kong	4.0
10	Kazakhstan	3.0	10	United Arab Emirates	3.3
11	Slovakia	3.0	11	Philippines	2.5
12	Turkey	2.9	12	Portugal	2.5
13	France	2.7	13	Indonesia	2.5
14	Austria	2.6	14	Singapore	2.3
15	Venezuela	2.5	15	Saudi Arabia	2.0

It can be seen from the above table that China was a major net importer of steel during 2003. However, with addition of new capacities, the net import during 2004 is reduced. In the early part of 2005, it has appeared to be a net exporter of steel products.

During this time, Asian countries will upgrade their steel making capacity and technology to match international quality. Asia led by China will hold the key to the growth of international economy.

FUTURE GLOBAL STEEL DYNAMICS

Between 2002 and 2004 steel production and consumption has grown at a rapid pace with frequent price rises. Following are the indications of movement of steel economy in the future time horizon.

Between 2005 and 2008, there will be a slow down in steel demand and the growth will be at the rate of 5 to 6% pa. There will also be major addition of new steel capacities through capital investment route. Over-supply of steel products will result in inventory build up with the major consumers. This will have a strong pressure on the prices of steel products. Competition will continue and prices of steel products may fall.

After 2008

To reduce the effect of price competition steel consolidation may take place among the major steel producers through merger and acquisition route. There will be pressure on steel prices and marginal steel producers may either close down their businesses or merge with a bigger entity. Technology and capacity will play a vital role to meet customers demand in terms of quality and cost.

Table 2.9: Major Steel-producing Companies in 2003 and 2004

2004		2003		Company
Rank	Qty	Rank	Qty	
1	46.9	1	42.8	Arcelor
2	42.8	2	35.3	Mittal Steel
3	32.4	3	31.3	Nippon Steel
4	31.6	4	30.2	JFE
5	30.2	5	28.9	POSCO
6	21.4	6	19.9	Shanghai Baosteel
7	20.8	8	17.9	US Steel
8	19.0	7	19.1	Corus Group
9	17.9	10	15.8	Nucro
10	17.6	9	16.1	Thyssenkrupp

(*contd.*)

2004		2003		Company
Rank	Qty	Rank	Qty	
11	16.7	11	15.7	Riva Acciao
12	16.1	18	10.6	ISG
13	14.6	14	12.3	Gerdau
14	13.0	12	12.8	Sumitomo
15	12.2	15	12.1	EvrazHolding
16	**12.1**	**13**	**12.4**	**SAIL**
17	11.3	19	10.2	Anshan
18	11.3	16	11.5	Magnitogorsk
19	10.9	17	10.8	China Steel
20	10.4	20	9.9	Severstal
21	9.3	22	8.4	Wuhan
22	9.1	21	8.9	Novolipetsk
23	8.7	25	7.8	Imidro
24	8.5	23	8.2	Shougang
25	8.1	24	8.0	Salzgitter
26	8.0	33	6.1	Maanshan
27	7.7	26	7.3	Kobe Steel
28	7.6	27	7.2	INI Steel
29	7.6	46	5.0	Jiangsu Shagang Group
30	7.1	28	7.1	Krivorozstal
31	7.1	43	5.2	Valin Steel Group
32	7.1	32	6.1	Tangshan
33	6.9	30	6.5	Mariupol (llyich)
34	6.9	45	5.1	Jinan
35	6.8	34	6.1	Handan
36	6.7	29	6.5	BlueScope
37	6.6	58	4.2	Laiwu
38	6.5	36	5.8	Duferco Group
39	6.2	49	4.9	Chelyabinsk (Mechel)
40	6.0	39	5.3	Panzhihua

(*contd.*)

2004		2003		Company
Rank	Qty	Rank	Qty	
41	5.9	35	5.8	Voestalpine
42	5.7	40	5.3	Azovstal
43	5.6	38	5.4	AK Steel
44	5.5	41	5.3	CSN
45	5.5	37	5.6	HKM 2
46	5.5	51	4.7	Benxi
47	5.4	42	5.3	Baotou
48	5.2	54	4.6	Anyang
49	5.2	47	5.0	Techint
50	5.1	65	3.7	Celsa
51	5.0	48	4.9	Erdemir Group
52	4.9	53	4.7	Stelco
53	4.7	53	4.6	USIMINAS
54	4.6	72	3.3	Nangang
55	4.5	55	4.6	Rautaruukki
56	4.5	56	4.4	Zaporizhstahl
57	4.4	59	4.2	Dofasco
58	**4.2**	**57**	**4.3**	**Tata Iron and Steel Co**
59	4.2	60	4.1	COSIPA
60	4.1	62	3.9	SSAB
61	4.0	73	3.3	Tangshan Guogfeng Steel
62	4.0	63	3.9	Nisshin Steel
63	4.0	70	3.4	EZZ
64	3.9	67	3.5	SIDOR
65	3.9	61	3.9	Hadeed
66	3.8	50	4.8	CST
67	3.8	68	3.5	Alchevsk
68	3.7	64	3.8	Lucchini
69	3.6	66	3.7	Tokyo Steel
70	3.6	69	3.4	Urals Steel

(*contd.*)

2004		2003		Company
Rank	Qty	Rank	Qty	
71	3.5	80	2.9	Shaoguan
72	3.4	77	3.1	Tianjin Tiantie
73	**3.4**	**71**	**3.4**	**RINL**
74	3.4	76	3.1	Lion Group
75	3.4	107	2.1	Commercial Metals
76	3.4	92	2.5	Hebei Jinxi
77	3.4	85	2.6	Tangshan Jianlong
78	3.3	82	2.8	Hylsamex
79	3.3	91	2.5	Xuanhua
80	3.3	86	2.6	Xinyu

INDIAN STEEL SCENARIO

With the onset of liberalization, the steel industry has to become competitive, not only to meet domestic competition, but also the global competition in terms of product range, quality and price. The growth of the steel sector is intricately linked with the growth of the Indian economy and especially the growth of the steel consuming sectors, India though is able to compensate for the domestic demand of steel but it has to look for more lucrative markets through exports and make itself a force in the steel sector. Production and production capacities should be increased through expansion and installation of new plants using secondary steel making route that are more cost effective and quality conscious. At the same time, productivity of our steel plants must be maintained at levels close to international standards. All in all, in order for the Steel Industry to become globally competitive it is important that strategies have to be made so that bottlenecks in the growth of this sector are removed and the companies are made more responsive to change.

The Indian steel industry has performed very well in recent years. The industry is able to meet to stringent international quality specifications for high end applications in sectors like construction, engineering, automobile and infrastructure, higher production of value-added products, capacity expansion, up gradation of production process achieving cost effective production in an environment friendly manner, have been the major thrust areas of the Indian steel producers in the recent times.

Market Scenario

- Steel industry that was facing a recession for some time has staged a turn around since the middle of 2002. The steel industry is buoyant due to strong growth in demand particularly by the demand for steel in China.
- Efforts are being made to boost demand domestically also, through various infrastructure projects taken up by the Government and encouragement given by the government for more FDI inflow into the new projects.
- There have been no shortages of iron and steel materials in the country. Imports have become quite competitive due to reduction in import duties on steel products.
- Apparent consumption of finished carbon steel increased from 14.84 million tons in 1991-92 to 33.370 million tones in 2004-05.
- China has been an important export destination for Indian steel products.

Production

- India is the 9th largest crude steel producer of steel in the world.
- In 2004-05, production of finished carbon steel was 38.385 million tones.
- The share of Main Producers (i.e SAIL, RINL, TISCO) and secondary producers in the total production of Finished (Carbon) steel was 39% and 61% respectively during the period April-June 2005.

- Past 4 years production of finished carbon steel is given below:

(in million tons)

Category	2001-02	2002-03	2003-04	2004-05
Pig Iron	4.08	5.28	3.764	3.171
Finished Carbon steel	30.63	33.67	36.957	38.385

(Source: Joint Plant Committee)

Imports

- India has been importing around 1.5 million tones of steel annually.
- Last five year's import of finished carbon steel is given below:

Year	Qty. (in MT)
2000-2001	1.417
2001-2002	1.271
2002-2003	1.510
2003-2004	1.540
2004-2005	**2.050**

Exports

Exports of finished carbon steel and pig iron during the past five years is given below:

(Qty. in million tons)

Year	Finished (Carbon) Steel	Pig Iron
2000-2001	2.664	0.232
2001-2002	2.704	0.312
2002-2003	4.506	0.629
2003-2004	4.835	0.518
2004-2005	**4.375**	**0.177**

Custom Duties

The peak rate of customs duty has been reduced sharply during the last 5 years. In the interim budget for 2004-05, the peak rate was reduced from 25% to 20%. In February 2004 the Customs Duty on carbon steel items and pig iron was further reduced to 15% and 10% respectively. In February end itself the customs duty on pig iron was further reduced from 10% to 5%.

Customs duty on several raw materials used by the steel sector like non-coking coal, metcoke and nickel has been reduced to 5%. Customs duty on coking coal has been reduced to 'nil'. In the Union Budget 2004-05 customs duty on raw material for refractory has been reduced from 20% to 15%.

THE NEW INDUSTRIAL POLICY REGIME

The new industrial policy has opened up the iron and steel sector for private investment by:

(a) Removing it from the list of industries reserved for public sector

(b) Exempting it from compulsory licensing.

While the existing units are being modernized/expanded, a large number of new/green field steel plants are setting up plants in different parts of the country based on modern, cost effective technologies. Globally reputed companies like POSCO, Mittal Steel have also signed MOUs with Orissa and Jharkhand Government to set up integrated steel plants in those regions.

At present, total (crude) steel making capacity is over 34 million tones and India is the 9th largest producer of steel in the world.

The major steel producers in India and their crude steel production figures are given below (Table 2.10):

Table 2.10: The major steel producers in India and their crude steel production

(million tonnes)

	2003	2004
SAIL	12.4	12.1
TISCO	4.3	4.2
RINL	3.4	3.4
Others	11.7	12.9
India	31.8	32.6
Mkt Share of SAIL	39%	37%

Table 2.11: Steel Consumption (India) during 2002-2004

(million tonnes)

	2002	2003	2004
Steel Consumption (India)	29.5	31	33

FUTURE OF INDIAN STEEL INDUSTRY

The New Industrial policy has opened up the iron and steel sector for private investment. The National Steel Policy has set an ambitious target of 60 Mt of steel production by 2010 and to 100 Mt by 2018. The major steel producers in India are planning to expand their capacities and new steel producers are targeting new production facilities in India. Even the global giants like POSCO and Mittal Steel have signed MOUs with State Governments of Orissa and Jharkhand to set up new production facilities in those States.

The Indian steel industry has a vision of attaining global standards by 2020. Today the country ranks among the top 10 steel producers of the world. India looks at attaining top three slots in terms of steel production in the world. What is worrying is the per capita consumption of steel in the country. With respect to per capita consumption, which is accepted as the norm for the socio-economic development of a nation, India lags behind other major nations. India's present per capita steel consumption stands at a low of 26 kg compared to the global average of 121 kg. China's per capita steel consumption is 128. This needs to change substantially in future with the growth of economy.

EXPANSION PLANS

To support India's vision, primary steel producers have lined up major capacity expansion. Tata Steel, the oldest integrated steel producer with a present capacity of 4 mtpa, has targeted to attain 15 mtpa by 2010. Public sector Steel Authority of India Ltd. is aiming at an overall capacity of 20 mtpa by 2011, from the present 12 mtpa. Rashtriya Ispat Nigam (Vizag Steel) has targeted a capacity of 10 mtpa by 2020, as against the current 3 mtpa. Other primary producers, Essar and Ispat Industries, have also lined up expansion plans. Global giants like POSCO and Mittal Steel have signed MOUs with State Governments of Orissa and Jharkhand to set up new production facilities in those States.

Electric Arc Furnace (EAF) based steel producers are also gearing up to meet the spiraling projected demand. In fact, EAF producers are expected to have a higher share of 50 per cent in total steel production by 2020, as against the current 35 per cent.

As India aspires to more than treble its steel capacity over the next 15 years, sustenance of this burgeoning capacity is becoming the core issues. The main obstacle to the steel industry's growth could be raw material availability, metallurgical coal/coke and scrap in particular.

With China, the largest supplier of metallurgical coke, stepping up its own consumption, worldwide supplies have come under tremendous pressure. Metallurgical coke prices have increased from $120 per ton in December 2002 to $465 per ton in 2004. Instead of direct imports, India could explore the option of acquiring mining rights in coal-rich countries like Australia. This way, production costs would remain fairly insular to the vagaries of international prices. India can also take steps towards forming barter arrangements with countries like Brazil and China, wherein India's surplus iron ore can be traded for metallurgical coke. Big producers like Steel Authority of India Ltd., TISCO are planning to acquire coalfields abroad to maintain consistent supply of coal, which will support the increased levels of production in the future. The natural gas grid, which will become a reality in future will support the increased energy requirement to meet higher levels of production. At the same time use of natural gas will make it the production process cost effective.

Imported scrap availability is shrinking following the sluggishness in the ship breaking industry. Domestic EAF (Electric Arc Furnace) units use scrap for steel making. They will face the problem of lesser scrap availability in the market. Scrap rates have also sky rocketed during this time. However, sponge iron is found to have replaced the shortage of scrap to a greater extent in the steel making process. On this front India is well placed, having recently emerged as the world's largest sponge iron producer ahead of Iran and Venezuela. From 6.53 million tones in 2002, sponge iron production is targeted to produce 10 million tones, by 2012.

The current buoyancy in steel consumption is largely driven by fast-developing China, which is expected to import around 30 million tones annually till 2008, ahead of the Olympics. Given the country's growth estimates, similar demand levels are likely to persist. However, during May 2005 to July 2005, the imports from China have slowed down and it has become net exporter of steel products. Even if it slows down on its imports, it is expected that there will be export opportunities from other developing Asian economies. In India, the demand is expected to come from the construction sector, increased outlay on infrastructure projects (roadways, shipping and power), automobiles and exports.

3

A Brief Profile of Rourkela Steel Plant

SAIL AND ROURKELA STEEL PLANT

Steel Authority of India Ltd. is the largest producer of Steel in the country. It is a fully integrated iron and steel maker producing both basic and special steels for construction, engineering, power, railways, automotive, defence industries and for exports too. Its Crude Steel Production capacity is 13 million tons. It has ranked 16th in the world in terms of crude steel production during 2004. Its products range from Long products to Flat products to special grade and alloy steel to stainless steel. Long products include bars, structures, channels, rails, railway wheels and axles, rods, joints etc. Flat product include Hot Rolled Coil (HR Coil), Plate, Cold rolled coil/sheet (CR Coil/Sheet), Galvanized - plain and corrugated Coil/Sheet (GP/GC) etc. special products like Electrolytic Tin Plate (ETP), Cold rolled grain non oriented (CRNO), Electric resistance welded (ERW) pipe, Spiral Welded (SW) pipe etc. are also produced by the company.

The SAIL produces iron and steel at four integrated steel plants and three special steel plants. The integrated steel plants are situated close to the raw material sources in the East and Central regions of the country. The integrated steel plants are Rourkela Steel Plant (RSP), Bhilai Steel Plant (BSP), Bokaro Steel Ltd. (BSL) and Durgapur Steel Plant (DSP).

Ranked among the top ten companies in the country, it achieved highest ever turnover of Rs. 31800 crores and net profit of Rs. 6817 crores during the financial year 2004-05, which is a landmark by itself.

It has got its captive iron ore mines meeting the total requirement of raw materials in its integrated steel plants at present. It has a wide marketing network connecting around 35 stock yards through out the country managed by its marketing arm (CMO) (Central Marketing Organization) and the exports are managed through its International Trade Division (ITD).

FUTURE PLANS

It is expected that the steel market will grow at the rate of 8% per annum in the coming decade. India has set a target of doubling its capacity by 2012 and trebling by 2018. In line with this, SAIL is also geared up to double its capacity by the year 2012. It has prepared a long-term plan called, which provides a direction for the company's growth in the coming years, in line with a growing market.

By 2012, the consumption of steel in India is expected to reach around 55 to 60 million tons (MT), nearly double the current level. The Center for Policy Research, in its November 2002 report dealing with perspectives up to 2025, indicates that the Construction, Cold-reducing and Oil and Gas Transportation segments are poised for major growth in India. TMT Bars and Rods, Structural, HR/CR Coils, Plates and Pipes have been identified as the key growth products for the domestic steel industry. For SAIL, which is an established and significant player in these product segments, the scenario holds a huge potential for growth.

Long-term Plan of SAIL envisages increasing its domestic market share from a level of around 26% to around 27%. For realistic achievement and investments in stages, the plan has been split into two stages - Stage 1 pertaining to the period up to 2006-07 and Stage 2 up to 2011-12.

As part of this plan, SAIL will increase hot metal production from its plants to a level of about 20 million tones per annum (MTPA) by 2012 against the current level of 13 MT. Plant-wise break-up of hot metal production is shown in Table 3.1.

Table 3.1: Plant-wise break-up of hot metal production

Integrated Steel Plant	Current level (2003-04)	Projected level (2011-12)
Bhilai Steel Plant (BSP)	4.9	7
Durgapur Steel Plant (DSP)	1.98	3.2
Rourkela Steel Plant (RSP)	1.73	3
Bokaro Steel Plant (BSL)	4.1	6.5
Total	12.71	19.7

Based on the above, crude steel production by SAIL is planned to reach a level of 18.7 MTPA by 2012, leading to saleable steel production of 17.38 MTPA.

SAIL will give due emphasis to achieve quality and cost competitiveness. Cost competitiveness will be achieved through:

a) Reduction in fixed cost through volume growth, reduction in manpower cost and financial charges

b) Reduction in variable cost through technological interventions like elimination of ingot steel route, 100% Basic Oxygen Furnace and Continuous Casting, coke rate reduction via CDI/auxiliary fuel injection, and higher levels of process control computerisation/ automation, leading to enhancement of operating efficiency.

c) Business process improvements such as streamlining of supplies of key inputs of steel making through higher utilization of e-commerce, centralized procurement for select items, etc.

SAIL's plans may be revised from time to time, and further growth in terms of volume, products, etc., may be aimed through Greenfield investments, acquisitions/mergers etc.

On the raw material front SAIL will take up the following steps to meet the increased requirement in the future:

1) Development of iron ore mines
2) Exploring possibilities to obtain strategic partnership with/acquisition of coal fields abroad.

INVESTMENT

The SAIL has estimated that to achieve its long-term plan it will require investment in the region of Rs. 25,000 crore by 2011-12. The immediate priority schemes, to be taken/ completed by 2006-07, have been estimated to be around Rs. 4,300 crore. The capital expenditure envisaged will be financed mainly through internal accruals, and will be supplemented by market borrowing if the need arises. Company's debt-equity ratio will be maintained at, a level of 1:1.

The plan for capital expenditure covers up gradation/ modernisation of some existing assets as well as installation of some new facilities. The areas broadly identified for investment pertain to:

- Development of iron ore mines to support additional production volume
- Rebuilding Coke Oven Batteries at BSP, DSP
- Revamping of iron and steel making facilities at BSP, DSP and BSL
- Installation of one blast furnace at RSP
- Installation of auxiliary fuel injection systems in all blast furnaces in a phased manner
- Installation of new finishing mills.

ROURKELA STEEL PLANT

Rourkela Steel Plant (RSP) is an integrated steel plant in the family of SAIL with a capacity of 2 million tonnes of Hot Metal Production. The RSP is referred to as the torch-bearer for the public sector integrated steel plant and carried the banner of revolution in steel making in the country. It was the first plant to be commissioned in the public sector after Government of India decided to set up three plants in the Second Five-year Plan. The steel plant, now a unit of the Steel Authority of India Limited (SAIL), started during the mid- fifties of the 20th century, in collaboration with leading steel makers from the Federal Republic of Germany. Consultancy for the plant started in the year 1948 and agreement with M/s. IKGD was made in the year 1953 to set up a 0.5 million tons steel plant. In the year 1956 decision was taken for setting up the steel plant with 1 million-ton capacity instead of 0.5 million tons per year. The 1st Blast Furnace (BF No.1) was commissioned on 27th Jan. 1959. Subsequently, other 2 Blast Furnaces (BF No-II and BF No-III) were commissioned on 12th Jan. 1960 and 8th Jan 1962 respectively. The units at the 1.0 Mt stage were commissioned between December 1958 and early part of 1962. With a view to meeting the additional demand for flat products in the country, it was decided to increase the capacity of the Blooming and Slabbing Mill, Hot Strip Mill and Plate Mill at RSP. Accordingly, capacity of ingot steel was increased from 1.0 MT to 1.8 MT between the year 1965 and 1969. Besides expansion of the capacity of the existing units, the scheme also envisaged addition of new units like Electrical Sheet Mill (For dynamo and transformer grade steel) and Galvanising Lines (for corrugated and plane galvanized sheets). Subsequent to expansion of the steel plant, a number of units were added to enhance the product quality, production and productivity, profitability and to meet the market needs. These units included Desulphurisation in Blast Furnaces; Spiral welded Pipe Plants, Silicon Steel Mill, Captive Power Plant-II, Mechanical Shop, Structural and Fabrication Shop, Heavy Loco Repair Shop, Slag Granulation Plant and Coke Ovens – Battery No.5.

In order to overcome technological obsolescence and to continue to remain competitive in the market place, RSP went in for modernisation, which was conceived in the year 1988. Phase-I of modernisation, which emphasized on improving the quality of raw material consisted of a Raw Material Handling System, Coal Handling Plant (in Coke-Ovens), new Oxygen Plant, upgradation Schemes for Blast Furnaces, Dolomite Brick Plant, Cast House SGP at BF-IV, and Power Distribution System, was completed in the year 1994. phase-II consisted of a new Sinter Plant, Basic oxygen Furnace and Slab Casting Shop in Steel Melting Shop-II, modification of Plate Mill and Hot Strip Mill, and installation of Slab Casting Shop in SMS-I. Except for Hot Strip mill, which was completed in the year 1999, all the other areas were completed in the year 1997. After modernization, the capacities have been enhanced to 2 MT of Hot Metal, 1.9 Mt of Continuous Cast Slabs and 1.671 Mt of Saleable Steel.

Table 3.2: Production after modernization

Item	Capacity
Hot Metal	2.0 Million tons/yr
Crude Steel	1.9 Million tons/yr
Saleable Steel	1.671 Million tons/yr

The RSP produces a wide variety of special purpose steels, the use of its plates in Ship building and high pressure vessels, Silicon Steel in the electrical industries, Corrugated Galvanized Sheets for roofing including industrial roofing, pipes in the oil and Gas sectors, Tin Plates in packaging industry and spherical plates in the defence of the nation are well known. Its steel production is totally through continuous cast route of steel, which is considered to be a cost effective process. RSP has also implemented ISO: 9001 in almost all the major shops under it.

The product range of RSP and the key segments of its application are given in Table 3.3.

Table 3.3: The product range of RSP and the key segments of its application

Main Products	Key Segment
Plate	Structural, Construction, Fabrication, Boiler Industry, Ship Building, Automobiles, Railways, Pipe Making, Galvanizing pots etc.
HR Coils	Tube/Pipe making, Cold reducing, Cold forming, Hamilton poles, Cycle Industry, LPG, Railways, Automobiles, Industrial flooring etc.
CR Sheet/Coil	Furniture, Household appliances, Fabrication, Cold forming, Drum and Barrels, Tube Making Cycle Industries, Railways, Agricultural Equipment, Packaging, Coating etc.
Galvanised Plain/ Corrugated Sheets	Furniture, Household appliances, Cooler body, Air conditioning duct, Roofing, Storage bins/Silos, Fabrication, construction etc.
CRNO	Electric Motors, Relays, Transformers, Rotating Electrical Machineries, Laminations etc.
Tin Plates	Oil Cans
ERW Pipes	Oil and water transportation, Slurry Transportation, Ash handling, Construction etc.
SW Pipes	Oil and Water transportation, Sewerage etc.

ORGANIZATION STRUCTURE AND MANAGEMENT

The RSP functions under the aegis of SAIL. The unit is generally headed by a Managing Director, who is also a part of the Board of the Directors of the Navaratna Steel behemoth, SAIL. This gives the head a substantial amount of freedom and independence in taking decisions for the plant. Among the Direct Reporting Officers to the M.D are ED (Works), GM

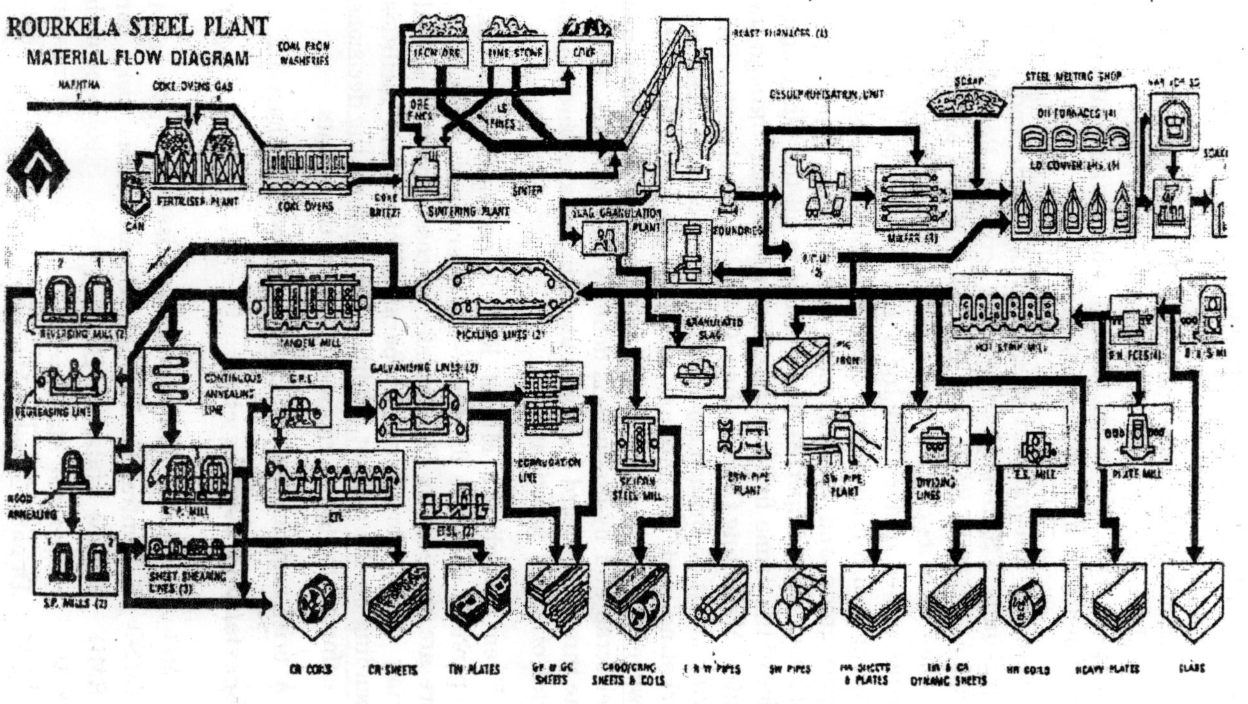

Chart 3.1: The Process Flow Diagram of RSP

(Projects), ED (Personnel), ED (Material Management), GM (Finance and accounts) etc. They look after the key functions of the company. They have one or multiple Departments under them. There are General Managers (GM), Deputy General Managers (DGM) under them, who head individual departments or an important section.

Being an integral part of SAIL, RSP also depends on the central units of SAIL for its day-to-day activities. Raw Material Division (RMD) of SAIL does the raw material allocation to the plant from its captive mines. Indigenous Coal supply from various mines under Coal India Ltd. is handled by CCSO (Central Coal Supply Orgn.) a central unit under SAIL. Coal Import group and the transport and shipping group under SAIL look after imported coal souring to all the plant units. Sales of the prime finished steel material is done through the Central Marketing Organisation (CMO), a central unit of SAIL having about 35 Branch sales offices in the country. The total marketing and promotional activities are done by CMO. However the sales of secondary and steel products, iron and steel scrap and by-products is done by RSP directly. This is done through forward auction route using e-sales through the portal of Metal junction.

Even though the MD of RSP is empowered to take independent decisions for day-to-day operations of the plant, there are some areas like transfer prices, allocation of coal during crisis, operation/non operation of certain facilities depending on the market conditions etc., where the decisions are enforced by the Corporate office on the plants.

A brief organisation structure is shown in Chart-3.2.

Abbreviations used in chart

CMO = Central Marketing Organisation
CCSO = Central Coal Supply Organisation
RMD = Raw Materials Division
GM = General Manager
DGM = Deputy General Manager
AGM = Assistant General Manager

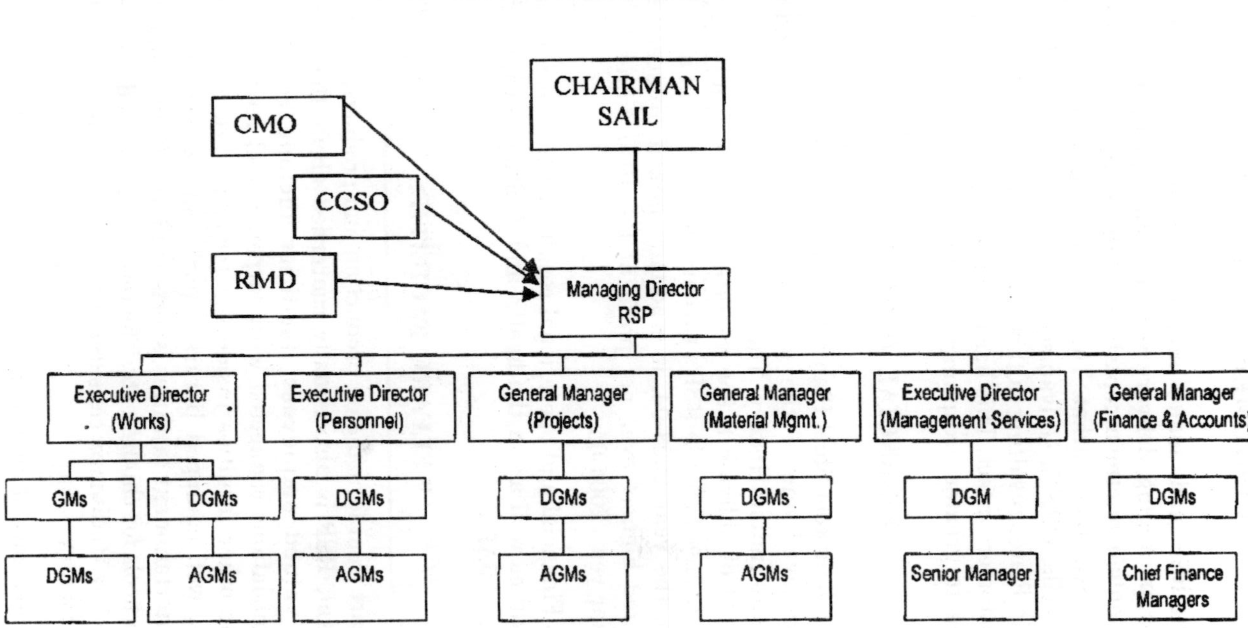

Chart-3.2: Organisation Chart

CUSTOMER SATISFACTION

The RSP made major improvements in the areas of steel quality, packaging, delivery and customer satisfaction thereby vastly enhancing the acceptability of its products in the highly competitive steel market. Thrust was given to the packaging of HR coils, CRNO, Galvanised Plain and Corrugated sheets and Tin Plates resulting in this value added products reaching the customers intact. This has enhanced customer satisfaction leading to greater acceptance of RSP's products.

FINANCIAL PERFORMANCE

The Rourkela Steel Plant, in around two and a half years, has achieved one of the most dramatic turnarounds in Corporate Indian History. The Steel Plant, which was on the threshold of oblivion a few years ago, is now firmly on the net profit mode. While RSP's turnaround started on a modest note in the year 2003-04, it gradually picked up speed and registered highest ever net profit of Rs. 1045 crores in the financial year 2004-05.

Its Financial and operational results depend upon its own potential as well as on the health and decisions of its parent company, SAIL.

WELFARE FACILITIES

Apart from focusing on production and productivity inside the plant, RSP is also equally concerned about the welfare of its valued employees. facilities include residential accommodations connected with carpeted road length of 340 km. the other facilities inside the township are community centres, well equipped libraries, parks and zoos with up to date entertainment facilities, sports stadiums (indoor and out door), schools for children etc. The recently completed synthetic turf hockey stadium is considered to be one of the best in the entire country today.

To take care of health of the employees, RSP has 685 beds hospital called Ispat General Hospital, which is the largest hospital in the region with modern equipments and specialist doctors. It is the only comprehensive hospital in Orissa with the facilities like Burn centre, Intensive care unit, nuclear medicines, city scan, blood transmission centre, dialysis unit, Bio-medical waste management, ultrasound. The RSP is the first steel plant in the steel Industry to have full-fledged occupational health service centre.

HR EXERCISE

Over the past four years, a series of communication exercises, workshops and interaction sessions have been conducted involving employees' participation in large and small groups. Deliberations are held for continual improvement in the performance of plant in open sessions in which the employees participate in large numbers expressing their commitment and dedication for the plant. The themes in these lively sessions range from "Sharing Concern" where the financial details of the plant are discussed threadbare, to "Reducing the Distance between minds" by "Bringing Closeness" where the problems of internal customers are analyzed and debated along with supplier departments for achieving organizational goals. Of all the HR interventions initiated in the plant the one that has created the greatest impact is the "The Mass Contact Exercise" (MCE). In each session around five hundred employees interact in an open forum with the Managing Director on various issues of concern to the organisation. The average workman could air his work related problems to the Chief Executive himself. A patient hearing and a quick redressal was always on the cards and in many cases the employees came back and using the same forum expressed their happiness at their issue being resolved quickly.

CORPORATE SOCIAL RESPONSIBILITY

An exclusive cell has been started by RSP for taking care of periphery Development. The various facilities extended by RSP to its periphery include:

* Drinking Water facilities by providing Dug wells, Tube wells and Dhobi Ghats
* Health Care facilities – RSP runs 2 numbers medical aid centres for mentally challenged children, 1 No. pathological diagnostic centre, 1 No. dispensary, organises regularly health check up camps.
* Education Care by Construction of classrooms, Merit awards to students.
* Communication Construction of Roads and bridge.

4

Rourkela Steel Plant
An Analytical Study

INTRODUCTION

Rourkela Steel Plant (RSP) is an integrated steel plant in the family of SAIL with a present capacity of 2 million tonnes of Hot Metal Production. It is a producer of flat and special steel products, which include the following saleable steel items:

1. Plates
2. Hot rolled coil (HR Coil)
3. Hot rolled Plate (HR Plate)
4. Cold rolled coil (CR Coil)
5. Cold rolled Sheet (CR Sheet)
6. Galvanized Plate and Galvanized Corrugated sheet (GP/GC)
7. Electrolytic Tin Plate (ETP): Used for preparation of cans
8. Cold rolled Non oriented (ETP): Used in the electric appliances
9. Electric Resistance welded pipe (ERW Pipe)

10. Spiral welded Pipe (SW Pipe)
11. Slab
12. Spade, Jackal, Target Steel and other special steel products mostly for Defense use.

Its financial and operational results depend upon its own potential as well as on the health and decisions of its parent company, SAIL as described below:

— On Own Potential: Improvements in the following areas are possible:

  a) Production volume
  b) Quality of products
  c) Better Techno economic parameters and operational efficiency
  d) Better maintenance practices and optimum utilization of stores and spares
  e) Better culture through out the organisation.

— Dependence in on SAIL is there in the following areas:

  a) Raw material linkage
  b) Allocation of coal
  c) Sources of fund allocation during capital investment
  d) Other key decisions affecting production/sales activities.

An analysis of strengths and weaknesses of RSP is done below, which gives an idea about its positioning today vis-à-vis its competitors in the market place.

SWOT ANALYSIS OF RSP

Strength:

- 100% continuous casting route
- more number of value added products

- Iron ore supply from captive mines of SAIL
- Nearer to the Iron ore mines
- Modernised plant.

Weakness:

- Quality
- High Manpower

Opportunity:

- Good steel market for flat products and market is expected to grow in future too.
- Better product mix with value added products in the product range. In a depressed market, more concentration on production of value added items where fall in sales price is comparatively much less, will improve the profit margin of the company.

Threat:

- More number of competitors
- Smaller capacity
- New grass root Projects, likely to be set up by Indian firms and MNCs with latest technology will give tough competition.
- Higher imported coal price

The above analysis shows that RSP has advantage of sourcing iron ore from the captive sources which provides a shield against price rises, continuous casting route of steel making, special steel production facilities. But its concerns are quality, low capacity and high manpower. It may address these issues in future so as to remain viable in the market. Further details of financial analysis are done in the subsequent pages. Prior to this, the behaviours of sales price and input prices affecting the profitability of the company are analysed in Table 4.1.

Table 4.1: The behaviors of sales price and input prices and the profitability of the company

(Rs. per ton)

Product	Period				
	2000-01	2001-02	2002-03	2003-04	2004-05
Plates	14000	12600	15000	19000	25600
HR Plate	13000	11000	14700	18600	25100
HR Coil	12600	10500	14300	16700	23200
CR Coil	15000	12200	16600	19900	25900
CR Sheet	16000	13000	16700	20000	25200
GP/GC	20000	16700	19500	22700	29000
ERW Pipe	16000	14700	16400	18000	25000
SW Pipe	18000	16000	15100	19400	27500
ETP	27000	24700	26400	29000	34800
CRNO	28000	23400	25600	29300	36000
Average Saleable Steel	15000	12800	16100	19200	25800
% Increase		-15%	26%	19%	34%

BEHAVIOUR OF SALES PRICE

Net Sales price for various products were depressed during the financial year 2001-02, after which it started improving. This is shown in the tabular and graphical forms below:

It can be seen from Charts 4.1 and 4.2 and Table 4.1 that the sales prices have improved after 2001-02. The maximum jump of 34% in the price took place during the financial year 2004-05 in which the company recorded a highest ever turnover of Rs. 4674 crores and profit of Rs. 1045 crores.

A temporary down ward pressure on the sales price front in seen during May 2005 to Jul 2005. During this time, there has been a reduction of about 10 to 15% in the sales prices

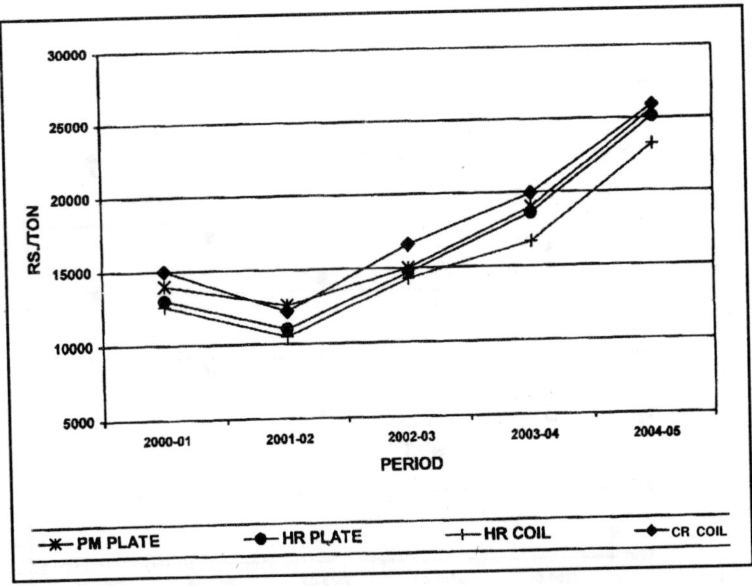

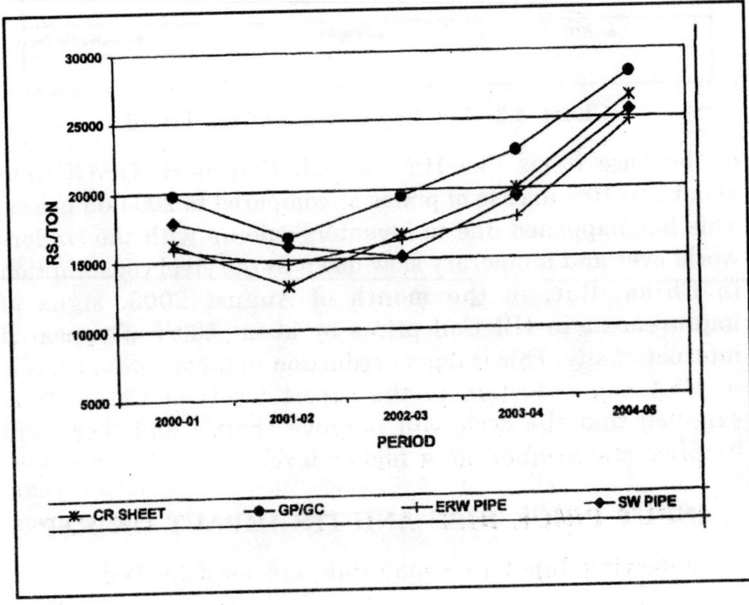

Chart 4.1: Net Sales Realisation Trend

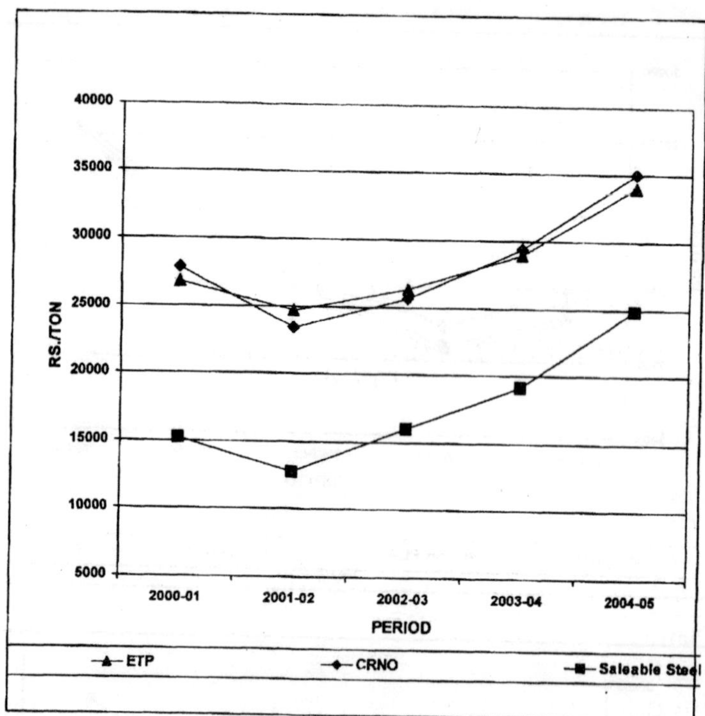

Chart 4.2: Net Sales Realisation Trend

of the base items like HR coil, CR Coil/sheet, GP/GC and about 5 to 10% in case of plates as compared to 2004-05 prices. This has happened due to inventory pile up with the traders world over and temporary slow down in the steel consumption in China. But, in the month of August 2005, signs of improvement in HR Coil prices by about $30/Ton appeared internationally. This is due to reduction in the inventory levels in USA and reduction in the export levels of China. It is expected that the cycle will improve shortly and there will be price stabilization at a higher level.

INPUT PRICE RISE AND ITS IMPACT ON RSP

Following Input raw materials are used by RSP.

- Coal

- Iron ore
- Lime stone
- Dolomite
- Ferro Alloys
- Aluminum
- Copper
- Boiler Coal
- Coke

PERCENTAGE CHANGE IN NSR OVER PAST PERIOD

Table 4.2: Percentage Change in NSR During 2001-01 to 2004-05

Product	Period			
	2001-02	2002-03	2003-04	2004-05
Plates	-9%	20%	25%	35%
HR Plate	-14%	32%	27%	35%
HR Coil	-17%	37%	17%	39%
CR Coil	-20%	36%	20%	30%
CR Sheet	-19%	28%	19%	26%
GP/GC	-16%	17%	16%	28%
ERW Pipe	-7%	11%	9%	39%
SW Pipe	-10%	-5%	28%	42%
ETP	-8%	7%	10%	20%
CRNO	-16%	9%	15%	23%
Saleable Steel	-17%	26%	19%	34%

Out of the above coal, ferro alloys, Aluminum, Copper Boiler coal are purchased by RSP. Coal is a major raw material, which accounts for about 20% of the total expenditure of the company. The input purchase rates between 2000-01 and 2004-05 are tabulated below. This shows an increase in price in almost all the items. Stiff increase is there in case of coal.

Coal shortage in the international market due to increased demand has resulted in this hike.

Table 4.3: The input purchase rates between 2000-01 and 2004-05

(*Rs. Per Ton*)

Raw Material (Purchase)	Period				
	2000-01	2001-02	2002-03	2003-04	2004-05
Coal - Indigenous	2200	2600	2700	2900	3500
Coal - Imported	3100	3400	3600	3700	5100
Ferro Manganese	20500	21400	22100	24000	28800
Ferro Silicon	31600	30500	31700	33800	39300
Silico Manganese	21600	21600	21000	22400	36000
Aluminium	83700	83800	81200	83600	91700
Coke	-	-	5900	9100	14500

Percentage Change in Purchase Price Over Last Period

Raw Material (Purchase)	Period			
	2001-02	2002-03	2003-04	2004-05
Coal - Indigenous	14%	7%	5%	21%
Coal - Imported	9%	7%	2%	38%
Ferro Manganese	4%	3%	8%	20%
Ferro Silicon	-3%	4%	6%	16%
Silico Manganese	0%	-3%	7%	61%
Aluminium	0%	-3%	3%	10%
Coke	-	-	55%	59%

Iron ore is another major raw material accounting for 5% of total expenditure of the company. This is generated by the captive mines of the group company SAIL and is transferred for consumption on cost of generation. Thus it is insulated from the variations in the market price.

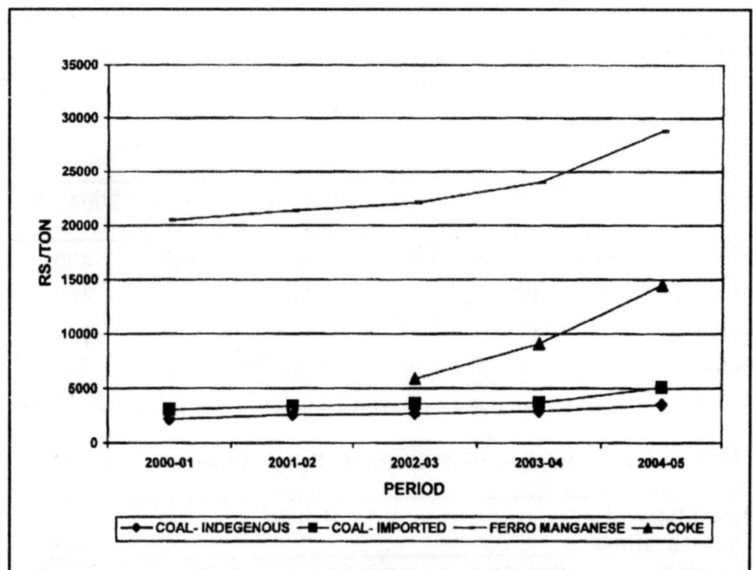

Chart 4.3: Input Price Trend

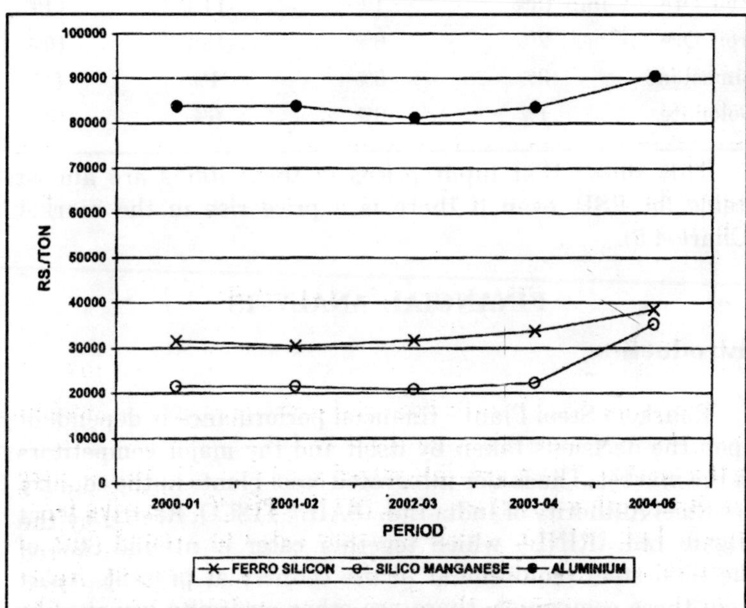

Chart 4.4: Input Price Trend

The input pries of these items are tabulated in Table 4.4.

Table 4.4: The input pries major raw materials (2001-02 to 2004-05)

Raw Materials (Captive Mines of SAIL)	Period				
	2000-01	2001-02	2002-03	2003-04	2004-05
Iron Ore - Lump	440	490	495	440	490
Iron Ore - Fines	430	440	470	420	460
Limestone	1520	1560	1640	1620	1700
Dolomite	315	320	320	300	340

Percentage Change in Purchase Price Over Last Period

Raw Material (Captive Mines of SAIL)	Period			
	2001-02	2002-03	2003-04	2004-05
Iron Ore - Lump	13%	1%	-11%	11%
Iron Ore - Fines	2%	6%	-10%	10%
Limestone	3%	5%	-1%	5%
Dolomite	1%	0%	-6%	13%

This shows that input prices of these items are almost stable for RSP, even if there is a price rise in the market (Chart 4.5).

FINANCIAL ANALYSIS

Introduction

Rourkela Steel Plant's financial performance is dependent upon the decisions taken by itself and the major competitors in the market. The major integrated steel plants in the country are Steel Authority of India Ltd. (SAIL), TISCO, Rastriya Ispat Nigam Ltd. (RINL), which together cater to around 60% of the total steel requirement in the country at present. Apart from these companies, there are other emerging private like

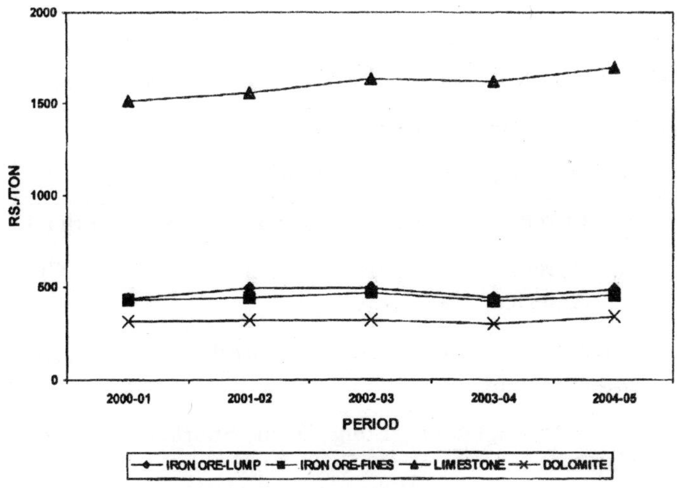

Chart 4.5: Input Price Trend

Jindal group, Ispat group etc. which will increase the steel production capacity in the country in future. Multi National Companies like Mittal Steel and POSCO have also geared up their activities to set up new integrated steel plants in the country.

Therefore, financial analysis of RSP is required to be done along with that of major players in the country so as to judge the performance of the company and be able to benchmark the key parameters for future achievement. As a part of this research, three companies namely RSP, SAIL and TISCO are considered to carry out the financial analysis. SAIL is the biggest public sector steel company in the country, RSP is one of the main steel plants of SAIL and TISCO is the biggest private sector steel company in the country at present. Performance of RSP is compared with those of SAIL and TISCO and suggestions for future improvement are worked out. Different models have been used in the course of financial anlaysis.

Rourkela Steel Plant (RSP) is an integrated steel plant and is one of the four major steel producing units of SAIL.

Some of the major business and financial decisions of RSP are also taken by the Corporate Office, Central Units (like Raw material Division, Central Marketing Organisation etc.) and the Board Directors of SAIL. These are as follows:

1. Raw material linkage:
   a) Sourcing from captive mines
   b) Purchase of indigenous coal from Coal India Ltd.
   c) Purchase of imported coal from Australia, China, America, Canada etc.
2. Sales of Prime products and key customers management.
3. Loan arrangement (Long Term, Short Term/Working Capital).
4. Funds management.
5. Investment decisions.

Most of the financial trends of RSP can be best understood form the financial analysis in conjunction with those of its parent company SAIL. Certain financial analysis like Working capital, cash/funds flow of RSP is inconclusive without considering those of SAIL too. This is because of the fact that balance sheet entries like sundry debtors (to the extent of prime sales through Central Marketing organization of SAIL), sundry creditors of raw materials, Borrowings are operated through IUCA (Inter-unit Current Accounts) transactions. This has been elaborated in details in the relevant sub chapters. Analysis of working capital, financial statements, break even, cash flow, ratios are detailed below.

WORKING CAPITAL ANLAYSIS

Companies need cash to meet expenses for day-to-day activities. They have to pay wages, pay for raw materials, pay bills etc. money available to them to do this is known as the firms' working capital. The main sources of working capital are the current assets as these are the short-term assets that the firm can use to generate cash. These assets have a high liquidity. However, the firm also has current liabilities and so these have to be taken into account while working out working capital at the firm's disposal. It is important for a firm to have sufficient working capital to meet all its requirements like paying for raw materials, day to day bills, wages etc.

Working capital can be described as:

Working Capital =	Current Assets –	Current liabilities
	||	||
	Stock+debtors + short term securities + cash	Creditors + Advances from customers+ short term provisions

Thus working capital is also equal to net current assets, and forms an important part of the firm's balance sheet. Many businesses have gone under difficult times, not because they were unprofitable, but because they suffered from shortages of working capital.

Since working capital is net of Current assts and current liabilities, it can be both positive and negative at any point of time. A positive working capital arises when current assets are more than current liabilities. A negative working capital arises when current liabilities are more than the current assets.

Only current assets is also called as Gross Working Capital of the firm. Like long-term loan is taken for funding capital investments to meet the shortfall in the fund requirement, short-term loans are taken by the firm to meet shortfall in cash requirement for investing in current assets. This is otherwise known as Working Capital Loan.

Thus a judicious decision in respect of investment in current assets is very important for the company to avoid taking more working capital loan from Banks resulting in more interest pay outs. The amount of investment in current assets depends on the nature of business of the firm. If there is a considerable lead-time between procurement of raw materials and making finished goods and or if sundry debtors are very high due to the market condition, then investment in current assets is high. For traders, this is very low.

In case of an integrated Steel Plan, working capital requirement is more. Inventory of finished goods needs to be maintained at a comfortable level to avoid stock out situation at any point of time. However the stock of semi-finished goods can be reduced through ingenuous production planning between processes. This will ease the working capital requirement of the firm.

Working capital can also be high due to high sundry debtors and excess cash of the firm. Sundry debtors level depends on the market condition as well as collection efforts. In today's steel market, where demand outweighs supply, fresh sundry debtors are also nil for the steel manufacturers. Excessive cash situation, if any, in the balance sheet either due to more profit or idling of long-term loans taken by the company is not a good sign for the company. Idle cash is costly. It needs to be invested or utilized for loan repayment etc. that will be profitable for the firm.

Sundry creditors management depending on the gross working capital position is very important to manage the working capital requirement of the firm.

Net working capital can be both positive and negative. Analysis of the same from an integrated steel plant is elucidated below:

Very high positive working capital is not good for the health of the firm, since this means that either there is surplus idle cash and/or huge quantity of inventory or poorly managed high debtors for the firm.

At the same time negative working capital may not be desirable for the health of the company. This may arise due to any one or all of the following reasons:

- High levels of sundry creditors in the books, even when investment requirement in current assets is minimal. It will dissatisfy the suppliers because their payments are held much beyond the due date. This will damage the image of the firm among the key suppliers and may result in less supply of quality materials.

- A very low level of finished goods inventory: This may lead to non-fulfillment of supply against booked orders from the customers within due date. Thus it will damage the brand image of the firm in the market place.

Thus a minimum amount of working capital is required to be held by the firm to meet its day-to-day requirements. This is known as permanence working capital. This is very much required in case of an integrated steel plant like Steel Authority of India Ltd. and one of its main producing unit "Rourkela Steel Plant". Estimation of this is governed by working capital policy, which is dealt with in the next pages in details.

Working capital management is very important for a firm. Abnormal fluctuation of working capital during an accounting period is dangerous.

WORKING CAPITAL CYCLE

Working capital is vital to a business. The working capital takes care of current assets and current liabilities of the firm. It is very important for a company to manage its working capital carefully. This is particularly true where there is a substantial time lag between making the product and receiving the money for it. In this situation, the company has paid out all the costs associated with making the product (labour, raw materials and so on) but not yet got any money for it. The firm must therefore ensure that it has enough cash to run the business.

The way working capital moves around the business is modeled by the **working capital cycle**. This shows the cash coming into the business, its transformation during the business operations and then its outflow. A simple working capital cycle may look something like:

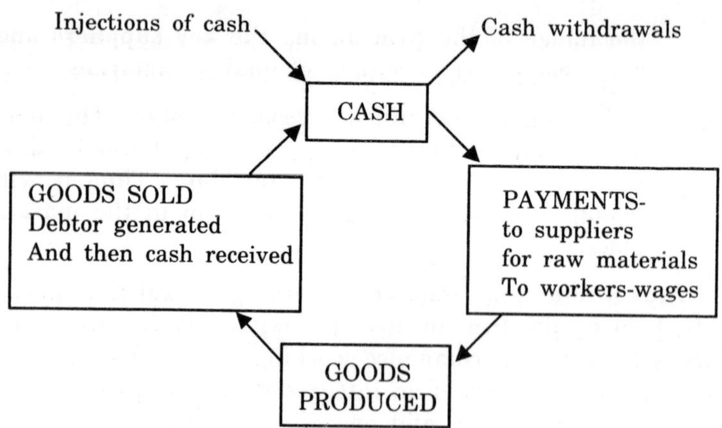

Chart 4.6: the working capital cycle

Between each stage of this working capital cycle there is a time delay. For some businesses this will be very long where it takes them a long time to make and sell the product. Thus these businesses need a substantial amount of working capital to survive. Others that receive cash very quickly after paying out for raw materials etc., need less working capital.

A schematic diagram of operating cycle suitable for an integrated steel plant is shown below.

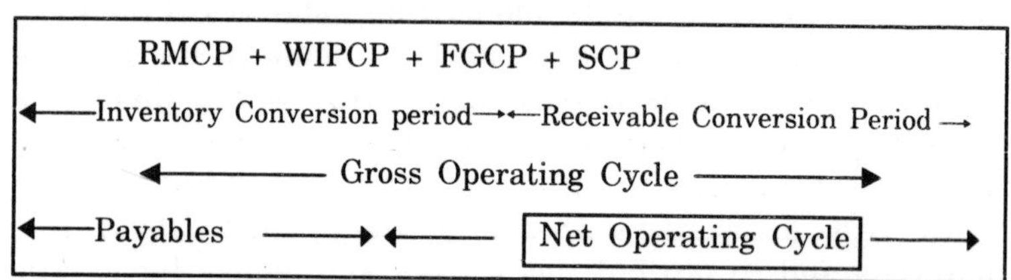

Chart 4.7: Operating cycle of an Integrated Steel Plant

The various terminologies used for described below:

RMCP = Raw Material Conversion Period.

WIPCP = Work in Progress Conversion Period.

FGCP = Finished Goods Conversion Period.

SCP = Stores and Spares Consumption Period.

WORKING CAPITAL CALCULATION FOR RSP

The relevant data for calculation of working capital for RSP is tabulated in Table 4.5 for ten years to make an analysis on the changes during this period.

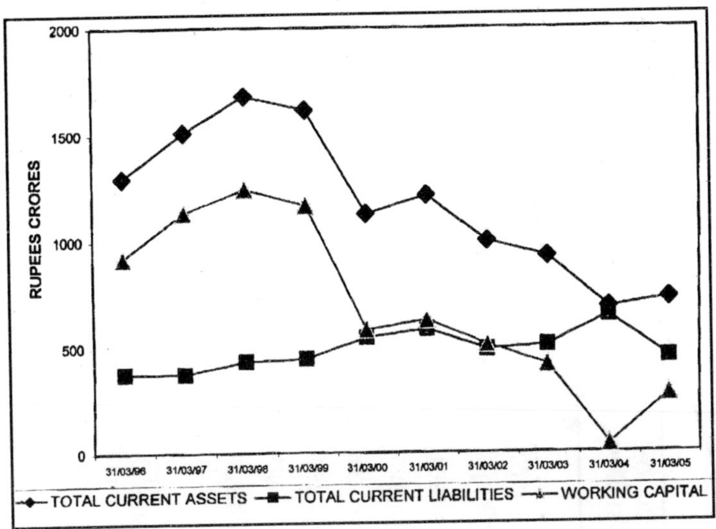

Chart 4.8: Working Capital Trend in RSP

The observations are as follows:

1. Net working capital was on a decline till the year 2003-04. It has again increased during 2004-05.
2. Current assets were falling till 2003-04. As on 31st March 2005, current asset is higher as compared to last year. Current liability has also fallen as on 31st March 2005. The reasons are analyzed in the next pages.
3. The trend flows the pattern of its group company SAIL.

The observations are as follows:

1. Semi-Finished and Finished goods stock was the highest as on 31/03/98. But there after there has been

Table 4.5: The working capital for RSP

(Rs. in crores)

	As On 31/03/96	As On 31/03/97	As On 31/03/98	As On 31/03/99	As On 31/03/00	As On 31/03/01	As On 31/03/02	As On 31/03/03	As On 31/03/04	As On 31/03/05
A) Current Assets:										
Cash and Bank	1.86	0.06	1.06	0.07	0.04	0.10	0.14	0.14	0.12	15.75
Raw Materials	153	165	96	59	75	65	71	80	60	122
Stores and Spares	275	267	227	261	210	160	154	161	156	167
Semi/Finished	510	715	1013	925	508	634	514	449	252	212
Sy. Debtors	31	52	28	31	38	28	8	9	9	12
Loans and Adv	310	293	284	290	262	299	226	214	200	196
Interest Receivable	12	18	29	47	34	25	23	11	10	3
Total Current Assets	1293	1509	1678	1613	1127	1211	997	924	686	727
B) Current Liabilities										
Sy. Creditors	160	148	238	219	207	218	237	230	249	239
Security and Other Deposits	35	41	45	44	47	42	45	45	41	35

Others	180	186	151	185	177	179	160	177	106	127
Provision*	0	0	0	0	115	145	47	57	253	51
Total Current Liabilities	375	375	434	447	545	583	488	508	648	452
C) Working Capital = (A-B)	918	1134	1244	1166	582	628	510	416	38	275

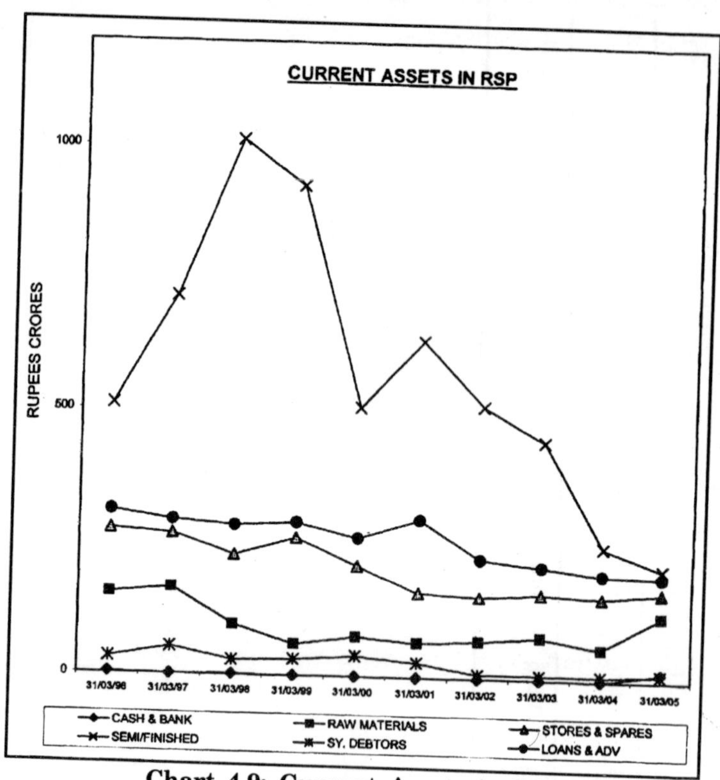

Chart 4.9: Current Assets in RSP

a steep fall in the stock till 31st March, 2004. This has eased the working capital requirement of the plant considerably.

2. There is also a reduction in Stores and Spares stock over the years, but still the figure is quite high.

3. Raw material stock has also increased considerably as on 31st March 2005 as compared to the previous year. This was due to maintaining a high stock of imported coal to take care future requirements of the plant.

4. Sundry debtors in RSP books of accounts reflect only the portion of the Defective Iron and Steel products, scrap and byproducts sold at the plant. The major

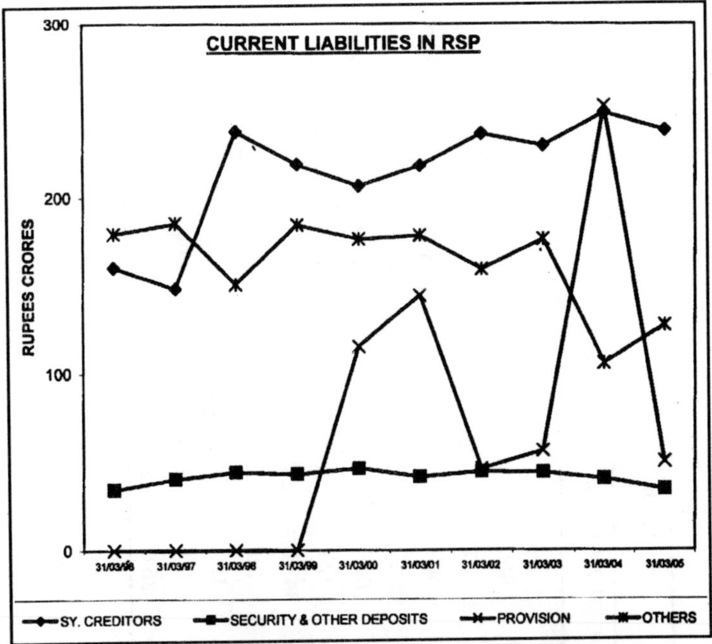

Chart 4.10: Current Liabilities in RSP

chunk of the sundry debtors, which is from prime products sold through Central Marketing Organisation of SAIL does not appear under the heading "Sundry debtors". The accounting entry for this is done through Inter Unit Current Account (IUCA) code. Since sundry debtors of SAIL appears to be on a declining trend over the years, the same trend can also be assumed true in case of RSP.

The observations are as follows:

1. Sundry creditor has gone up over the years. The figure is little less in 2004-05 compared to 2003-04.
2. Provisions are high after 1999. It is the highest as on 31st March, 2004. The reason for this is the pay revision arrear dues of the employees of the plant. However, provision figure as on 31st March, 2005 is

Table 4.6: Number of days holding

(Rs. in crores)

	As on									
	31/03/96	31/03/97	31/03/98	31/03/99	31/03/00	31/03/01	31/03/02	31/03/03	31/03/04	31/03/05
RM Stock	153	165	96	59	75	65	71	80	60	122
M CONSMN.	1147	1148	1071	966	880	1035	998	1132	1176	1277
O. of Days	48	52	32	22	31	23	26	26	18	24
Semi/Fin Stock	510	715	1013	925	508	634	514	449	252	212
Ost of Goods Old	2075	2203	2150	2810	3017	2558	2942	3215	3350	3018
Losing Stk	510	715	1013	925	508	634	514	449	252	212
Pening Stk	492	510	715	1013	925	508	634	514	449	252
Cost of Prod.	2057	1998	1853	2897	3434	2432	3062	3280	3548	3058
O. of Days	89	129	197	115	53	94	60	49	26	25
Stores/Spares	275	267	227	261	210	160	154	161	156	167
Stores/Spares Consmn.	336	350	352	339	300	276	232	292	292	299
No. of Days	294	274	233	277	251	209	239	199	192	200

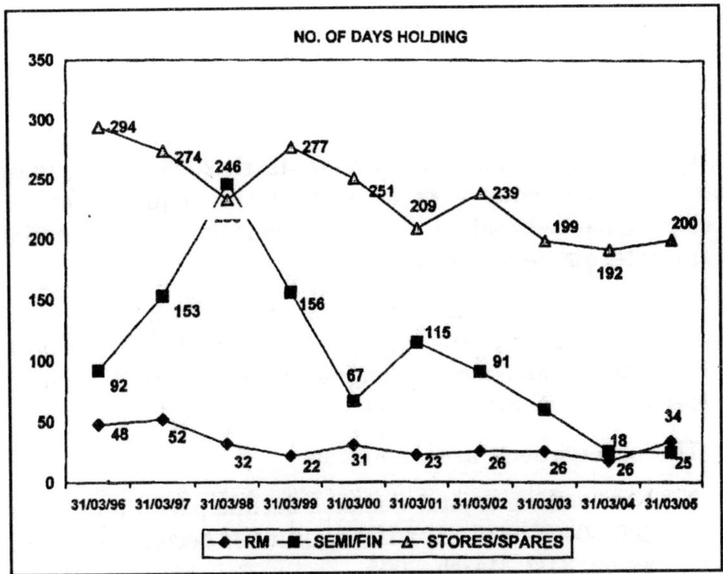

Chart 4.11: No. of Days Holding

much less compared the previous year. This is the reason for a fall in total liabilities figure as on 31st March 2005 as compared to the previous year's figure.

Number of days holding:

1. RM: Raw Material Inventory/(Raw material consumption/360).
2. WIP: Work-in-Process inventory/(Cost of Prodcution/ 360).
3. FG: Finished Goods Inventory/(Cost of Goods sold/360).
4. Stores and Spares: Stores and Spares Inventory/(Stores and Spares consumption/360).

ANALYSIS

There is a remarkable improvement in the Semi/Finished stock. The stock has declined rapidly during 2002-03 and 2003-04 with improvement in steel market during this period. This has certainly reduced the working capital requirement for the plant during the difficult times. However the figure of 31st March 2005 appears to be more than that of 31st March, 2004.

Raw material holding as on 31st March 2005 is more than that of the previous year because of the requirement for stocking imported coal on the face a shortage of the material in the international market.

There is reduction in stores and spares stock during this time. But as on 31st March, 2005 the stock is of 200 days, which is more than 6 months holding. This needs to be reduced to less than 3 months holding.

The observations are as follows:

1. Net working capital was on a decline path till the year 2003-04 (Chart 4.12). However it has become very high as on 31st March 2005.
2. Current liabilities have gone up steadily.

The reasons are analyzed in details from its various elements in the next pages.

It is evident from the Chart 4.13 that:

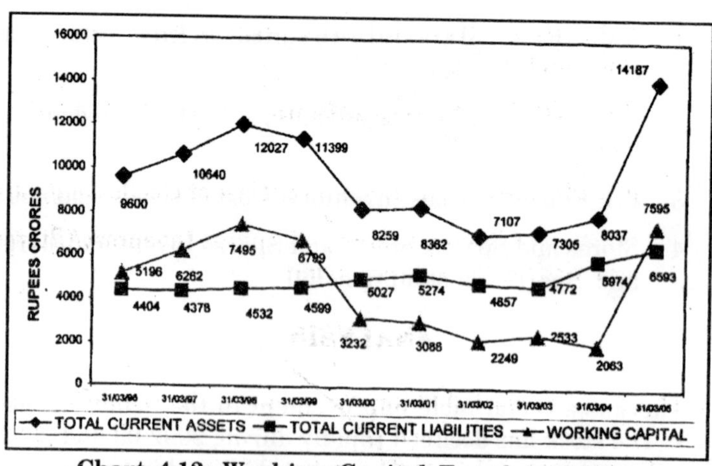

Chart 4.12: Working Capital Trend in SAIL

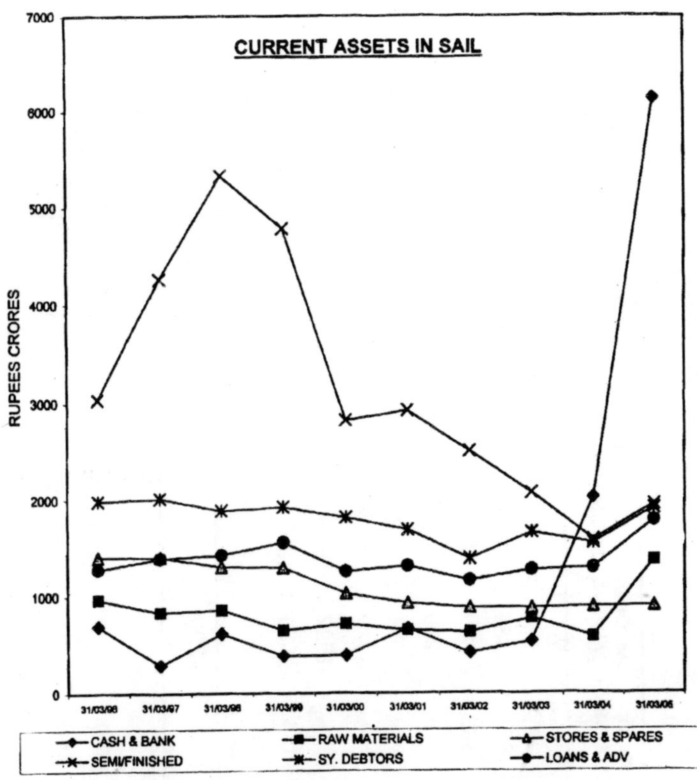

Chart 4.13: Current Assets in SAIL

1. Cash and Bank balance has increased considerably after 31st March, 2003. The balance as on 31st March 2005 is to take care of the total outstanding loan amount of the company.

2. Raw material stock has also increased considerably as on 31st March 2005 as compared to the previous year. This was due to maintaining a high stock of imported coal to take care future requirements of the plant units, as availability of coal from imported source was a problem for some time.

3. Semi-finished and Finished goods stock had increased during 1996 to 1999, but is steadily decreasing after

Table 4.7: Working Capital Calculation for SAIL

(*Rs. in crores*)

	As On 31/03/96	As On 31/03/97	As On 31/03/98	As On 31/03/99	As On 31/03/00	As On 31/03/01	As On 31/03/02	As On 31/03/03	As On 31/03/04	As On 31/3/05
Current Assets										
Cash and Bank	694	292	621	384	393	667	416	535	2017	6132
Raw Materials	970	839	866	652	720	650	633	775	581	1370
Stores and Spares	1410	1409	1313	1298	1032	929	887	881	895	902
Scrapped Assets	16	21	60	64	52	17	22	22	24	0
Semi/Finished	3035	4264	5324	4782	2819	2923	2500	2067	1581	1949
Sy. Debtors	1985	2017	1889	1922	1817	1688	1389	1660	1550	1908
Loans and Advances	1281	1397	1433	1558	1262	1313	1165	1274	1296	1784
Interest Receivable	209	401	521	740	164	175	94	91	92	142
Total Current Assets	9600	10640	12027	11399	8259	8362	1707	7305	8037	14187
Current Liabilities										
Sy. Creditors	1121	1113	1459	1475	1660	1930	1853	1733	1953	2503
Security and Other Deposits	145	155	170	161	172	173	183	192	192	210

Interest Accrued but not due	1317	1504	1615	1708	1475	1240	1082	998	840	528
Others	1471	1415	1184	1221	1192	1231	1282	1357	1248	1310
Provision*	350	191	104	34	528	699	458	492	1741	2043
Total Current Liabilities	4404	4378	4532	4599	5027	5274	4857	4772	5974	6593
Working Capital	5196	6262	7495	6799	3232	3088	2249	2533	2063	7595

*Provisions on account of gratuity leave encashment, post retirement medical benefits are not considered in the working capital calculation.

that. However, the figure as on March 2005 is little more than previous year.

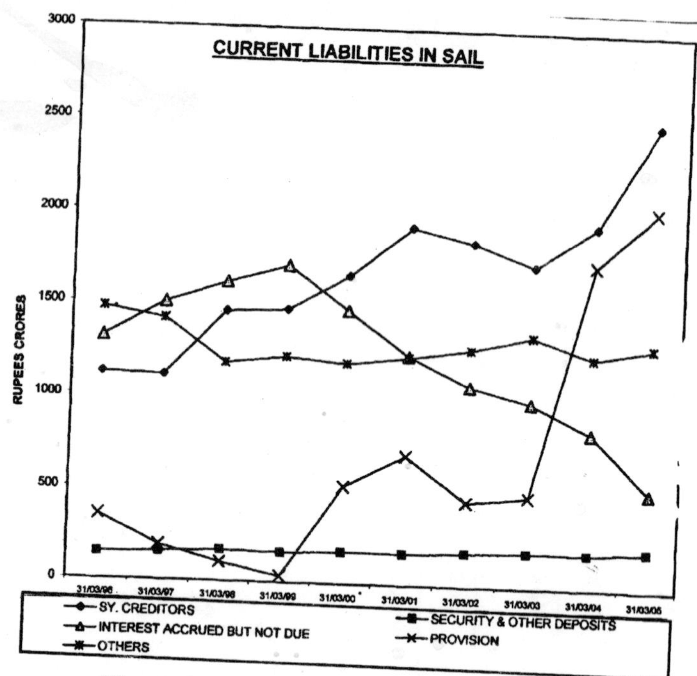

Chart 4.14: Current Liabilities in SAIL

The observations are as follows:

1. Sundry–creditors have gone up over the years.
2. Interest accrued had increased during 1996 to 1999, but is steadily decreasing after that.
3. Provisions have increased steadily after 1999. Percentage increase is the highest as on 31st March, 2004. The reason for this is the wage revision arrear provision. It has further increased as on 31st March 2005 on account of tax and dividend provisions made after a long time.

Thus it can be concluded that net working capital as on 31st March 2005 is high because of a high level of cash and bank balance held by the Firm.

NUMBER OF DAYS HOLDING IN SAIL

The nomenclatures used for the analysis and their descriptions are given below:

1. RM: Raw Material Inventory/(Raw material comnsumption/360)
2. WIP: Work-in-Process inventory/(Cost of Prodcution/ 360)
3. FG: Finished Goods Inventory/(Cost of Goods sold/360)
4. Stores and Spares: Stores and Spares Inventory/(Stores and Spares Consumption/360)

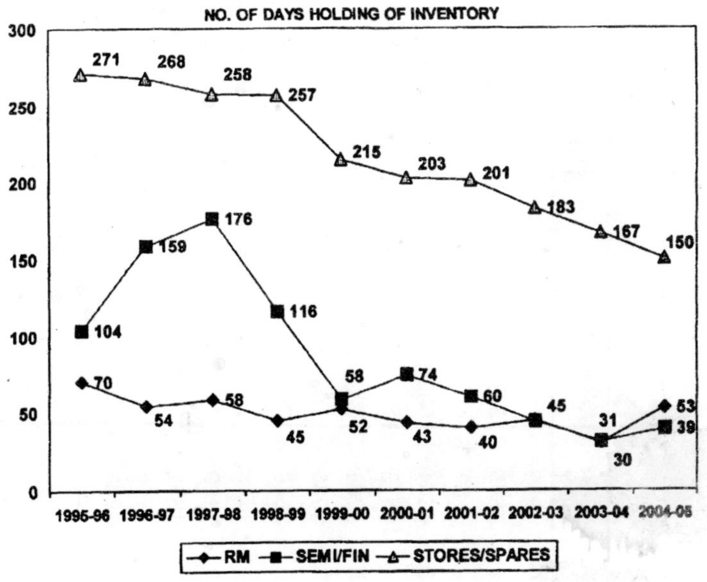

Chart 4.15: No. of days Holding of Inventory

Analysis

Number of days holding of stores and spares stock has declined over the years, as is clearly evident from Chart 4.15.

Table 4.8: Number of Days Holding in SAIL

(Rs. in crores)

	As on									
	31/03/96	31/03/97	31/03/98	31/03/99	31/03/00	31/03/01	31/03/02	31/03/03	31/03/04	31/3/05
RM Stock	970	839	866	652	720	650	633	775	581	1370
RM Consmn.	5012	5585	5411	5224	4976	5420	5645	6226	6892	9351
No. of Days	70	54	58	45	52	43	40	45	30	53
Semi/Fin Stock	3035	4264	5324	4782	2819	2923	2500	2067	1581	1949
Cost of Goods Sold	10867	10875	11948	14244	15503	14269	14635	16588	18062	18301
C/G Stk	3035	4264	5324	4782	2819	2923	2500	2067	1581	1949
O/G Stk	2707	3035	4264	5324	4782	2819	2923	2500	2067	1581
Cost of Prodn	10539	9646	10888	14786	17466	14165	15058	17021	18548	17933
No. of Days	104	159	176	116	58	74	60	44	31	39
Stores/Spares	1410	1409	1313	1298	1032	929	887	881	895	902
Stores/Spares Consmn.	1876	1892	1834	1817	1730	1650	1586	1734	1925	2164
No. of Days	271	268	258	257	215	203	201	183	167	150

Semi-finished and finished stock has declined rapidly during 2002-03 and 2003-04. This has also become possible with improvement in market situation during this period.

The raw material stock has increased towards the end of the financial year 2004-05 mostly on account of imported coal, which is in short supply through out the world. Thus there was a requirement to stock this material to meet the future requirement of the plant units till the normal supply of coal is restored.

WORKING CAPITAL CALCULATION FOR TISCO

The observations are as follows:

1. Net working capital is on a decline over the years (Chart 4.16).
2. Current Liabilities have gone up steadily. The reasons are analyzed in the next pages.

It is evident from Chart 4.17 that:

1. Semi-finished and finished goods stock has increased a son 31st March, 2004 as compared to 31st March 2003.
2. Loans and advances are on the rise and is very high as on 31st March, 2004. This is on account of a higher advance tax payment against taxes as on 31st March, 2004. This trend is also visible in the tax provision in the liability side, which is analyzed in the next pages.
3. Sundry debtors are on a decline and there is a substantial reduction as on 31st March, 2004 compared to that on 31st March, 2003.

The observations are as follows (Chart 4.18):

1. Sundry creditor has gone up over the years.
2. Provisions have increased steadily after 2002. It is the highest as on 31st March, 2004. The reason for this is the higher tax provision kept as on 31st March, 2004. The corresponding increase is also visible in the

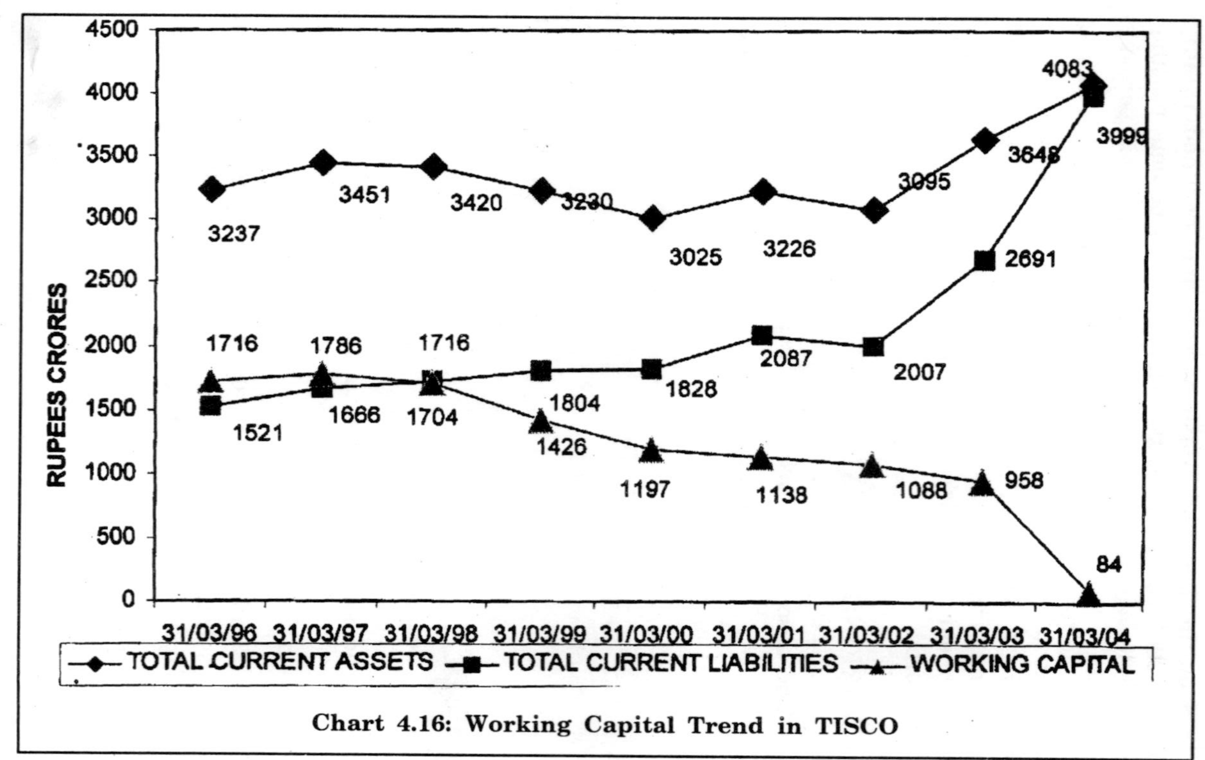

Chart 4.16: Working Capital Trend in TISCO

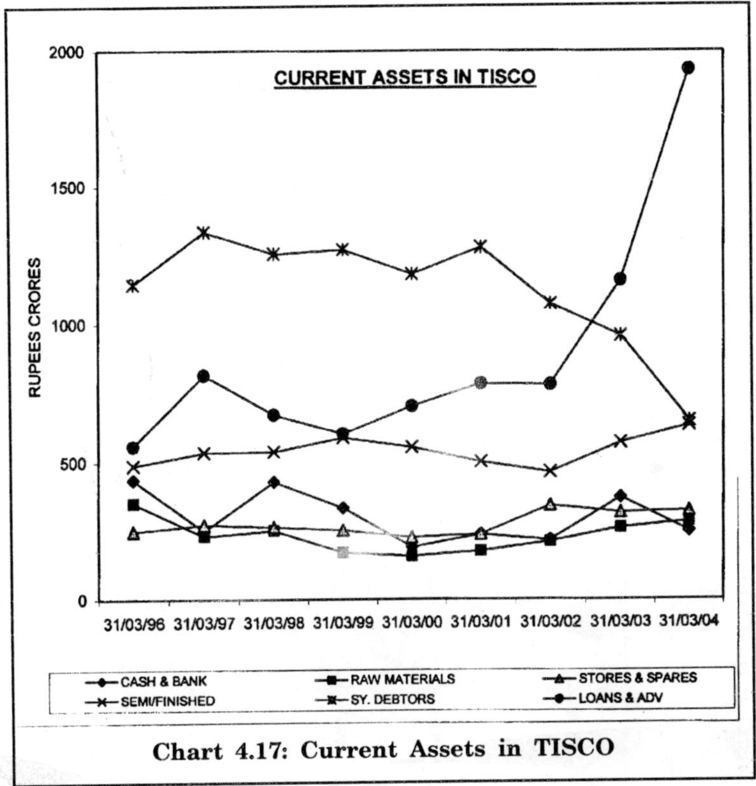

Chart 4.17: Current Assets in TISCO

advances against tax payment in the current asset side.

NUMBER OF DAYS HOLDING

1. RM: Raw Material Inventory/(raw material consumption/360)
2. WIP: Work-in-Process inventory/(Cost of Prodcution/ 360)
3. FG: Finished Goods Inventory/(Cost of Goods sold/360)
4. Stores and Spares: Stores and Spares Inventory/(Stores and Spares Consumption/360)

Table 4.9: Working Capital Calculation for TISCO

(Rs. in crores)

	As On									
	31/03/95	31/03/96	31/03/97	31/03/98	31/03/99	31/03/00	31/03/01	31/03/02	31/03/03	31/03/04
Current Assets										
Cash and Bank	140.88	437.09	251.38	429.41	336.19	193.38	239.23	219.20	373.12	250.74
Raw Materials	231.43	353.57	231.24	253.49	172.87	160.44	179.26	212.15	262.30	287.02
Stores and Spares	226.50	249.35	274.10	265.64	254.03	228.66	239.49	344.00	319.22	326.17
Semi/Finished	422.95	488.99	535.06	539.19	589.61	555.75	503.02	465.44	571.43	635.89
Sy. Debtors	920.50	1144.35	1335.77	1256.08	1271.34	1182.65	1279.31	1073.66	958.47	651.30
Loans and Adv	405.57	558.78	816.41	672.36	604.78	704.18	785.21	780.84	1160.67	1931.69
Interest Receivable	0.26	5.16	7.29	3.97	1.46	0.05	0.09	0.10	2.89	0.20
Total Current Assets	2348.09	3237.29	3451.25	3420.14	3230.28	3025.11	3225.61	3095.39	3648.10	4083.01

Current Liabilities										
Sy. Creditors	1104.23	1169.09	1152.99	1269.86	1245.41	1334.34	1582.96	1511.64	1746.29	1997.14
Security and Other Deposits	91.40	92.71	106.91	87.00	79.87	111.10	83.40	83.01	95.74	133.59
Others	189.51	64.95	125.41	57.64	137.87	60.01	46.02	72.90	75.46	87.64
Provision	142.83	194.28	280.41	301.37	341.27	322.78	374.75	339.64	773.09	1780.41
Total Current Liabilities	1527.97	1521.03	1665.72	1715.87	1804.42	1828.23	2087.13	2007.19	2690.58	3998.78
Working Capital	820.12	1716.26	1785.53	1704.27	1425.86	1196.88	1138.48	1088.20	957.52	84.23

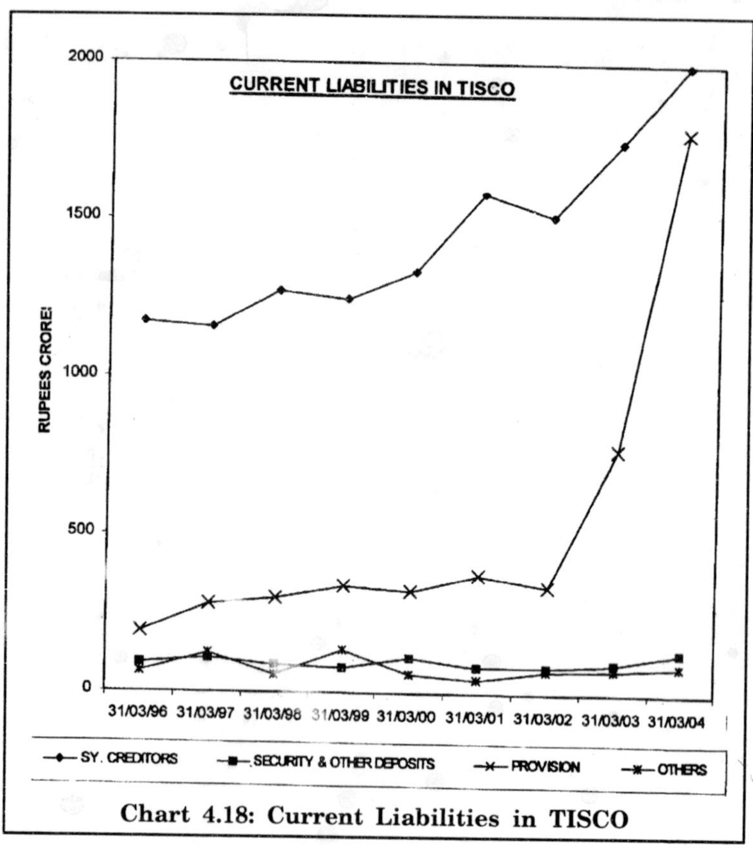

Chart 4.18: Current Liabilities in TISCO

Analysis

Number of days holding for raw material stock, semi finished and finished stock and stores and spares stock have declined over the years, as is clearly evident from the above graph. Semi finished and finished stock has been maintained quite low over the years. This indicates coherence between sales and production plans. A good steel market during the last three years has also helped in rapid reduction in the stock.

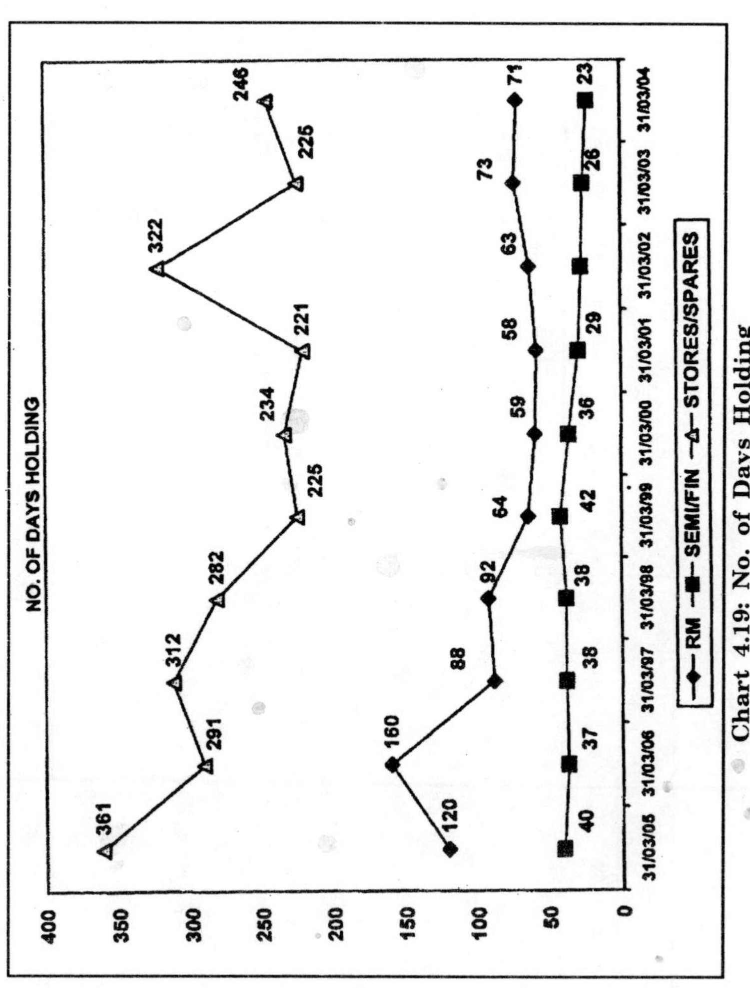

Chart 4.19: No. of Days Holding

Table 4.10: Number of days holding

(Rs. in crores)

	As On									
	31/03/95	31/03/96	31/03/97	31/03/98	31/03/99	31/03/00	31/03/01	31/03/02	31/03/03	31/03/04
RM Stock	231	354	231	253	173	160	179	212	262	287
RM Consmn.	697	798	947	991	972	986	1111	1216	1291	1462
No. of Days	120	160	88	92	64	59	58	63	73	71
Semi + Fin Stock	423	489	535	539	590	556	503	465	571	636
Cost of Goods Sold	3799	4773	5120	5165	5056	5539	6260	6145	8025	9954
C/G Stk	423	489	535	539	590	556	503	465	571	636
O/G Stk	438	423	489	535	539	590	556	503	465	571
Cost of Prodn	3814	4707	5074	5161	5006	5573	6313	6183	7919	9890
No. of Days	40	37	38	38	42	36	29	27	26	23
Stores/Spares	227	249	274	266	254	229	239	344	319	326
Stores/Spares Consmn.	226	309	316	339	406	352	391	385	511	478
No. of Days	361	291	312	282	225	234	221	322	225	246

RAW MATERIAL HOLDING (NO. OF DAYS)

	31/03/96	31/03/97	31/03/98	31/03/99	31/03/00	31/03/01	31/03/02	31/03/03	31/3/2004
TISCO	160	88	92	64	59	58	63	73	71
SAIL	70	54	58	45	52	43	40	45	30
RSP	48	52	32	22	31	23	26	26	18

Raw material holding is the least in case of RSP. It was very high during 1996-97. Since then there has been a continuous decrease in the holding, which is a good sign.

Semi/Finished Stock (No. of Days)

	31/03/96	31/03/97	31/03/98	31/03/99	31/03/00	31/03/01	31/03/02	31/03/03	31/3/2004
TISCO	37	38	38	42	36	29	27	26	23
SAIL	104	159	176	116	58	74	60	44	31
RSP	92	153	246	156	67	115	91	60	26

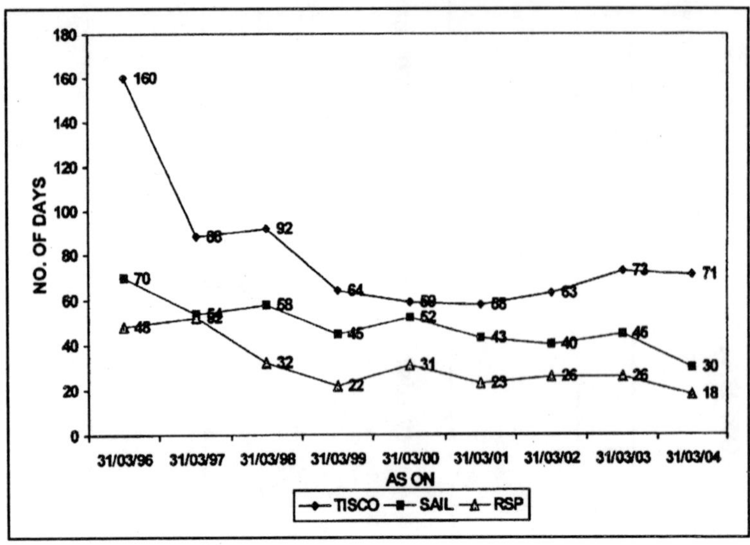

Chart 4.20: Comparison: RSP, SAIL and TISCO

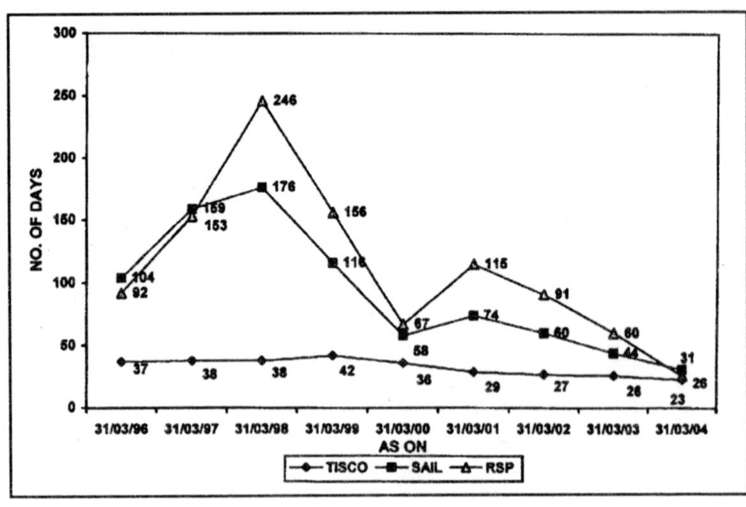

Chart 4.21: Semi/Finished Material Holding (No. of Days)

Semi-finished and finished stock holding is high in case of RSP and SAIL. It was very high during the financial years 1997-98, 1998-99 and 2001-02. Number of days stock holding in RSP was higher than that of SAIL. This was because of poor market condition and may be due to mismatch between sales order and production planning, which resulted in specific grades and sizes of products not having immediate marketability. This affected the working capital position of RSP and SAIL to a greater extent.

However the situation started improving from 2002-03 onwards, especially with improvement of steel market. Present No. of days of stock holding is quite comfortable in case of RSP and SAIL, which is closer to that of TSICO too.

TISCO on the other hand could manage the stock holding within a comfortable level of around one month in all these years. It was little high during 1998-99 when market situation was bad. But with proper planning and sustained efforts in the areas of customer satisfaction, quality improvement etc., stock holding could be maintained at a lower level.

Substantial improvement in the inventory holding is observed in case of RSP after 2001-02 due to improvement in quality of products as well as proper production planning and control. This needs to be maintained in future (Table 4.13).

Number of Days Holding of Stores/Spares in RSP is more compared to the average figure of SAIL. However, it is less compared to TISCO and there is also signs of improvement over the years. Still there is lot of scope for improvement in this area. The comfortable level should be one month holding, though the ideal number is zero (just in time). But, since some quantities of spares are required in the stock to take care of break down and emergency situations, zero holding is practically not possible.

To reduce the number of days of holding from the present 6 months to even 3 months, emphasis on further reduction in average processing time of indents, vendor development, proper spares requirement planning to avoid creating non moving stock may be given.

Stores/Spares Stock (No. of Days)

	31/03/96	31/03/97	31/03/98	31/03/99	31/03/00	31/03/01	31/03/02	31/03/03	31/03/04
TISCO	291	312	282	225	234	221	322	225	246
SAIL	271	268	258	257	215	203	201	183	167
RSP	294	274	233	277	251	209	239	199	192

SUMMARY

The RSP can set an optimistic target for itself, which could be as follows:

Item	Target (No. Of Days)	Present Position (No. of Days)
Raw Material	15	34
Semi/Finished	15	25
Stores/Spares	30	200

The company has decreased the holding period considerably over the years. Input raw material stock though is quite high in 2004-05 due to imported coal problem; in the previous yeas the figures were under control. However there is a scope for improvement in the areas of Semi/Finished inventory and Stores/Spares inventory.

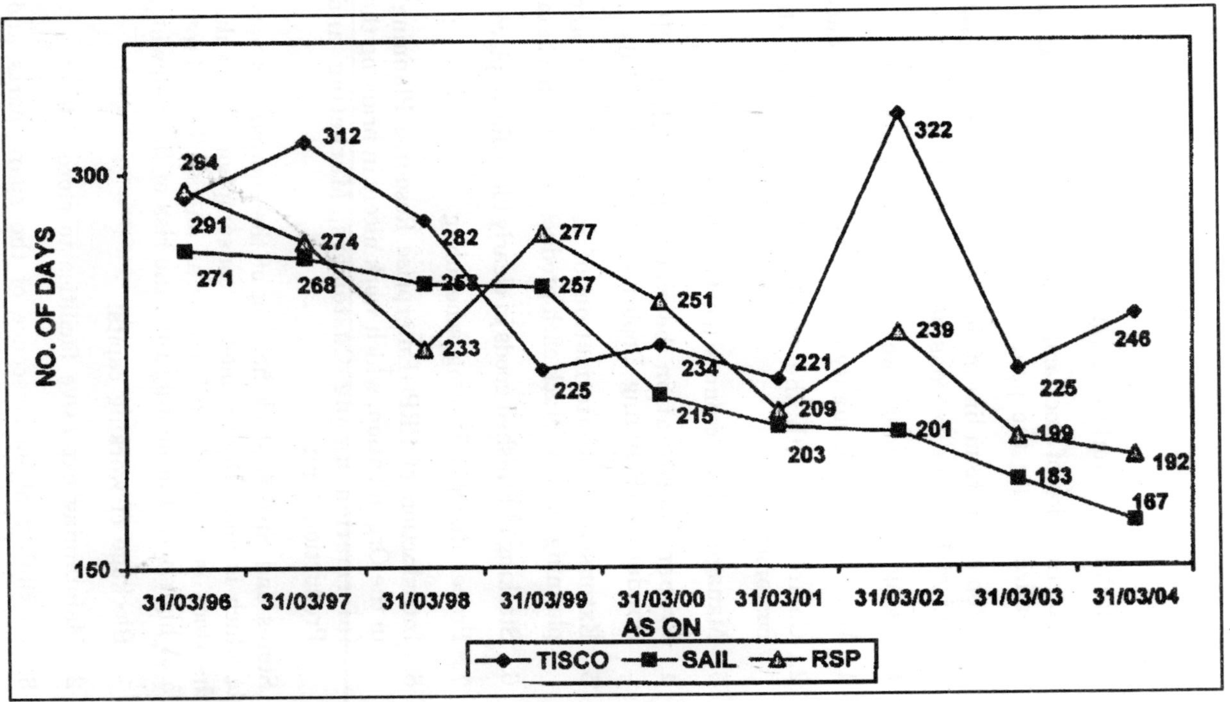

Chart 4.22: Stores/Spares Holding (No. of Days)

Semi/Finished inventory value is quite high for the company. It is in the range of Rs. 212 crores. This needs to be brought under control. Maintaining a high inventory runs the risk of:

1. Blockage of working capital.
2. Deterioration of stock and consequent decline in market realization for the product.

Thus top and bottom line of the company gets hit severely on account of both the reasons as cited above.

Following action plants can improve the situation:

1. Improvement in quality and packaging of the product.
2. Compliance with the specifications given by the customers.
3. Managing key accounts (customers) properly.
4. Proper coordination between marketing, PPC (Production Planning Department) and the Mills.
5. Extensive computerization of material flow and planning, so as to track each product in its value chain.
6. Stacking of Finished goods in clearly identifiable places.
7. Proper dispatch/loading scheduling.
8. Introduction of ERP (Enterprise Resource Planning) in the Organization, which work nicely in bridging the information among Customers, Marketing and Production Units.

Stores and Spares stock holding of the company is very high, which is more than 6 months consumption. The value of the stock is about Rs. 167 crores as on the 31st March, 2005. A high period of holding runs the risk of the following,

1. Blockage of working capital.
2. Maintaining extensive facilities to store this.
3. Possibility of obsolescence of the spare parts and consequential rejection of the items

All of the above will have a telling effect on the profitability of the company.

The company may look forward to a considerable improvement in this regard. At present due to the revision of the guidelines of the company regarding identification of non-moving /obsolete spares, provisions are being made towards these categories of spares for partial write off of value each year. However there is a need to arrest the generation of such stocks in future.

Emphasis on the following action points can ease the situation:

1. Reduction of lead-time between indenting and receipt of the material in the stores. This is possible if the user departments do proper planning before indenting.
2. RSP may adopt Supply Chain Management in the company for procurement of stores and spares. Key vendors can be identified; long-term relationship is to be developed with them. The objective is to receive quality spares at short notice.
3. RSP can improve its preventive maintenance and house keeping activities further so as to achieve zero breakdowns in the shops. This will not only reduce the requirement of spare parts by the shops but also will give quality time to concentrate on proper planning for procurement of materials for future requirement.

FINANCIAL STATEMENT ANALYSIS OF RSP

Analysis of Financial Statement of RSP, SAIL and TISCO reveals the strength and weaknesses of the companies. The Profit and Loss Accounts and Balance-sheets are analyzed in details and the behaviours of the key factors like net profit, operating profit, net worth, reserve and surplus, Capital employed etc. have been captured. Data relating to these factors are tabulated and analyzed below:

Rourkela Steel Plant

Data for past 10 years for RSP are tabulated and analyzed in Table 4.11.

The pattern appearing in case of RSP in the chart above is more or less similar to that of its group company SAIL, which is shown in the next pages. Depreciation kept on increasing from the year 1995-96 to 1998-99 on account of capitalization of new assets commissioned through modernization in the various production units of RSP. Major capitalization of modernized units took place in the year 1998-99. Depreciation increased by about 102% during that period compared to the previous year, which is evident from the above graph. There after depreciation remained almost steady. This indicated that major capitalization of commissioned capital schemes took place in the year 1998-99 and after that capital investment in the various production units has been negligible.

Interest was also on an increasing tend from 1995-96 to 1998-99. The increase in the interest amount between 1998-99 and 1995-96 was Rs. 314 crores, an increase of 157%. The increase in 1998-99 over 1997-98 was a whopping 54%. This was on account of more borrowing during this period for funding the on-going capital projects in various production units of RSP. However, there after the interest burden gradually declined, which is evident form the above graph. This reduction in interest has taken place in different periods due to various reasons. Interest reduced by 21% during 1999-00 over 1998-99 on account of waiver of a major chunk of SDF loan utilized in the modernization of the plants, as a part of the Financial Restructuring approved by the Government of India. Interest also reduced between 2000-01 and 2002-03. This was on account of repayment of costly loans with the help of cheaper loans from the market. After 2002-03, there has been a steady decline in the interest between 30 to 40% during 2003-04 and 2004-05 over the previous years. This has happened owing to a better steel market during that time, which resulted in an improved profit and cash position for the company. In these years, the company managed to pay the debt repayment obligation from its own fund. Thus total

Table 4.11: Data for past 10 years for RSP

	1995-96	1996-97	1997-98	1998-99	1999-00	2000-01	2001-02	2002-03	2003-04	2004-05
PBDIT	238	86	86	5	-34	281	-367	52	421	1472
Interest	200	282	333	514	405	444	390	365	256	151
Depreciation	95	120	127	256	265	282	279	280	274	276
Tax	0	0	0	0	0	0	0	0	0	0
Pat	-57	-316	-374	-765	-704	-445	-1036	-593	-109	-1045
Equity Capital	490	490	490	490	490	490	490	490	490	490
Reserve/Surplus	260	-34	-380	-1177	-1960	-2383	-3445	-4028	-4111	-3057
Net Worth	**750**	**456**	**110**	**-687**	**-1470**	**-1893**	**-2955**	**-3538**	**-3621**	**-2567**
Capital Employed	2567	3122	3866	6171	4990	4842	4484	4176	3774	3890
Borrowings	2100	2496	2700	3244	1519	1582	1349	1495	1577	900

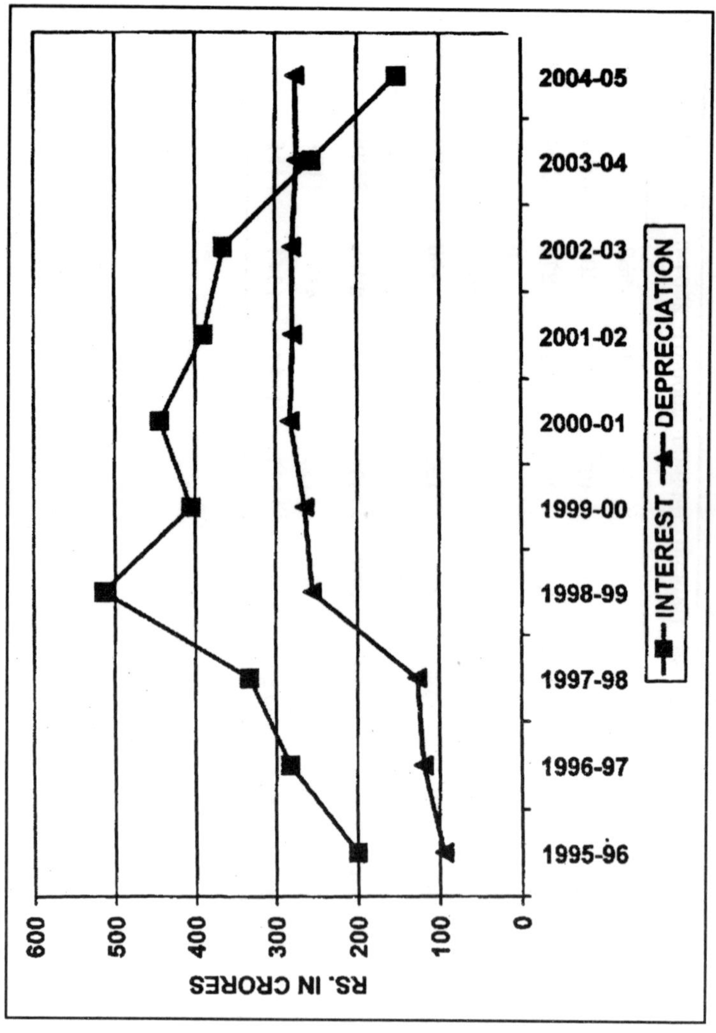

Chart 4.23: Interest and Depreciation Trend

outstanding borrowings have been reduced drastically during this period too.

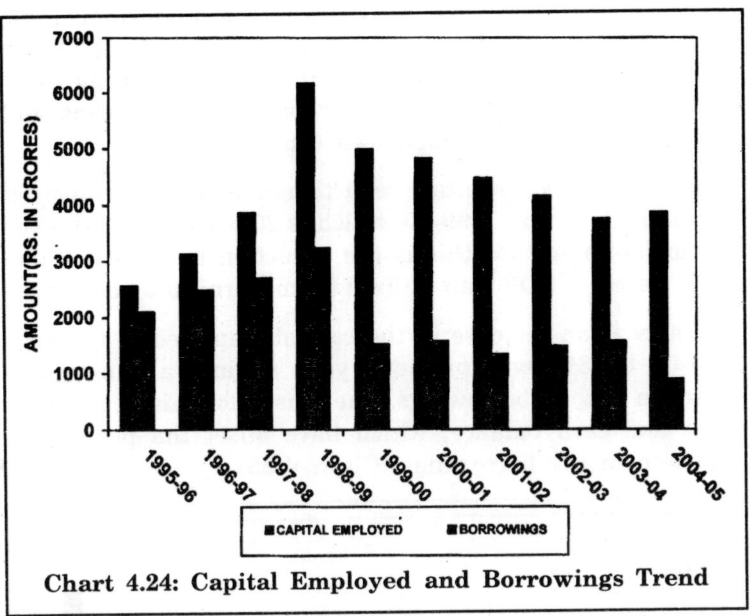

Chart 4.24: Capital Employed and Borrowings Trend

The total borrowings and capital employed are plotted in the form of a bar chart 4.24. It is evident that the capital employed trend follows the trend in the total borrowings for the company in all other years except 2004-05.

There has been an increase in the figures up to the year 1998-99. There after there is a gradual decline in capital employed till 2003-04. During this time total borrowings figures are almost steady. In the year 2004-05 borrowings have reduced, but the capital employed has increased. These are analyzed in details below.

The increase in total borrowings and capital employed between 1995-96 and 1998-99 is attributed to more funding for the on going capital schemes in various Departments of RSP through borrowings and increase in net block due to capitalization of new assets.

Percentage reduction in the total borrowings is quite high during 1999-00. This was on account of waiver of SDP loan utilized for modernization activities in the production units, as a part of the financial restructuring process for SAIL. There was also about 40% reduction in total borrowings during 2004-05. The reason for this is, better profit for the plant and repayment of loans through own fund.

Similarly, the percentage reduction in the Capital employed is quite high during 1999-00, which is 20% over the last year. The major reason for this is the reduction in net block due to the waiver of SDF loan utilized for modernization activities.

There is an increase in the capital employed in the year 2004-05 by 3% over previous year against a substantial reduction in total borrowings. The reason for this is, a higher profit and cash balance, which have offset the percentage reduction in the borrowings (Chart 4.25).

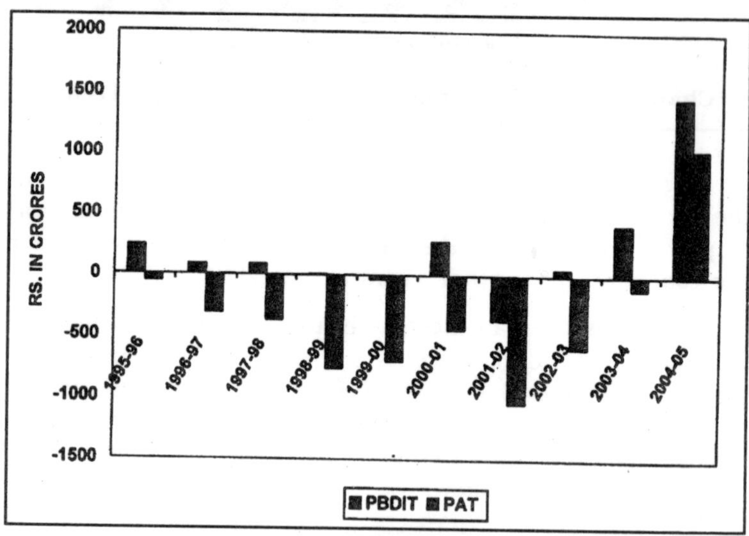

Chart 4.25: Profit Trend

Profit Before Depreciation, Interest and Tax (PBDIT) has been positive for the company in all other years except 1999-00 and 2001-02. However these figures were low between 1995-96 and 2002-03. PBDIT for the years 1998-99, 1999-00 and

2001-02 were very low. With improvement of steel market from 2002-03 and reduction in interest, PBDIT started increasing from 2002-03 on wards and so also the net profit (PAT). In the year 2004-05, PBDIT increased considerably by 250% over 2003-04 and net profit (PAT) achieved an impressive Rs. 1045 crores. This has been possible due to a good market (domestic as well as international) through out the year, better cash realization, lower interest, economy of scale and improved capacity utilization (Chart 4.26).

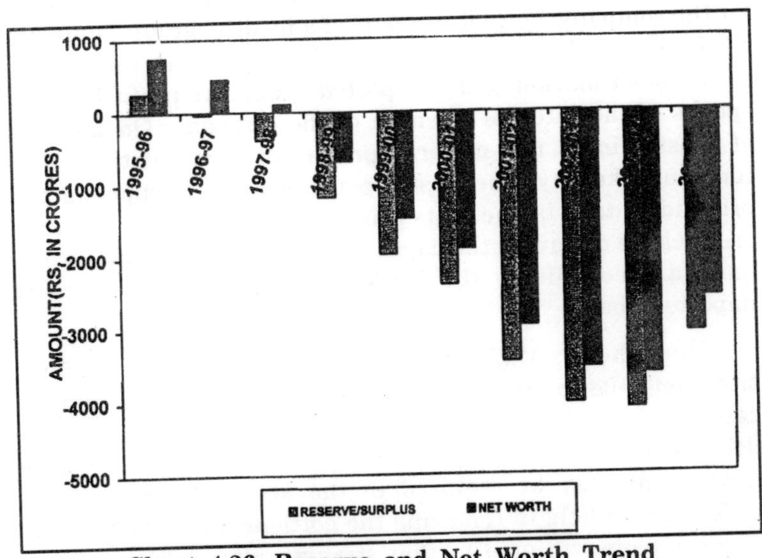

Chart 4.26: Reserve and Net Worth Trend

Reserves started depleting after 1996-97 and the trend continued till 2003-04. This has been negative since 1996-97, which started eroding the share capital and from 1998-99 on wards, Net worth of the firm also became negative. The firm has borne huge losses from 1998-99 till 2002-03. Bottom line started looking up fro, 2003-04 on wards. Loss of the firm got substantially reduced during 2003-04 and there has been a huge Net Profit for the firm during 2004-05. But this is not sufficient to wipe out the accumulated losses of the firm. At the end of the Financial Year 2004-05, Reserve and Surplus as well as Net worth of the firm are still negative. However there has been am improvement of 26% in Reserve/Surplus and 29% in the Net worth of the firm during the Financial Year 2004-05 as compared to the previous year. The firm needs to make Net profit at this rate for few more years to be able to achieve positive Net worth.

Summary

Looking at the risk factor of the Firm, it can be seen that in spite of having a negative Net worth, there is no threat for the company, since it is a part of a healthy group company, SAIL. The company has shown resilience during the upturn in the steel market and has posted a healthy profit level. It speaks of the internal strength of the company. On the face of a rising input raw material prices in the recent times, the company like any other sister plant of SAIL is enjoying the price advantage in one of its principal raw materials, i.e. Iron ore because of having the captive mines. However, the bottom line has been hit by the increase in procurement price of imported coal.

Step ahead: Major Weakness of the Firm in today's situation is its capacity and capacity utilization. The company can try to achieve 100% capacity utilization through debottlenecking in the logistics and planning processes. A little investment may be required in the areas of technological difficulties to help in removing the bottlenecks in the process. The company will gain further strength after achieving this. It may also try to augment its capacity at least by 100% to secure its viability in the form of an individual integrated steel plant in the future. The investment for capacity expansion need to be financed mostly from the current and future profits of the company (i.e. from internal accruals of SAIL). At the same time, timely project execution and implementation also play a vital role in the success of the Firm.

SAIL

Data for past 10 years for SAIL are tabulated and analyzed in Table 4.12.

Table 4.12: Data for past 10 years for SAIL

	1995-96	1996-97	1997-98	1998-99	1999-00	2000-01	2001-02	2002-03	2003-04	2004-05
PBDIT	2712	2461	2498	1547	1202	2167	1011	2177	4652	11097
Interest	808	1179	1554	2017	1789	1752	1562	1334	899	605
Depreciation	585	691	795	1104	1133	1144	1156	1147	1123	1127
Tax	0	76	16	0	0	0	0	0	118	2548
Pat	1319	515	133	-1574	-1720	-729	-1707	-304	2512	6817
Equity Capital	4130	4130	4130	4130	4130	4130	4130	4130	4130	4130
Reserve/Surplus	3807	3868	4359	2756	635	34	-1878	-2141	529	5881
Net Worth	**7937**	**7988**	**8489**	**6886**	**4765**	**4164**	**2252**	**1989**	**4659**	**10011**
Capital Employed	**21950**	**24993**	**27787**	**27415**	**20580**	**19486**	**17611**	**16920**	**15599**	**20430**
Borrowings	**14574**	**17421**	**20015**	**21018**	**15083**	**14250**	**14019**	**12928**	**8689**	**5770**

The various elements in the above tables have been plotted in the graphs shown in the next pages and their behaviours have been analyzed.

Depreciation kept on increasing from the year 1995-96 to 1998-99 steadily on account of capitalization of new assets commissioned through modernization in the various plants units of SAIL. The depreciation figure during 1998-99 was Rs. 1104 crores, a growth of 89% over 1995-96. There after it remained almost steady. This indicates that major capitalization of commissioned capital schemes took place between the year 1995-96 and 1998-99. After that capital investment in the various plants have been negligible (Chart 4.27).

Interest also increased from 1995-96 to 1998-99 by Rs. 1209 crores, an increase of 150% over 1995-96. This is on account of more borrowings during this period for funding the on-going capital projects in various plant units of SAIL. There after the interest burden gradually declined, which is evident from the above graph. This reduction in interest has taken place in different periods due to various reasons. It reduced by 11% during 1999-00 over 1998-99 on account of waiver of a major chunk of SDF loan utilized in the modernization of the plants, as a part of the Financial Restructuring approved by the Government of India. Interest also reduced by 11% between 2000-01 and 2001-02, 15% between 2001-02 and 2002-03. This was on account of repayment of costly loans with the help of cheaper loans from the market. After 2002-03, there has been a steady decline in the interest by 33% during 2003-04 and 2004-05 over the last years. This has happened owing to a better market situation, which resulted in an improved profit and cash position for the company. In these years, the company managed to pay the debt repayment obligation from its own fund. Thus total outstanding borrowings have been reduced drastically during this period.

The total borrowings and capital employed figures are plotted in the form of a bar chart above. It is seen that the capital employed trend followed the borrowings trend except in the year 2004-05. There is an increase in the pattern up

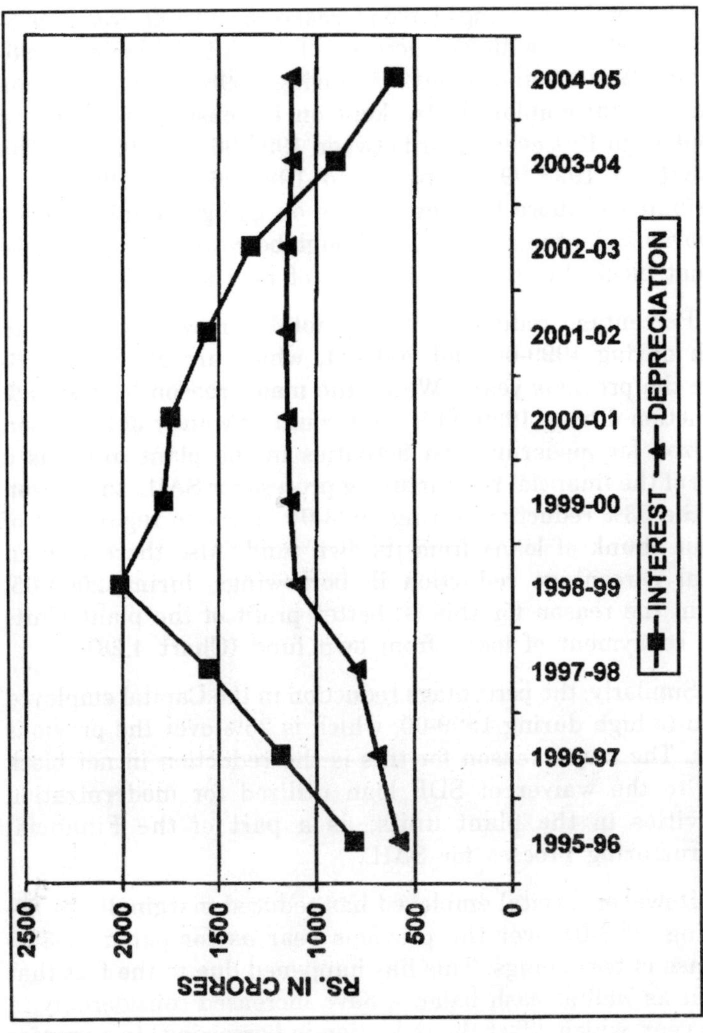

Chart 4.27: Interest and Depreciation Trend

to the year 1998-99. After that, there is a gradual decline in both the figures till 2003-04. In 2004-05 while there is a reduction in borrowings, the capital employed has increased. These have been analyzed in details below.

The total borrowings have increased by 44% between 1995-96 and 1998-99 with an increase of 15 to 20% during 1996-97 and 1997-98 and about 5% during 1998-99. At the same time Capital employed also kept on increasing at a pace of about 10 to 15% every year between 1995-96 and 1997-98. The growth in 1998-99 compared to 1995-96 and 1998-99 is attributed to more funding for the on going capital schemes in various plant units of SAIL through borrowings and increase in net block due to capitalization of new assets.

Percentage reductions in the total borrowings are quite high during 1999-00 and 2003-04, which are 28% and 33% over the previous years. While, the major reason for the 28% reduction during 1999-00 is on account of waiver of SDF loan utilized for modernization activities in the plant units as a part of the financial restructuring process for SAIL, the reason for the 33% reduction during 2003-04 is due to repayment of major chunk of loans from its own fund. Also there was an equal percentage reduction in borrowings during 2004-05. Again the reason for this is, better profit of the plant Units and repayment of loans from own fund (Chart 4.28).

Similarly, the percentage reduction in the Capital employed is quite high during 1999-00, which is 25% over the previous year. The major reason for this is the reduction in net block due to the waiver of SDF loan utilized for modernization activities in the plant units, as a part of the Financial restructuring process for SAIL.

However, capital employed has reduced marginally by 8% during 2003-04 over the previous year as compared to 33% in case of borrowings. This has happened due to the fact that profit as well as cash balance have increased considerably in this year, which offset the reduction in borrowings to a greater extent. There was also an increase of 31% in capital employed during 2004-05 over previous year against a substantial reduction in total borrowings. The reason for this is again a

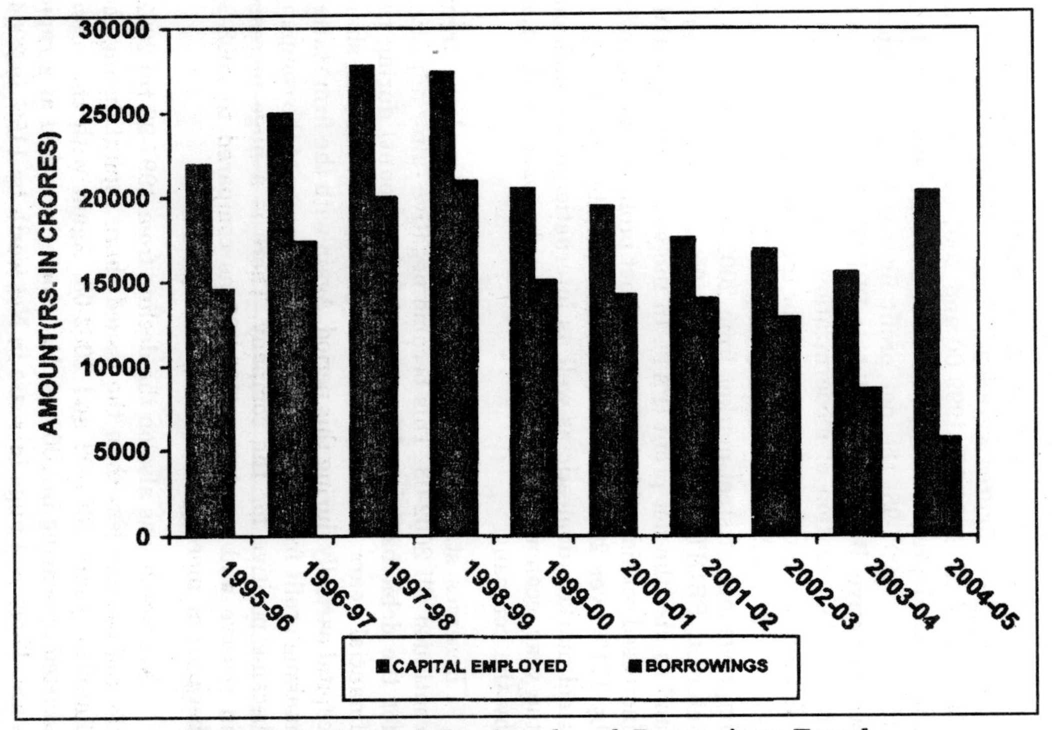

Chart 4.28: Capital Employed and Borrowings Trend

higher profit and cash balance during that year, which have offset the percentage reduction in the borrowings (Chart 4.29).

Profit Before Depreciation, Interest and Tax (PBDIT) has been positive for the company in these 10 years period. However these figures were low between 1995-096 and 2002-03. PBDIT for 1998-99, 1999-00 and 2001-02 were very low. Since the depreciation and interest burdens were less from 1995-96 to 1997-98, the net profit figures for the company were positive. But with the slide in PBDIT after that and with major capitalization of modernization facilities along with a high interest burden, the net loss for the Company from 1998-99 to 2001-02 become very high. However, with the improvement of steel market from 2002-03 and reduction in interest, PBDIT started increasing from 2002-03 on wards and so also the net profit (PAT). In the year 2004-05, PBDIT increased considerably by 139% and net profit (PAT) improved by 171% over 2003-04. This has been possible due to a good steel market (domestic as well as international) through out the year, economy of scale and improved capacity utilization by the company.

Reserves started depleting after 1997-98 and the trend continued till 2002-03. This became negative (after adjusting for the debit balance of profit and loss account) during the financial years 2001-02, 2002-03 and thus eroded the share capital partially during this period. Again with the firm started making profit from, 2003-04 onwards, reserves of the company became positive for the company. There is a huge increase in reserve and surplus in 2004-05 as compared to 2003-04 because of more profit during that year.

Net worth was also on the decline from 1997-98 till 2002-03 and became less than the issued share capital during the financial years 2001-02 and 2002-03. Again with the profit started appearing in 2003-04, Net worth increased at a rapid pace. There is a huge increase in Net worth by 115% in 2004-05 as compared to 2003-04 (Chart 4.30).

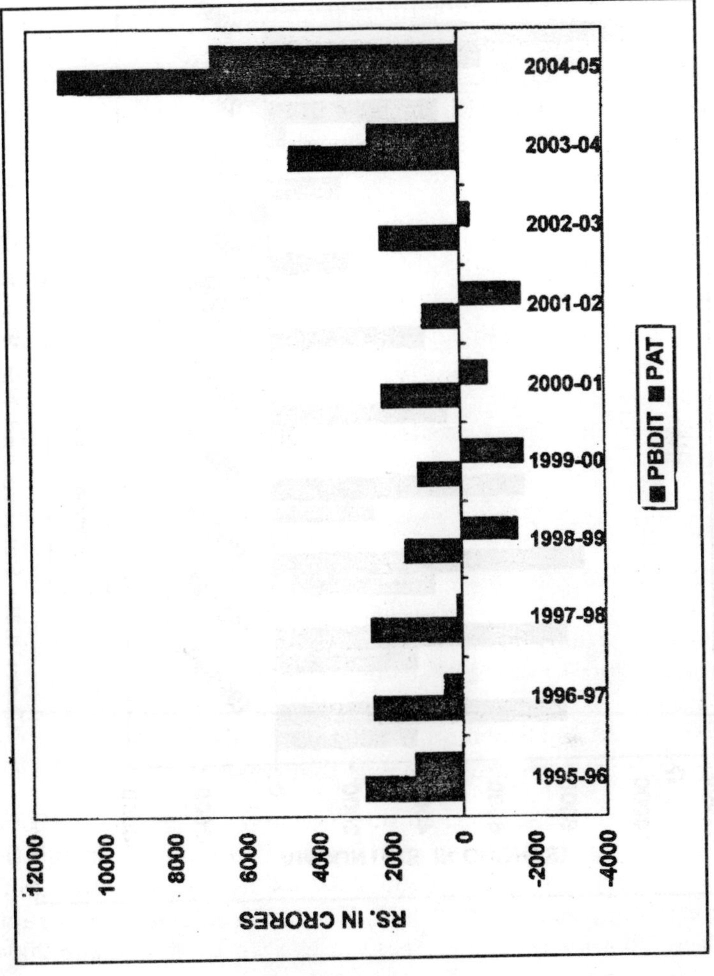

Chart 4.29: Profit Trend

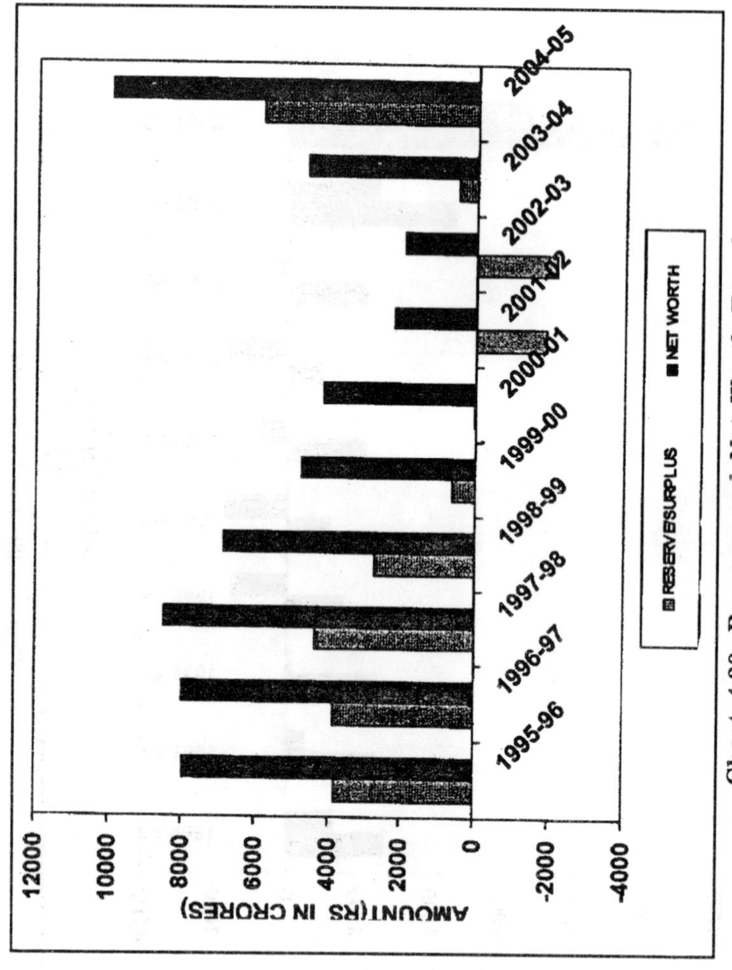

Chart 4.30: Reserve and Net Worth Trend

Summary

The parent company SAIL had difficult times from 1998-99 to 2001-02, during which the capitalization impact of new assets affected the accounts coupled with a slow down in the steel market resulting in increasing losses for the company.

However, the aggressive cost control measures taken by the management across all the SAIL Units during this time has yielded huge savings for the company. SAIL was also awarded by ICWAI in recognition of the cost control steps taken by it. Apart from this, better loan management, improved domestic as well as international steel market, economy of scale, captive iron ore mines, better capacity utilization and reduction in inventory have helped the company in improving the bottom line drastically. Today, SAIL is a vibrant, forward-looking company with a clean balance sheet.

Step ahead: With the boom in the steel sector still continuing, there is a mad rush of big steel companies to start new steel making facilities attached with captive mines as well as to consolidate steel strength through mergers and acquisitions. Steel sector in India being totally open, competition in future will be quite fierce. SAIL is the largest manufacturer of steel today in the country having captive iron ore mines. The company has to take bold steps in the areas of capacity expansion and more importantly expansion in the field of mining. The company should also explore possibilities of acquiring coalmines abroad or forming strategic partnership with them so as to maintain uninterrupted supply of imported metallurgical coal to the plant units. However, in the process of doing this, which requires a lot of capital outflow, SAIL should look at an optimum capital structure without sacrificing the health of the balance sheet much.

TISCO

Data for past 10 years for SAIL are tabulated and analyzed in Table 4.13.

Table 4.13: Data for past 10 years for SAIL

	1995-96	1996-97	1997-98	1998-99	1999-00	2000-01	2001-02	2002-03	2003-04	2004-05
PBDIT	1143	1143	966	999	1264	1471	1146	2122	4313	6045
Interest	279	274	260	302	360	377	370	305	122	129
Depreciation	298	327	343	382	427	492	525	555	625	619
Tax	0	73	41	33	54	49	46	250	920	1823
Pat	566	469	322	282	423	553	205	1012	1746	3474
Equity Capital	368	368	368	368	518	508	368	368	369	554
Reserve/Surplus	3206	3328	3681	3763	3999	4343	3078	2818	3991	7300
Net Worth	3574	3696	4049	4131	4517	4851	3446	3186	4360	7800
Capital Employed	7417	7778	8628	9070	9424	9523	9545	9696	10136	12500
Borrowings	3842	4083	4579	4938	4907	4672	4708	4226	3373	2500

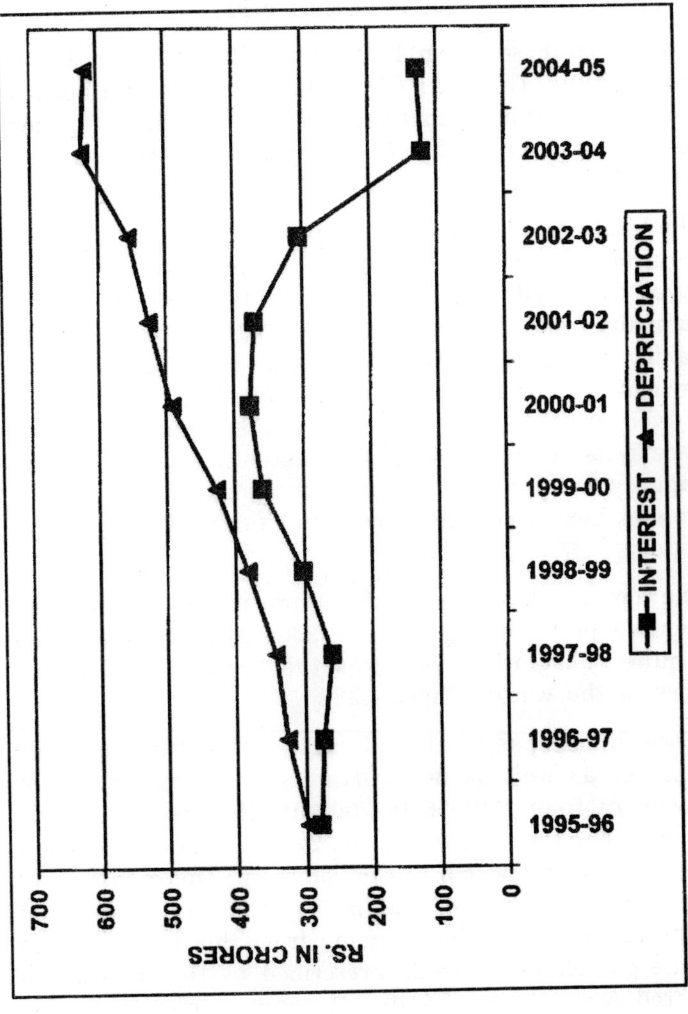

Chart-4.31: Interest and Depreciation Trend

Depreciation kept on increasing from the year 1995-96 till 2003-04 steadily. This is due to capitalization of new assets in the process of expansion and modernization in phases. The depreciation figure during 2004-05 is Rs. 619 crores, a growth of 108% compared to 1995-96 (Chart 4.31).

Interest increased from 1998-99 to 2000-01. After that it started declining. There is a 60% reduction in interest burden in the year 2003-04 as compared to 2002-03. This has happened due to a substantial reduction in the borrowings of the company (Chart 4.31).

The total borrowings and capital employed are plotted in the form of a bar Chart 4.32. It is evident that the capital employed trend follows the trend in the total borrowings for the company from 1995-96 to 1999-00. After that, it is on an increasing trend contrary to a falling trend in the total borrowings. This is because the company has been making profit every year. Its increase in reserve is more than that of decrease in the total borrowings from 2000-01 to 2004-05. Thus the capital employed is found to be on an increasing path all these years. Increase is quite substantial during 2004-05 (Chart 4.32).

The company has been making profit all these years. The jump in net profit during 2002-03, 2003-04 and 2004-05 has been quite substantial. This was the time of Steel sector recovery in the world (Chart 4.33).

Since the company has made net profits all these years, its reserves as well as net worth have shown a trend of improvement from 1995-96 to 2000-01. However, there has been a slump in the reserves during 2001-02 and a consequent decrease in the net worth of the company. The reduction in the reserves is because of making deferred tax provision of Rs. 1390.35 crores for the company from this in accordance with the guidelines of AS-22 prescribed by the Institute of Chartered Accountants of India. It again started increasing after this year (Chart 4.34).

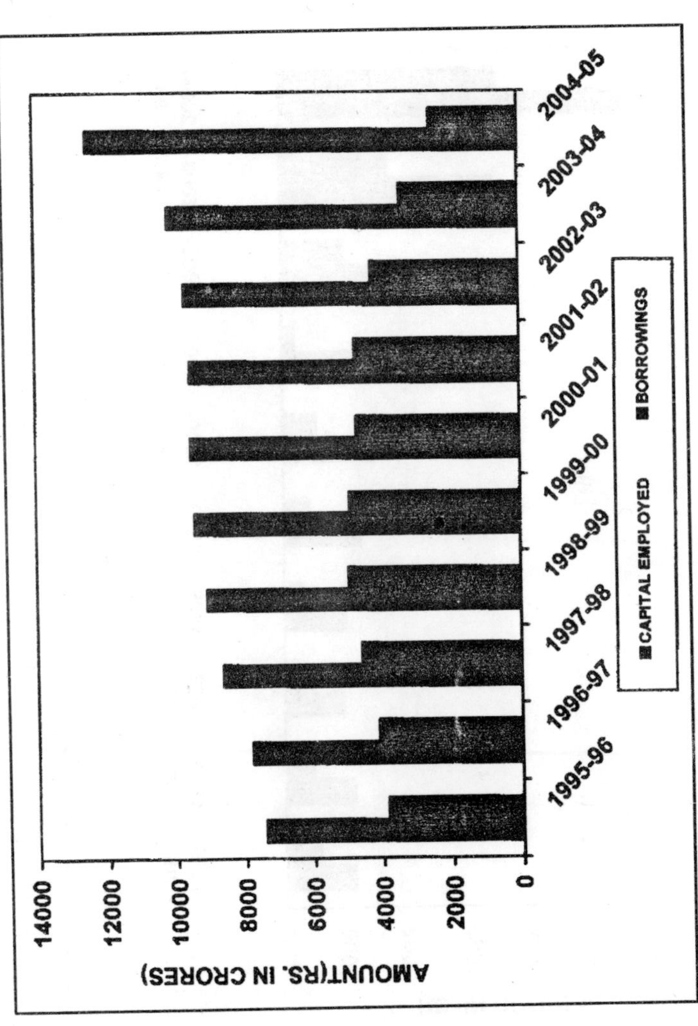

Chart 4.32: Capital Employed and Borrowings Trend

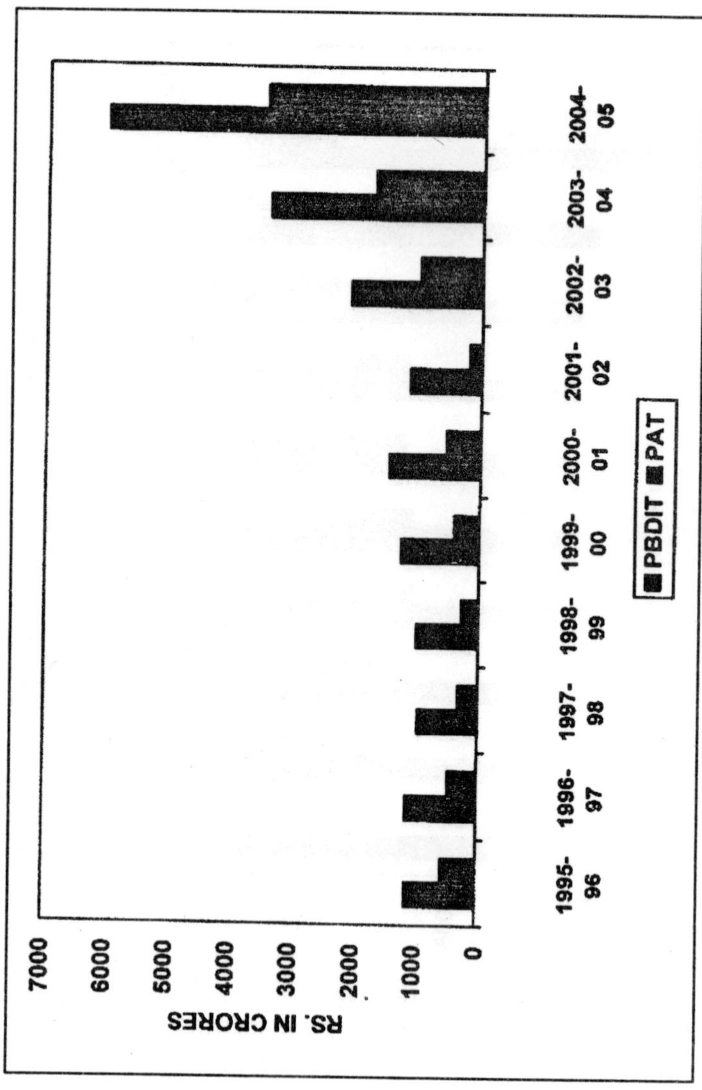

Chart 4.33: Profit Trend

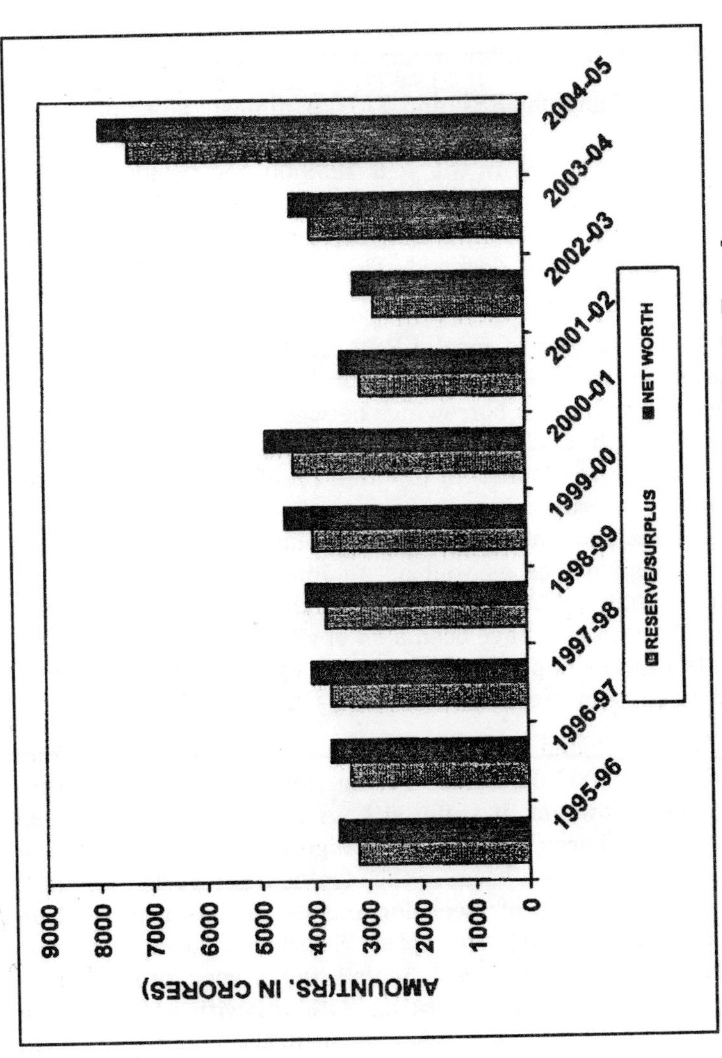

Chart 4.34: Reserve and Net Worth Trend

Summary of Analysis

Capital Employed and Borrowings trend for TISCO is quite smooth. While capital employed has slowly increased from 1995-96 to 2004-05, borrowing has increased from 1995-96 to 1999-00 and thereafter it has declined (Chart 4.35).

The pattern for RSP and SAIL is almost the same. There is a steep rise in borrowings as well as capital employed from 1995-96 to 1998-99. In the year 1999-00, the trend has taken a sudden dip and figures continued to decline till 2003-04. In the year 2004-05, capital employed started increasing, whereas borrowing has still declined. This is due to high net profits during that year (Chart 4.36).

The gradients in case of RSP and SAIL are quite high as compared to TISCO. This is because of a huge capital investment through borrowings between 1995-96 and 1998-99 coupled with a slump in the steel market, poor capacity utilization and consequent dip in net profit of the Firms. After financial restructuring, the figures have started improving. Thereafter prudent treasury management, better operations, cost control drives as well as an improvement in the steel market from 2002-03 has reversed the gradient. Thus it is evident that there have been a lot of vibrations in the financial health of the company, which is also, clear from the net profit and net worth trend as shown in Chart 4.37.

The RSP had been making losses all these years from 1995-96 till 2003-04. Losses during 1995-96 and 2003-04 were very less. However, it suffered huge net losses form 1998-99 to 2002-03. There has been a change in the situation in the year 2004-05 with a boom in the steel market world over. RSP got the advantage of steel demand as well as price of Iron ore because of having the captive mines with Group Company SAIL. It has bounced back registering a good profit during this time in spite of achieving 94% capacity utilization in Saleable Steel and 83% capacity utilization in Crude Steel (Chert 4.38).

Net worth of the Firm became negative from 1998-99 on wards. This is the year, in which world steel market started

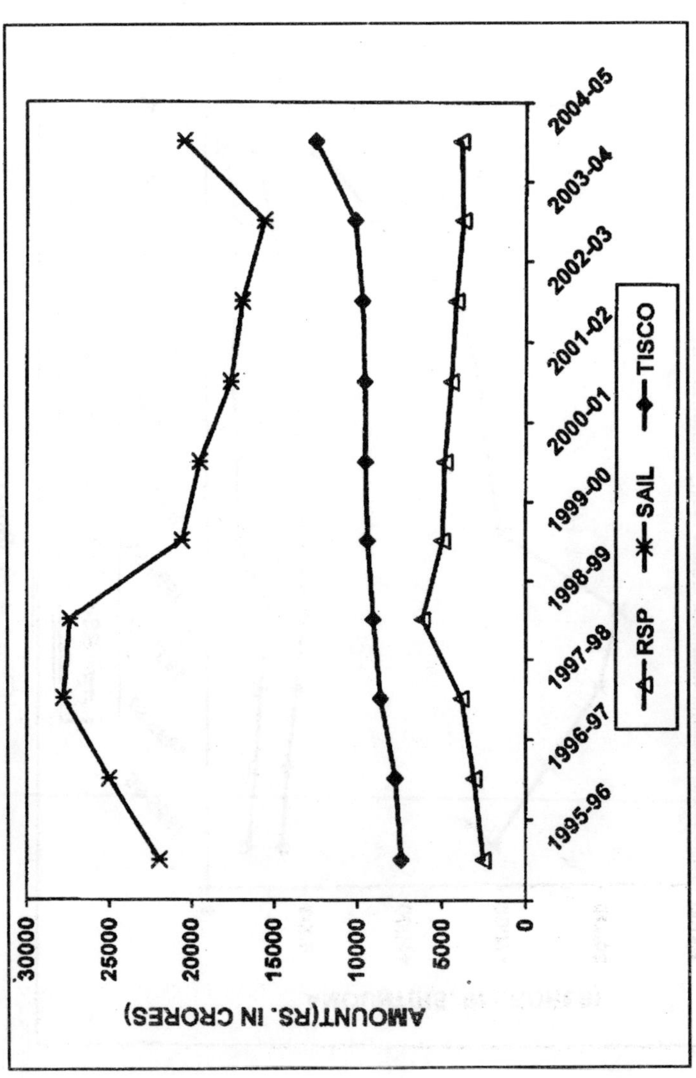

Chart-4.35: Capital Employed

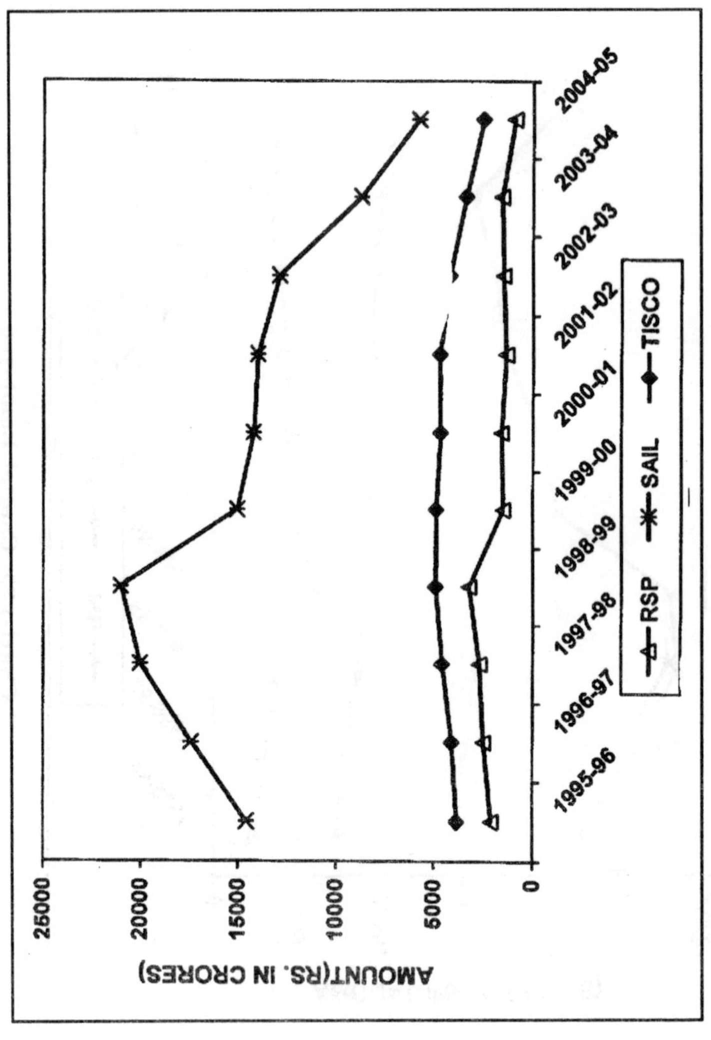

Chart 4.36: Borrowings

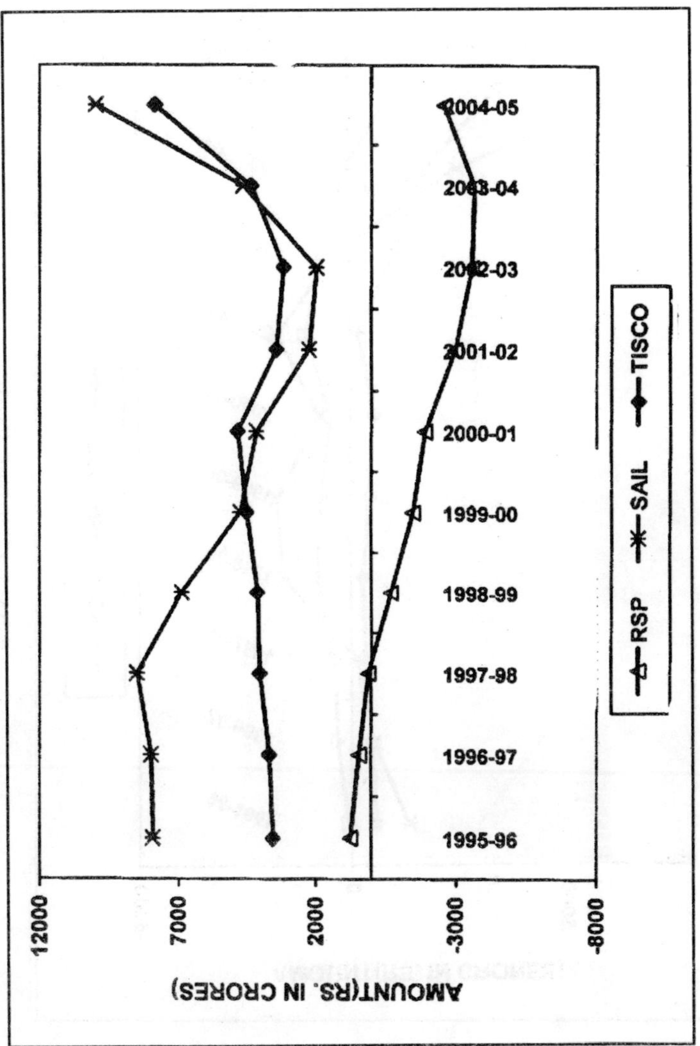

Chart 4.37: Net Worth

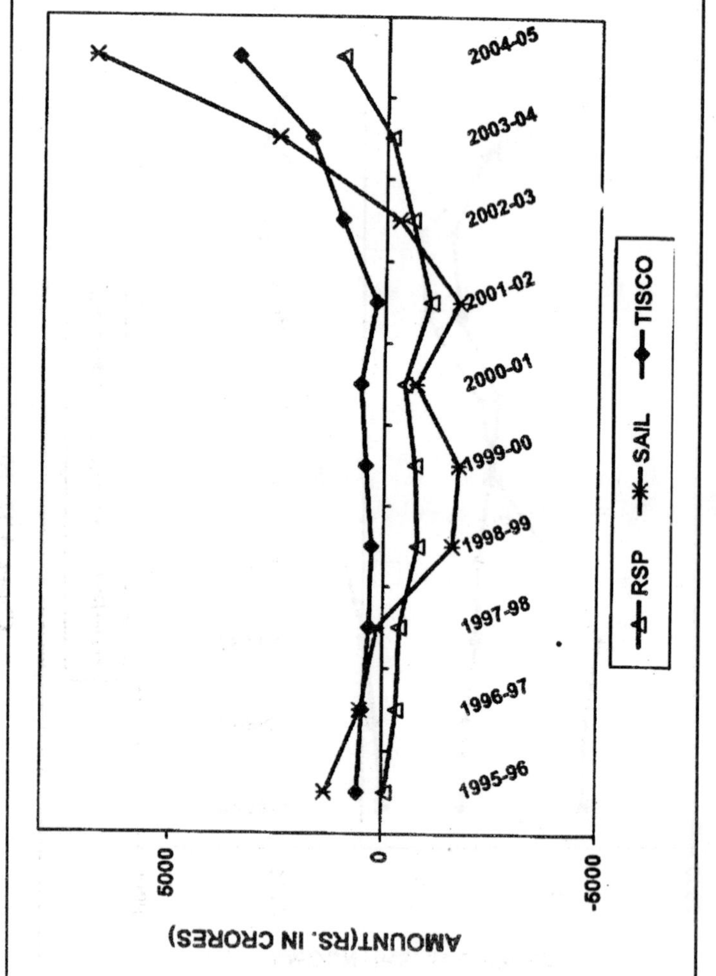

Chart-4.38: Net Profit

slowing down for few years. Steel production was cut by the Steel Producers world over to clear the stockpile and there was continuous stress on the sales price of Steel products from 1998-99 to 2001-02. The net worth as on 31st March, 2005 is also negative for RSP, even if there has been substantial improvement during 2004-05.

At this point of time, in spite of having a negative net worth, the company doesn't have any risk, because of being a part of a healthy group company, SAIL, which is a virtually zero debt company (net of borrowings and cash in hand/Bank).

But to correct its fundamentals and balance sheet, RSP may take some of the aggressive steps:

- Achievement of 100% capacity utilization in crude steel.
- Zero dependence on Inter Plant transfer of semi finished steel materials.
- Improvement of quality of steel products in the down stream mills.
- Proper advertisement and creating dealer network for its special products.
- Reduction in manpower so as to reduce the fixed cost in the long-run.

To achieve 100% capacity utilization as well as quality standards, little investment in required in the coming 2 to 3 years to meet the technical requirements in the shops, mills and related areas.

These are the short-term measures required for viability of the firm for next 2 to 3 years. The firm should be able to make more profit year after year during this time.

However to make the firm vibrant and progressive in future, there needs to be an effort to enhance the capacity from the present level in the long-run. The capacity of the Plant can be doubled from the existing 2.00 million tons of hot metal to 4.00 million tons. The investment for this should be gradual, partly from the accumulated profits and partly from fresh borrowings. Debt to equity ratio needs to be kept under control at any point of time.

BREAK-EVEN ANALYSIS

Introduction

Profit is the most important concern of a Business Organization. All the efforts of the management are geared up towards maximizing profit. The profit element depends on the production volume, sales volume, sales price and product mix for a multi-product firm. So it is very important to understand Break-even sales and production volume for the Organization. This is not a fixed point. This depends on the sales price, input rates, and other fixed expenditures of the firm. Fixed cost plays a vital role in determining the Break-even point of an Organization. It is not really fixed in the organization. This is variable depending the decisions of the management and other situational factors.

The analytical tool used for this is the CVP (Cost, Volume, Profit) analysis. Break-even point analysis is the most popular CVP tool.

With the help of this tool a firm can determine the following for its decision-making:

* Minimum level of sales volume required
* Optimum product mix
* Sales volume and product mix requirement for achieving the target profit.
* New break-even point under the changing sales price, mix, input rate scenario
* New break-even point after plant expansion or modernization
* Profitability potential of the products
* Shut down decision.

The break-even analysis brings relationship between sales revenue and cost with respect to the volume of operation. The volume, which brings equilibrium between sales and cost, is called the break-even point for the firm. This is the point at which the Firm has no profit and no loss situation.

Sales revenue is the reflection of turnover of a company. It is important to study the cost of the firm too. The company derives the cost from the revenue expenditures made in a specified period.

Cost by its nature has two components. They are:

* Variable Cost: It is that cost which varies linearly with Production volume.
* Fixed Cost: It is that cost which remains fixed with respect to changes in the production volume. However, Fixed cost also varies depending on the critical decisions taken by the management or extraneous factors affecting this.

Total Variable Cost is variable with respect to Volume of Production. But Per Unit Variable Cost is constant with respect to Volume of Production. This is shown in Chart 4.39.

Break-even point for a firm will reach when total sales revenue covers the total variable and fixed cost components.

It is very important to calculate and interpret B.E.P. (Break-even point) for a firm. This can be calculated based on two approaches.

- Formula Approach and
- Chart Approach.

Analysis of break-even point in case of Steel sector has been done in details in the next pages using Formula approach.

Break-even point can be indicated in terms of Number of Units, Percentage Capacity or in terms of Sales revenue in Rupee or Dollar.

Per Unit Sales Price of a product covers its own Variable Cost and leaves a remainder, which is known as Contribution. This contribution is supposed to cover the Fixed Cost per Unit of the product to make the product profitable. Going by this concept, it is evident that if per unit contribution is equal to per Unit Fixed Cost of the product, then there is Break-even.

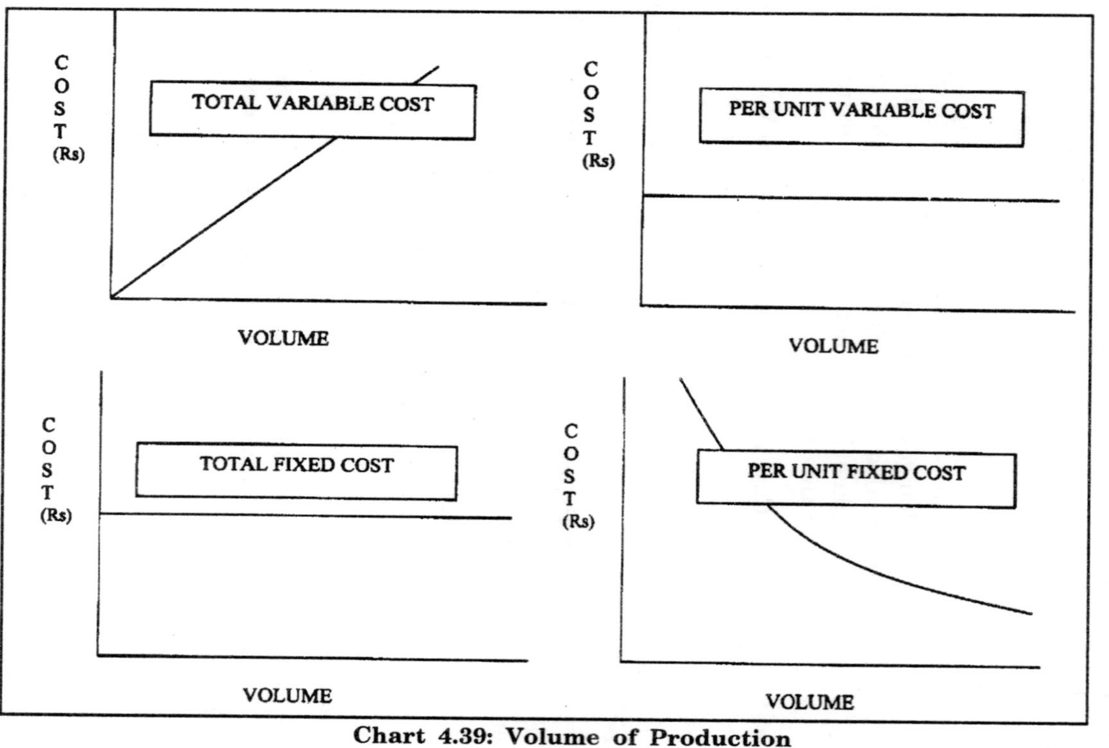

Chart 4.39: Volume of Production

If the firm produces a single product, this volume becomes the B.E.P (Break-even Point) for the firm.

However, if the firm produces multiple products, then this volume becomes the break-even point for that particular product. The Firm has to decide the optimum product mix so as to maximize total contribution. Thus prioritization of production needs to be based on the contribution potential of the products in the basket. Overall Break-even point for a Firm having a multiple product scenario depends on the product mix, which means that with the optimum product mix, B.E.P. will be low and with a bad product mix, B.E.P will be higher.

Unit Selling price – Unit Variable cost = Unit Contribution

Unit Contribution * Units Sold = Total contribution

Total Contribution – Total Fixed Cost = Profit

At the break-even point, profit will be zero. Thus total contribution will be equal to total fixed cost of the firm.

$$\text{B.E.P (Units)} = \frac{\text{Total Fixed Cost}}{(\text{Unit Selling Price} - \text{Unit Variable Cost} = \text{Unit Contribution})}$$

A detailed analysis on Break Even Point for RSP, its parent company SAIL and competitor TISCO is given in the next pages.

METHODOLOGY

The calculation is based on the data collected and tabulated from Annual Profit and Loss Accounts of M/s Steel Authority of India Ltd., M/s Rourkela Steel Plant, M/s Tata Iron and Steel Company Ltd.

Income and Expenditure Data

Tables 4.14, 4.15, 4.16 contain detailed item-wise data from Profit and Loss Accounts of the companies. The grouping and assumptions considered while tabulating data in the table is as follows.

Sales related items are tabulated under Sales group and net sales revenue is calculated after subtracting Excise duty, Freight and stockyard margins (if any appearing separately) from the Turnover of the firm.

Expenditure items are grouped under Variable and Fixed heads. Specific Percentages based on a study have been adopted to break items like Stores and Spares consumption and Employee remuneration and Benefits into Variable and Fixed components. The detail of this is narrated below:

- Variable portion of the Stores and Spares used as operating consumable in the plant is considered at 50% of the total figure appearing in the Profit and Loss Accounts under the head Stores and Spares Consumption. This percentage is based on an item wise study done in case of Rourkela Steel Plant. Operating Consumable Percentage varies from 48 to 53% of the total stores and spares consumption. Thus an average 50% is taken for the following calculation and analysis.
- A major portion of the Employee Remuneration and Benefit is fixed, since almost all the employees of the companies (RSP, SAIL and TISCO) are permanent in nature. The variable portion of the employee remuneration and benefits is mostly on account of Production and productivity related incentive and bonus amounts given to the employees as a motivational tool every month. It is considered at 10% of the total figure appearing in the Profit and Loss Accounts under the head employee remuneration and benefits. This percentage is based on an item wise study done in case of Rourkela Steel Plant. The Percentage varies from 6 to 10% of the Salary paid. The upper band of 10% is considered for calculation purpose.

Abnormal items like Profit on sale of Power Plant and/ or any division of the plant appearing under other revenue in the P/L Account is not considered for calculation. Items not relevant to this calculation like Stock Accretion/Decretion, Prior period adjustments etc. are also not considered.

Net expenditure is calculated after adding all the expenditure items as appearing in Table 4.14, 4.15, 4.16 and subtracting interest earned and other revenue figures from this. Tables 4.14, 4.15, 4.16 are shown in the next pages.

BREAK-EVEN POINT (B.E.P.) CALCULATION

Per Unit Calculation of Net Sales Price, Variable Cost, fixed Cost as well as calculation of Break Even Point (B.E.P) is shown in Tables 4.17, 4.18, 4.19 in the next page.

Saleable Steel Sales quantity, Production quantity and Capacity figures are adopted from the Notes to Accounts of Annual Accounts. Last 10 years figures from Annual Accounts is tabulated in Tables 4.17, 4.18, 4.19

Adjustment for Stock effect due to accretion/decretion of finished and Semi finished inventory of the firm is given to the Variable as well as Fixed Cost. Decretion of Finished stock has a positive impact on the bottom Line of the firm, where as Decretion of Semi-finished stock has a negative impact on the bottom line and *vise versa*. This positive or negative stock impact is given to the variable as well as Fixed Cost in their ratios as appearing in Tables 4.17, 4.18, 4.19. After that adjusted Variable Cost and adjusted Fixed Cost are calculated. Calculation of this is shown in Tables 4.17, 4.18, 4.19.

Per Unit Variable Cost (Rs./Ton) is calculated by dividing Adjusted Variable Expenditure from Tables 4.17, 4.18, 4.19 with Production quantity. Per Unit Contribution (Rs./Ton) is derived by subtracting Unit Variable Cost from Unit Sales Price of Saleable Steel as appearing in Tables 4.17, 4.18, 4.19. Per Unit Sales (Rs./Ton) is calculated by dividing Net sales revenue with Sales quantity.

RSP

Table 4.14: Income and Cost Data

(Rs. in crores)

Items	2004-05	2003-04	2002-03	2001-02	2000-01	1999-00	1998-99	1997-98	1996-97	1995-96
Sales										
Sales turn over (Excl. Chemicals & Scrap)	4635	3694	3001	2175	2321	2433	2189	1941	2055	2335
Less:										
Excise Duty	508	472	415	306	362	312	317	333	328	318
Freight	103	101	108	98	90	76	75	93	83	84
Stock Yard Margin	28	34	38	32	32	28	31	23	21	24
Net Sales Revenue	**3996**	**3086**	**2441**	**1739**	**1837**	**2016**	**1766**	**1493**	**1623**	**1909**
Expenditure										
Variable										
Raw Materials	1277	1176	1132	998	1035	880	966	1071	1148	1147
Variable Portion of Employee Remuneration and Benefits	59	73	56	49	47	42	37	35	34	35
Power and Fuel	297	318	358	303	217	194	238	287	262	224

Operating consumables	150	146	146	116	138	150	169	176	175	168
Total Variable Cost	**1783**	**1714**	**1692**	**1466**	**1437**	**1266**	**1410**	**1569**	**1619**	**1573**
Fixed										
Depreciation	276	274	280	279	282	265	256	127	120	95
Interest	151	258	365	390	444	405	514	333	282	200
Repair & Maintenance	35	28	32	25	24	22	28	31	35	39
Other Expenses	164	167	181	147	120	163	87	87	96	101
Maintenance Consumables and Spares	150	146	146	116	138	150	169	176	175	168
Fixed Portion of Employee Remuneration and Benefits	549	681	520	453	434	391	343	325	316	324
Head Office Expenses	36	33	31	29	26	27	22	22	22	0
Less:										
Inter Account Adjustment	15	17	19	16	14	11	48	98	101	78
Interest Earned and Other Revenue	81	83	67	59	55	59	45	50	52	93
Total Fixed Cost	**1264**	**1486**	**1470**	**1364**	**1399**	**1353**	**1325**	**953**	**893**	**755**
Net Expenditure	**3047**	**3200**	**3162**	**2830**	**2836**	**2619**	**2735**	**2522**	**2512**	**2329**

SAIL

Table 4.15: Income and Cost Data

(Rs. in crores)

Items	2004-05	2003-04	2002-03	2001-02	2000-01	1999-00	1998-99	1997-98	1996-97	1995-96
Sales turn over (Excl. Chemicals and Scrap)										
Sales turn over	31035	23138	18327	14635	15137	14747	13375	12914	12675	13566
Less:										
Excise Duty	3455	2882	2371	1983	2123	1939	1856	1915	1969	1813
Freight	679	528	512	553	531	475	479	605	648	585
Net Sales Revenue	**26902**	**19729**	**15445**	**12099**	**12482**	**12333**	**11039**	**10394**	**10058**	**11168**
Expenditure										
Variable										
Raw Material	9359	6904	6234	5664	5462	5043	5329	5682	5619	5030
Variable Portion of Employee Remuneration and Benefits	371	463	362	316	302	266	232	214	206	205
Power and Fuel	2196	2159	2037	1710	1580	1465	1348	1468	1384	1163
Operating Consumables	1082	963	867	793	825	865	909	917	946	938
Total Variable Cost	**13008**	**10489**	**9500**	**8482**	**8169**	**7640**	**7818**	**8282**	**8154**	**7337**

Fixed										
Depreciation	1127	1123	1147	1156	1144	1133	1104	795	691	585
Interest	605	901	1334	1562	1752	1789	2017	1554	1179	808
Repair and Maintenance	240	195	188	162	186	170	188	183	201	235
Other Expenses	1276	1427	1456	1234	1098	1260	886	848	887	968
Maintenance Consumables and Spares	1082	963	867	793	825	865	909	917	946	938
Fixed Portion of Employee Remuneration and Benefits	3441	4295	3361	2933	2804	2469	2150	1987	1908	1902
Less:										
Inter Account Adjustment	921	893	856	799	782	744	827	825	988	760
Interest Earned and Other Revenue	772	605	541	535	296	334	491	462	608	417
Total Fixed Cost	**6077**	**7407**	**6955**	**6507**	**6730**	**6607**	**5936**	**4996**	**4216**	**4259**
Net Expenditure	**19085**	**17896**	**16455**	**14990**	**14899**	**14247**	**13754**	**13278**	**12371**	**11596**

TISCO

Table 4.16: Income and Cost Data (Rupees in crores)

Items	2003-04	2002-03	2001-02	2000-01	1999-00	1998-99	1997-98	1996-97	1995-96
Sales turn over (Excl. Chemicals and Scrap)									
Sales turn over	11332	9223	7123	7236	6463	5905	6117	6060	5624
Less:									
Excise Duty	1219	1072	900	921	797	710	724	696	593
Freight	748	696	562	578	555	509	544	535	488
Net Sales Revenue	**9365**	**7456**	**5662**	**5737**	**5111**	**4686**	**4849**	**4829**	**4544**
Expenditure									
Variable									
Raw Material	2078	1689	1357	1099	1024	1065	1258	1290	1120
Variable Portion of Employee Remuneration and Benefits	109	141	129	109	108	104	102	92	87
Power and Fuel	725	788	719	688	637	569	571	457	422
Operating Consumables	239	256	178	181	162	187	148	134	129
Total Variable Cost	**3150**	**2873**	**2383**	**2078**	**1931**	**1925**	**2079**	**1973**	**1758**

Fixed									
Depreciation	625	555	525	492	427	382	343	327	298
Interest	122	305	370	377	360	302	260	274	279
Repair & Maintenance	635	512	498	518	511	472	425	440	362
Other Expenses	1229	1020	837	907	820	734	692	676	670
Maintenance Consumables and Spares	730	256	178	181	162	187	148	134	129
Fixed Portion of Employee	1010	1306	1196	1015	1007	962	942	854	805
Remuneration and Benefits									
Less:									
Interest Earned and Other Revenue, Sales of Raw material, bearings etc.	2232	1666	1498	1478	1372	1592	1613	1889	1420
Total Fixed Cost	**2119**	**2289**	**2105**	**2012**	**1914**	**1447**	**1198**	**816**	**1123**
Net Expenditure	**5269**	**5163**	**4487**	**4089**	**3845**	**3372**	**3277**	**2790**	**2881**

Adjusted Fixed Cost amount is taken from Table 4.17, 4.18, 4.19 for calculation of Break Even Point.

Break Even Point Quantity is arrived at by dividing Adjusted Fixed cost of the firm with Unit Contribution of Saleable Steel. Break-even Point (%) is calculated as a percentage of B.E.P quantity w.r.t the Capacity of the firm as tabulated in Tables 4.17, 4.18, 4.19.

Arriving at the Profit/Loss of the Firm:

The Margin quantity is calculated from Tables 4.17, 4.18, 4.19, which is the difference between the B.E.P. quantity and the Production quantity of Saleable Steel. The data and detailed computation is shown in Tables 4.20, 4.21, 4.22. The Margin quantity can be both positive and negative depending on the B.E.P and Production Volume. Margin Contribution is the contribution share of the Margin quantity, which goes into the Profit/Loss of the firm. This is calculated by multiplying Margin Quantity with Unit Contribution from Tables 4.17, 4.18, 4.19. This has been shown in Table 4.20, 4.21, 4.22.

After that, adjustments are given for the following items to arrive at the Profit/Loss of the firm:

- Income/Expenditure items not considered in the above calculation. These are abnormal items like profit on Sale of a division of the firm, Prior Period Adjustments etc.

Tabulation of Data is given in the Tables 4.20, 4.21, 4.22 below. The summary of the calculation is shown in the next page for interpretation and analysis.

SUMMARY OF B.E.P. ANALYSIS

The summary of the data in the above tables used for working out Break-even points for the firms is shown below (Table 4.23). Analysis of the same is also done in the next pages.

Net Sales revenue as well as Net Expenditure has increased over the years. After 2001-02, Sales revenue has increased more than proportionate to the Expenditure; which has resulted in increased profit for the firm. The Net Expenditure is more than Net Sales between 1995-96 and 2003-04. The firm was making losses from 1995-96 to 2003-04. Loss figures were very high during the Financial Years 1998-99, 1999-00, 2001-02 (Chart 4.40).

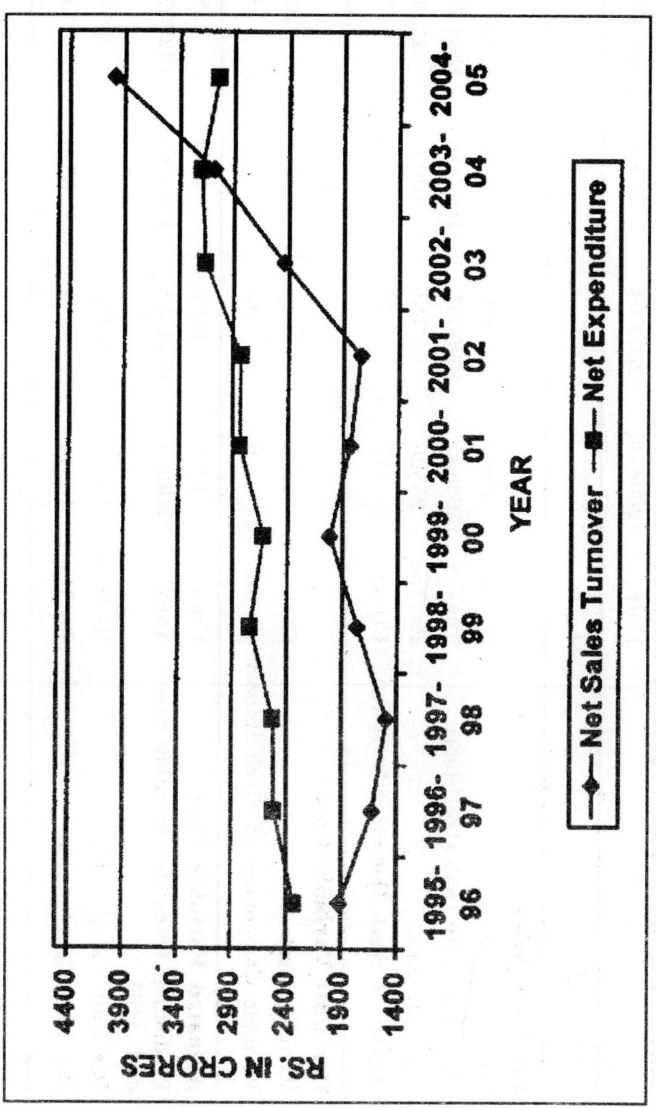

Chart 4.40: Sales Turnover and Net Expenditure

Rourkela Steel Plant

Table 4.17: Rourkela Steel Plant

	Unit	2004-05	2003-04	2002-03	2001-02	2000-01
0	1	2	3	4	5	6
Per Unit Sales						
Net Sales Revenue	crores	3996	3986	2441	1739	1837
Sales Quantity (Saleable Steel)	Tons	1565535	1595631	1522486	1364550	1203213
Per Unit Sales	Rs./Ton	25526	19343	16032	12742	15266
Impact of Stock Decretion/Accretion	Crores	-16	76	5	75	-34
Per Unit Variable Cost						
Variable Cost	Crores	1663	1542	1503	1293	1157
Variable Component of Stock Impact	Crores	-9	39	2	37	-15
Adjusted Variable Cost	Crores	1654	1581	1505	1330	1141
Production Quantity (Saleable Steel) excl. SSD	Tons	1543679	1532842	1484661	1329570	1263564
Per Unit Variable Cost	Rs./Ton	10712	10311	10140	10002	9033
Per Unit Contribution	Rs./Ton	14814	9032	5892	2740	6234

Fixed Cost						
Fixed Cost	Crores	1264	1486	1470	1364	1399
Fixed Component of Stock Impact	Crores	-7	37	2	39	-19
Adjusted Fixed Cost	Crores	1258	1523	1472	1403	1380
Break Even Point (B.E.P.)						
B.E.P. = Total Fixed Cost/Unit Contribution						
Capacity (Saleable Steel)	Tons	1671000	1671000	1671000	1671000	1671000
B.E.P. (Quantity)	Tons	848920	1686734	2498708	5118966	2214084
B.E.P (% Capacity)	%	51%	101%	150%	306%	133%

Table 4.17 (concld.)

	Unit	1999-00	1998-99	1997-98	1996-97	1995-96
0	1	7	8	9	10	11
Per Unit Sales						
Net Sales Revenue	Crores	2016	1766	1493	1623	1909
Sales Quantity (Saleable Steel)	Tons	1319122	1137641	982434	1045677	1104003
Per Unit Sales	Rs./Ton	15285	15522	15193	15517	17290
Impact of Stock Decretion/Accretion	Crores	146	0	-82	-92	-20
Per Unit Variable Cost						
Variable Cost	Crores	958	1118	1214	1248	1231
Variable Component of Stock Impact	Crores	61	0	-46	-54	-12
Adjusted Variable Cost	**Crores**	**1018**	**1118**	**1168**	**1194**	**1219**
Production Quantity (Saleable Steel)	Tons	1141665	1081644	1124361	1118733	1103029
Per Unit Variable Cost	Rs./Ton	8919	10337	10390	10674	11051
Per Unit Contribution	Rs./Ton	6366	5185	4803	4843	6239

Fixed Cost						
Fixed Cost	Crores	1353	1325	953	893	755
Fixed Component of Stock Impact	Crores	86	0	-36	-38	-7
Adjusted Fixed Cost	**Crores**	**1439**	**1325**	**917**	**854**	**748**
Break Even Point (B.E.P.)						
B.E.P. = Total Fixed Cost/Unit Contribution						
Capacity (Saleable Steel)	Tons	1671000	1671000	1225000	1225000	1225000
B.E.P. Tons		2259824	2556589	1908811	1763903	1198806
B.E.P (% Capacity)	%	135%	153%	156%	144%	98%

SAIL

Table 4.18: SAIL

	Unit	2004-05	2003-04	2002-03	2001-02	2000-01
0	1	2	3	4	5	6
Per Unit Sales						
Net Sales Revenue	Crores	26902	19729	15445	12099	12482
Sales Quantity (Saleable Steel)	Tons	11001591	10968987	10362939	9759446	9397165
Per Unit Sales	Rs./Ton	24452	17986	14904	12398	13283
Impact of Stock Decretion/Accretion	Crores	-608	373	271	222	66
Per Unit Variable Cost						
Variable Cost	Crores	11958	9217	8406	7434	6906
Variable Component of Stock Impact	Crores	-403	207	148	118	33
Adjusted Variable Cost	Crores	11555	9424	8555	7552	6939
Production Quantity (Saleable Steel) excl. SSD	Tons	10903674	10906312	10254113	9597866	9524951
Per Unit Variable Cost	Rs./Ton	10597	8641	8343	7868	7285
Per Unit Contribution	Rs./Ton	13855	9345	6562	4529	5998

Fixed Cost						
Fixed Cost	Crores	6077	7407	6955	6507	6730
Fixed Component of Stock Impact	Crores	-205	166	123	104	32
Adjusted Fixed Cost	**Crores**	**5873**	**7573**	**7078**	**6611**	**6762**
Break Even Point (B.E.P.)						
B.E.P. = Total Fixed Cost/Unit Contribution						
Capacity (Saleable Steel)	Tons	10625000	10625000	10625000	10625000	10625000
B.E.P.	Tons	4238614	8104145	10787529	14595234	11273476
B.E.P (% Capacity)	%	40%	76%	102%	137%	106%

Table 4.18 (concld.)

	Unit	1999-00	1998-99	1997-98	1996-97	1995-96
0	1	7	8	9	10	11
Per Unit Sales						
Net Sales Revenue	Crores	12333	11039	10394	10058	11168
Sales Quantity (Saleable Steel)	Tons	9624372	8723336	8052974	8089693	8502094
Per Unit Sales	Rs./Ton	12814	12655	12907	12433	13135
Impact of Stock Decretion/Accretion	Crores	1452	-191	-449	-312	1
Per Unit Variable Cost						
Variable Cost	Crores	5998	6098	6345	6515	5948
Variable Component of Stock Impact	Crores	691	-97	-251	-189	0
Adjusted Variable Cost	Crores	6689	6001	6093	6326	5949
Production Quantity (Saleable Steel)	Tons	9225571	8116505	8526348	8827922	8752452
Per Unit Variable Cost	Rs./Ton	7250	7394	7146	7166	6797
Per Unit Contribution	Rs./Ton	5564	5261	5761	5267	6338

Fixed Cost						
Fixed Cost	Crores	6607	5936	4996	4216	4259
Fixed Component of Stock Impact	Crores	761	-94	-198	-122	0
Adjusted Fixed Cost	Crores	7369	5841	4798	4094	4260
Break Even Point (B.E.P.)						
B.E.P. = Total Fixed Cost/Unit Contribution						
Capacity (Saleable Steel)	Tons	10625000	10001000	9478000	9478000	9026000
B.E.P. Tons		13243326	11103139	8328633	7773274	6720443
B.E.P (% Capacity)	%	125%	111%	88%	82%	74%

TISCO

Table 4.19: TISCO

	Unit	2003-04	2002-03	2001-02	2000-01
0	1	2	3	4	5
Per Unit Sales					
Net Sales Revenue	Crores	7815	6353	4691	4782
Sales Quantity (Saleable Steel)	Tons	4035043	4150745	3738587	3674891
Per Unit Sales	Rs./Ton	19367	15306	12547	13012
Impact of Stock Decretion/Accretion	Crores	55	-63	100	48
Per Unit Variable Cost					
Variable Cost	Crores	3079	2816	2324	2025
Variable Component of Stock Impact	Crores	33	-35	52	24
Adjusted Variable Cost	Crores	3112	2781	2376	2049
Production Quantity (Saleable Steel)	Tons	4089255	4119495	3809235	3601503
Per Unit Variable Cost	Rs./Ton	7611	6752	6237	5688
Per Unit Contribution	Rs./Ton	11756	8554	6310	7324

Fixed Cost					
Fixed Cost	Crores	2119	2289	2105	2012
Fixed Component of Stock Impact	Crores	23	-28	47	24
Adjusted Fixed Cost	Crores	2141	2261	2152	2035
Break Even Point (B.E.P.)					
B.E.P. = Total Fixed Cost/Unit Contribution					
Capacity (Saleable Steel)	Tons	3505000	3505000	3505000	3505000
B.E.P. (Quantity)	Tons	1821418	2643586	3410809	2779285
B.E.P (% Capacity)	%	52%	75%	97%	79%

Table 4.19 (concld.)

	Unit	1999-00	1998-99	1997-98	1996-97	1995-96
0	1	6	7	8	9	10
Per Unit Sales						
Net Sales Revenue	Crores	4201	3604	3606	3271	3361
Sales Quantity (Saleable Steel)	Tons	3432323	3125878	3068147	2939676	2729736
Per Unit Sales	Rs./Ton	12240	11529	11751	11127	12314
Impact of Stock Decretion/Accretion		31	132	118	-11	78
Per Unit Variable Cost						
Variable Cost	Crores	1903	1888	2049	1954	1739
Variable Component of Stock Impact	Crores	15	75	74	-8	47
Adjusted Variable Cost	Crores	1918	1963	2123	1946	1786
Production Quantity (Saleable Steel)	Tons	3430407	32804768	3172121	2967074	2847310
Per Unit Variable Cost	Rs./Ton	5592	5983	6693	6560	6274
Per Unit Contribution	Rs./Ton	6648	5546	5058	4567	6040

Fixed Cost						
Fixed Cost	Crores	1914	1447	1198	816	1123
Fixed Component of Stock Impact	Crores	15	57	43	-3	31
Adjusted Fixed Cost	Crores	1929	1504	1241	813	1154
Break Even Point (B.E.P.)						
B.E.P. = Total Fixed Cost/Unit Contribution						
Capacity (Saleable Steel)	Tons	3505000	2885000	2885000	2885000	2885000
B.E.P. Tons		2901560	2712279	2454196	1780712	1909889
B.E.P. (% Capacity)	%	83%	94%	85%	62%	66%

RSP

Table 4.20: Rourkela Steel Plant

	Unit	2004-05	2003-04	2002-03	2001-02	2000-01
0	1	2	3	4	5	6
B.E.P Quantity	Tons	848920	1686734	2498708	5118966	2214084
B.E.P (% Capacity)	%	51%	101%	150%	306%	133%
Margin Quantity	Tons	694759	-153892	-1014047	-3789396	-950520
Margin Contribution	Crores	1029	-139	-597	-1038	-593
Other adjustments	Crores	16	31	4	3	148*
Profit Before Tax	Crores	1045	-109	-593	-1036	-445

* Includes Rs. 144 crores of Profit on sale of Power Plant to form a Joint Venture Organisation

	Unit	1999-00	1998-99	1997-98	1996-97	1995-96
0	1	7	8	9	10	11
B.E.P Quantity	Tons	2259824	2556589	1908811	1763903	1198806
B.E.P (% Capacity)	%	135%	153%	156%	144%	98%
Margin Quantity	Tons	-1118159	-1474945	-784450	-645170	-95777
Margin Contribution	Crores	-712	-765	-377	-313	-59
Other adjustments	Crores	7.91	0	2.71	-3.48	2.83
Profit Before Tax	Crores	-704	-765	-374	-316	-57

SAIL

Table 4.21: SAIL

	Unit	2004-05	2003-04	2002-03	2001-02	2000-01
0	1	2	3	4	5	6
B.E.P. Quantity	Tons	4238614	8104145	10787529	14595234	11273476
B.E.P. (% Capacity)	%	40%	76%	102%	137%	106%
Margin Quantity	Tons	6665060	2802167	-533416	-4997368	-1748525
Margin Contribution	Crores	9235	2619	-350	-2264	-1049
Other adjustments	Crores	131	9	34	557*	320*
Profit Before Tax	Crores	9365	2628	-316	-1707	-729

*Profit on Sale of Power Plant during 2000-01 was Rs. 289.89 Crores and during 2001-02 was Rs. 490.58 Crores.

	Unit	1999-00	1998-99	1997-98	1996-97	1995-96
0	1	7	8	9	10	11
B.E.P. Quantity	Tons	13243326	11103139	8328633	7773274	6720443
B.E.P. (% Capacity)	%	125%	111%	88%	82%	74%
Margin Quantity	Tons	-4017755	-2986634	197715	1054648	2032009
Margin Contribution	Crores	-2236	-1572	114	555	1288
Other adjustments	Crores	516	-2	35	33	31
Profit Before Tax	Crores	-1720	-1574	149	588	1319

* Includes Cumulative Interest reduction of Rs. 506.91 Crores due to SDF Loan waiver approved by the Government

TISCO

Table 4.22: TISCO

	Unit	2003-04	2002-03	2001-02	2000-01
0	1	2	3	4	5
B.E.P. Quantity	Tons	1821418	2643586	3410809	2779285
B.E.P. (% Capacity)	%	52%	75%	97%	79%
Margin Quantity	Tons	2267837	1475909	398426	822218
Margin Contribution	Crores	2666	1263	251	602
Other adjustments	Crores	0	0	0	0
Profit Before Tax	Crores	2666	1263	251	602

	Unit	1999-00	1998-99	1997-98	1996-97	1995-96
0	1	6	7	8	9	10
B.E.P. Quantity	Tons	2901560	2712279	2454196	1780712	1909889
B.E.P. (% Capacity)	%	83%	94%	85%	62%	66%
Margin Quantity	Tons	528847	568489	717925	1186362	937421
Margin Contribution	Crores	352	315	363	542	566
Other adjustments	Crores	125*	0	0	0	0
Profit Before Tax	Crores	477	315	363	542	566

* Profit on Sale of Cement Division was Rs. 125.26 Crores.

RSP

Table 4.23: Rourkela Steel Plant

0	Unit	2004-05	2003-04	2002-03	2001-02	2000-01
	1	2	3	4	5	6
Net Sales Turnover	Rs./Crores	3996	3086	2441	1739	1837
Net Expenditure	Rs./Crores	3047	3200	3162	2830	2836
Production Capacity	Ton	1671000	1671000	1671000	1671000	1671000
Production Volume	Ton	1543679	1532842	1484661	1329570	1263564
Sales Volume	Ton	1565535	1595631	1522486	1364550	1203213
Unit Net Sales price	Rs./Ton	25526	19343	16032	12742	15266
Unit Cost	Rs./Ton	18859	20250	20056	20552	19955
- Variable Cost	Rs./Ton	10712	10311	10140	10002	9033
- Fixed Cost	Rs./Ton	8147	9939	9916	10551	10923
Unit Contribution	Rs./Ton	14814	9032	5892	2740	6234
B.E.P						
Percentage	%	51%	101%	150%	306%	133%
Volume	Ton	848920	1686734	2498708	5118966	2214084
Margin Available	Ton	694759	-153892	-1014047	-3789396	-950520
Profit (PBT)	Rs./Crores	1045	-109	-593	-1036	-445

	Unit	1999-00	1998-99	1997-98	1996-97	1995-96
0	1	7	8	9	10	11
Net Sales Turnover	Rs./Crores	2016	1766	1493	1623	1909
Net Expenditure	Rs./Crores	2619	2735	2522	2512	2329
Production Capacity	Ton	1671000	1671000	1225000	1225000	1225000
Production Volume	Ton	1141665	1081644	1124361	1118733	1103029
Sales Volume	Ton	1319122	1137641	982434	1045677	1104003
Unit Net Sales price	Rs./Ton	15285	15522	15193	15517	17290
Unit Cost	Rs./Ton	21520	22592	18544	18310	17832
- Variable Cost	Rs./Ton	8919	10337	10390	10674	11051
- Fixed Cost	Rs./Ton	12601	12254	8154	7636	6781
Unit Contribution	Rs./Ton	6366	5185	4803	4843	6239
B.E.P						
Percentage	%	135%	153%	156%	144%	98%
Volume	Ton	2259824	2556589	1908811	1763903	1198806
Margin Available	Ton	-1118159	-1474945	-784450	-645170	-95777
Profit (PBT)	Rs./Crores	-704	-765	-374	-316	-57

Production Capacity of the firm has increased after 1997-98 (Chart 4.41). During this time the Fixed Cost (Depreciation and Interest) burden of the firm has gone up substantially. It can also be seen from the graph (Chart 4.41) than, after addition of new capacities, capacity utilization has been less than 100% all these years. It slowly improved after 1998-99 after stabilization of the modernization facilities. Capacity Utilizations during 2003-04 and 2004-05 have been 92%.

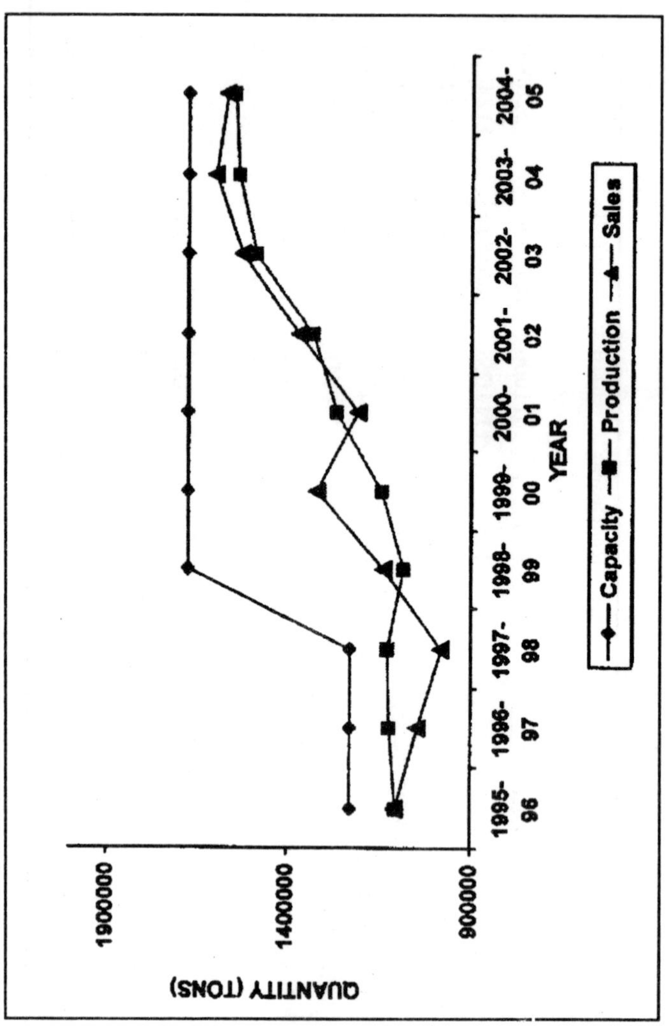

Chart-4.41: Capacity, Production and Sales

It is evident from the above graph (Chart 4.41) that, the company was making more losses during all these years prior to 2004-05 due to poor capacity utilization, higher fixed cost and lower sales price.

Cost of Production has been more that Net Sales Price all these years except 2004-05. After 2002-03, Net sales Price increased more than proportionate to the Cost of Production (Chart 4.42). Steel market improved during this time. Capacity utilisation also improved substantially.

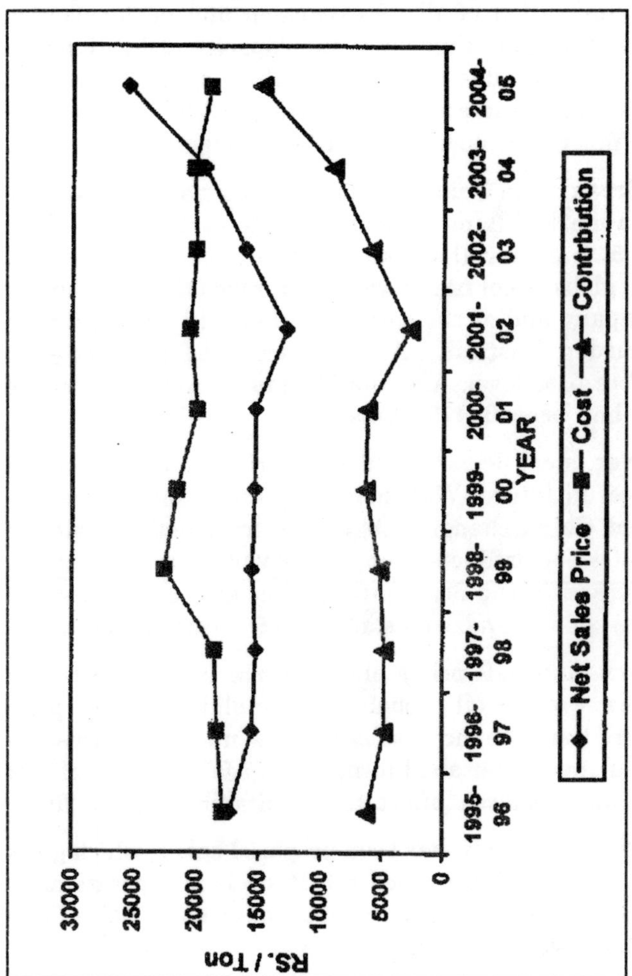

Chart 4.42: Average Sales Price, Cost and Contribution

Contribution in all these year has been positive, which saw a steady increase between the years 2001-02 and 2004-05. During this time losses were reduced and the firm registered a High Net Profit during 2004-05.

Break Even Points between the years 1996-97 and 2003-04 have been more than 100% Capacity of the firm. This is the period in which the firm was making losses. The firm registered a very high loss during the financial year 2001-02. The Fixed cost of the firm became very high after 1998-99 due to capitalization of all its expansion and modernization projects. At the same time since the capacity utilization was less than 100% and due to poor Sales Price of Steel products, the firm suffered successive losses till 2003-04. During this time, the margin of operation was also negative.

The Break Even Point during the financial year 2004-05 has seen a marked improvement over the earlier years. This has been 51% during this time. A strong steel demand has pushed up global steel prices, which improved the profitability of the company and at the same time helped in reducing the interest burden drastically. All these account for reduction in the B.E.P to 51% level. Also the Margin of operation during this time has been 694759 tons.

However, steel demand and steel prices may not remain at this level in future. With new steel units coming soon on stream and China changing its status from net importer to exporter of steel products soon, there will be a pressure on the steel prices in the near future. After that the prices will come down slowly and will stabilize at a certain level.

The raw materials prices may increase in the short-term period. How ever in all probability, the slide in Sales price will be more than the increase in the raw material prices. On the front of raw materials, the prices of coal, boiler coal and the Ferro alloys mostly affect the profitability of the firm.

A sensitivity analysis has been prepared below, which gives an indication about the revised B.E.P levels for operations of the firm to maintain its profit at different levels of Sales Price and Input Prices.

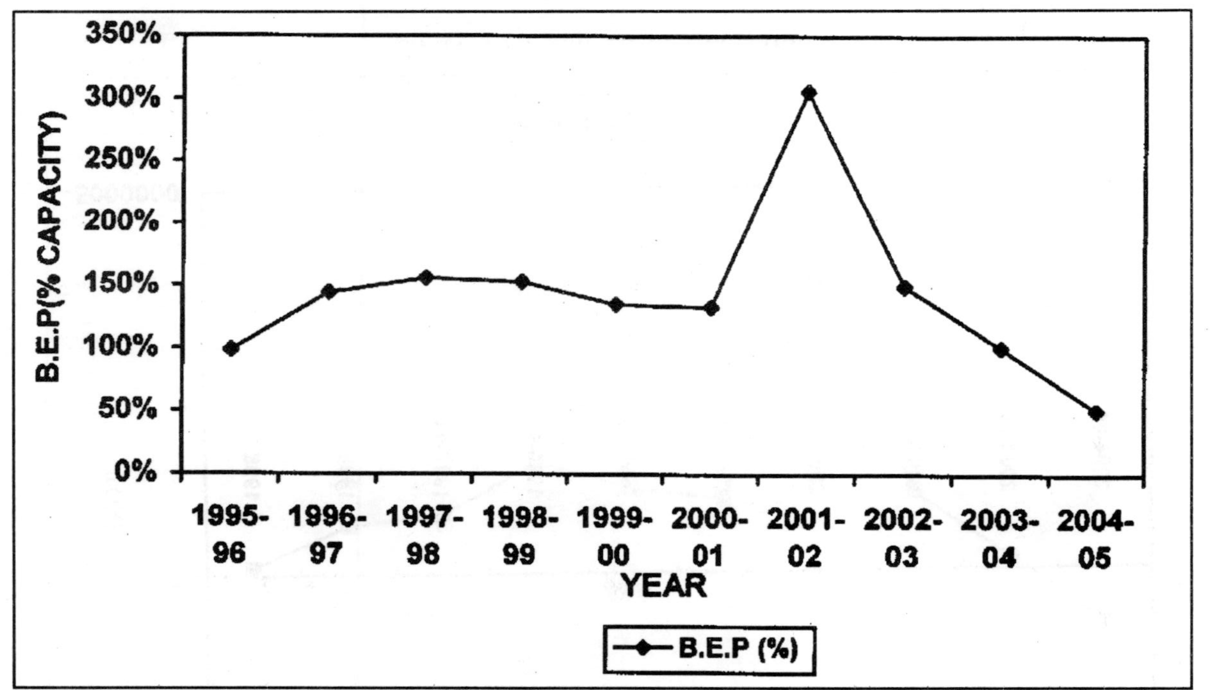

Chart 4.43: Break Even Point

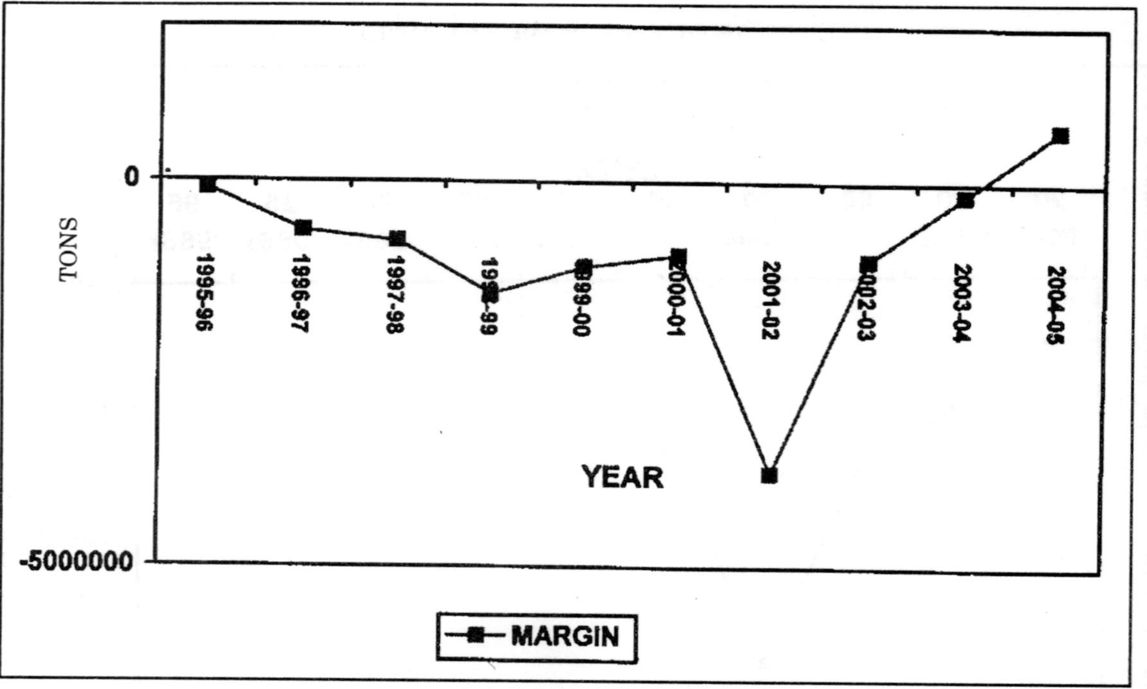

Chart 4.44: Margin of Operation

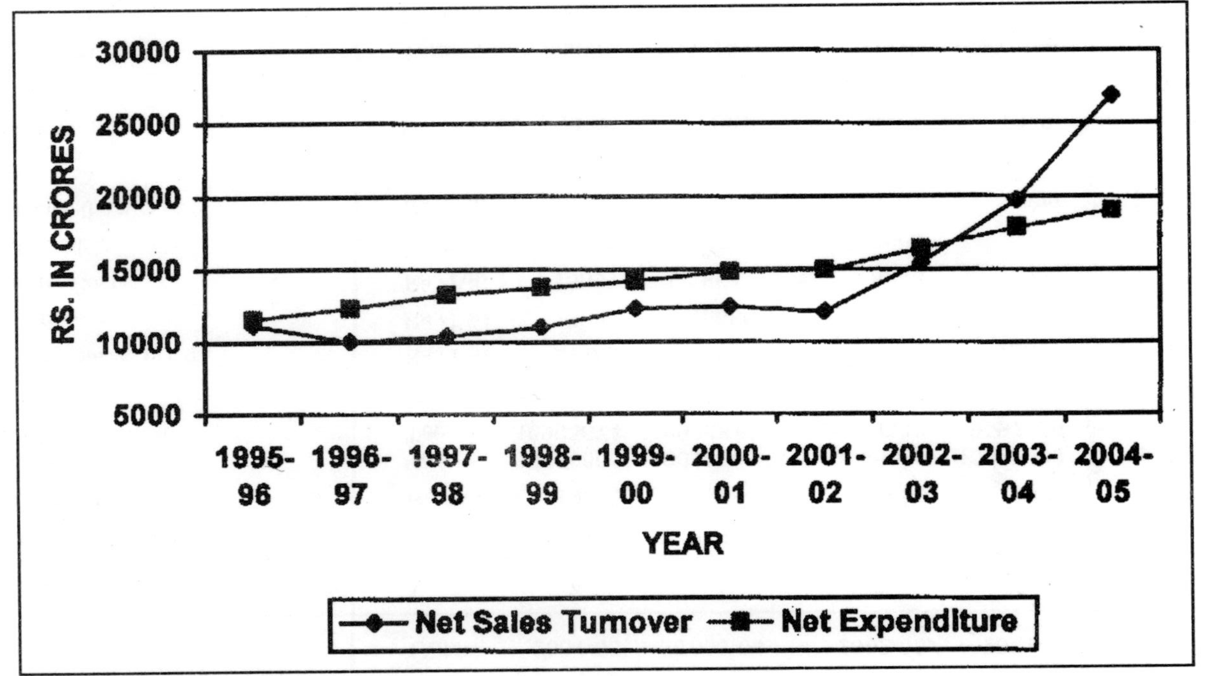

Chart 4.45: Sales Turnover and Expenditure

SAIL

Table 4.24

	Unit	2004-05	2003-04	2002-03	2001-02	2000-01
0	1	2	3	4	5	6
Net Sales Turnover	Rs./Crores	26902	19729	15445	12099	12482
Net Expenditure	Rs./Crores	19085	17896	16455	14990	14899
Production Capacity	Ton	10625000	10625000	10625000	10625000	10625000
Production Volume	Ton	10903674	10906312	10254113	9597866	9524951
Sales Volume	Ton	11001591	10968987	10362939	9759446	9524951
Unit Net Sales price	Rs./Ton	24452	17986	14904	12398	13283
Unit Cost	Rs./Ton	15983	15585	15246	14756	14384
-Variable Cost	Rs./Ton	10597	8641	8343	7868	7285
-Fixed Cost	Rs./Ton	5386	6944	6903	6888	7100
Unit Contribution	Rs./Ton	13855	9345	6562	4529	5998
B.E.P						
Percentage	%	40%	76%	102%	137%	106%
Volume	Ton	4238614	8104145	10787529	14595234	11273476
Margin Available	Ton	6665060	2802167	-533416	-4997368	-1748525
Profit (PBT)	Rs./Crores	9365	2628	-316	-1707	-729

	Unit	1999-00	1998-99	1997-98	1996-97	1995-96
0	1	7	8	9	10	11
Net Sales Turnover	Rs./Crores	12333	11039	10394	10058	11168
Net Expenditure	Rs./Crores	14247	13754	13278	12371	11596
Production Capacity	Ton	10625000	10001000	9478000	9478000	9026000
Production Volume	Ton	9225571	8116505	8526348	8827922	8752452
Sales Volume	Ton	9624372	8723336	8052974	8089693	8502094
Unit Net Sales price	Rs./Ton	12814	12655	12907	12433	13135
Unit Cost	Rs./Ton	15238	14591	12773	11804	11664
- Variable Cost	Rs./Ton	7250	7394	7146	7166	6797
- Fixed Cost	Rs./Ton	7987	7197	5627	4638	4867
Unit Contribution	Rs./Ton	5564	5261	5761	5267	6338
B.E.P						
Percentage	%	125%	111%	88%	82%	74%
Volume	Ton	13243326	11103139	8328633	7773274	6720443
Margin Available	Ton	-4017755	-2986634	197715	1054648	2032009
Profit (PBT)	Rs./Crores	-1720	-1574	149	588	1319

Net Sales revenue as well as Net Expenditure have increased over the years. After 2001-02, Sales revenue has increased more than proportionate to the Expenditure; which has resulted in increased profits for the firm. The Net expenditure is more than Net Sales between 1996-97 and 2002-03. From 1998-99 to 2002-03, the firm was making losses. Loss figure was very high during the Financial Years 1998-99, 1999-00, 2001-02. However, during 1996-97 and 1997-98 even if Net Expenditure is more than Net Sales, as is evident from the graph above, the firm recorded marginal profit. This is because the firm's production volume was more than Sales Volume resulting in Stock Accretion, which helped in creating profit. The graph in the next page describes this clearly.

Production Capacity of the firm has increased over the years. There is addition of capacity during the years 1996-97, 1998-99 and 1999-00. Most of the additional capacities have taken place between 1998-99 and 1999-00. During this time the Fixed Cost (Depreciation and Interest) burden of the firm has gone up substantially. This can also be seen from the Graph (Chart 4.46) that, after addition of capacities during this time, capacity utilization has been much less than 100% till the year 2003-04. This is because of more time required for stabilization of the additional facilities as well as a slow down in the market demand of Steel products from 1998-99 to 2001-02. Thus the company made more losses between 1998-99 and 2001-02 due to poor capacity utilization.

It can be also observed from the Graph (Chart 4.46) that the Production volume has been more than Sales Volume between the years 1995-96 and 1997-98.

Cost of Production has been more than Net Sales Price between 1998-99 and 2002-03. This is due to less capacity utilization after capitalization of the new Projects during this time, as well as a slow down in the Steel Market. However after 2002-03, Net Sales Price has increased more than proportionate to the Cost of Production. Steel market also improved during this time. Capacity Utilisation improved more than 100%.

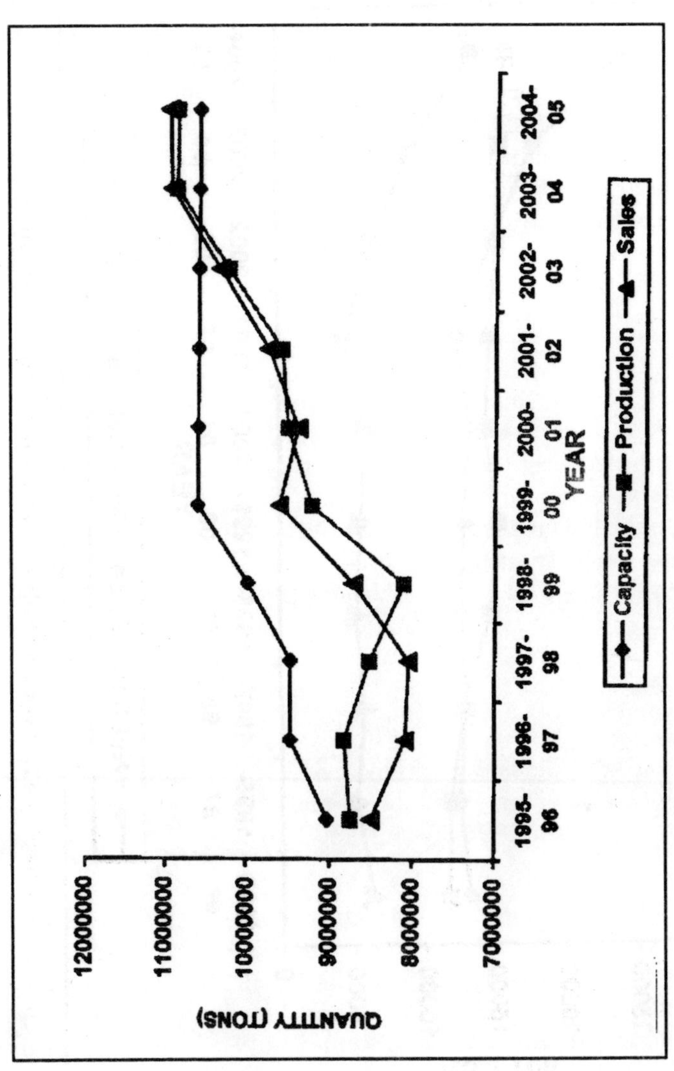

Chart 4.46: Capacity, Production and Sales

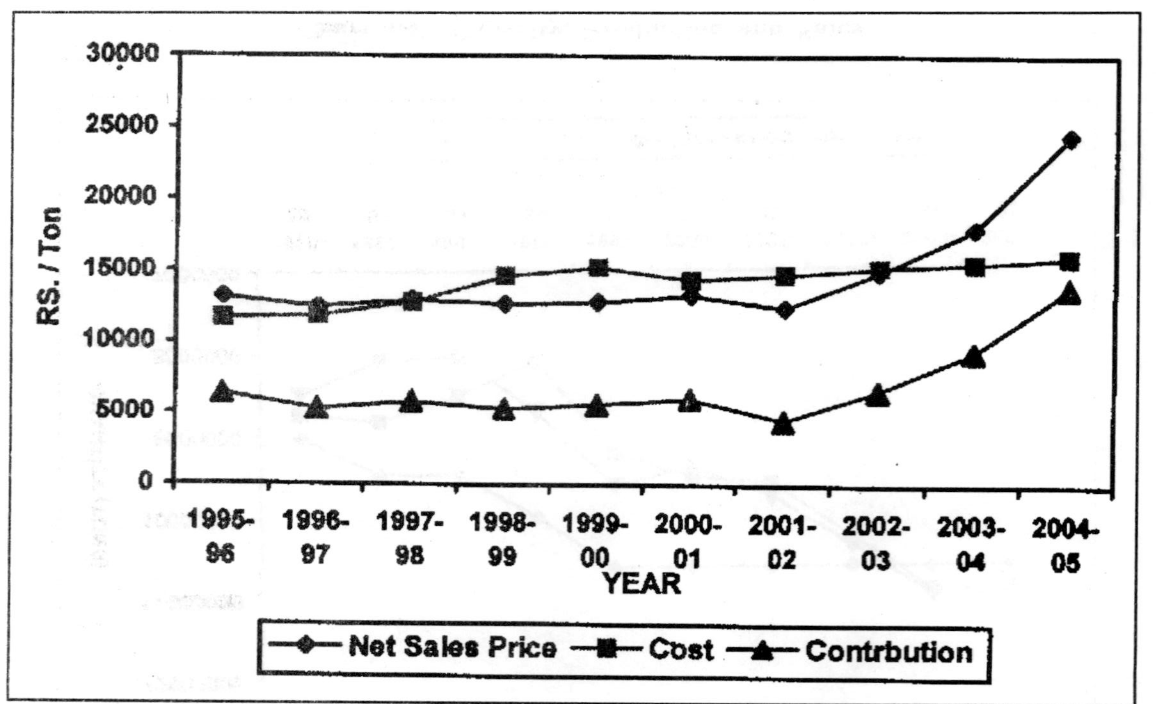

Chart 4.47: Average Sales Price, Cost and Contribution

Contribution in all these year has been positive, which saw a steady increase between the years 2001-02 and 2004-05. During this time losses were reduced and the firm registered net profit from 2003-04 on wards.

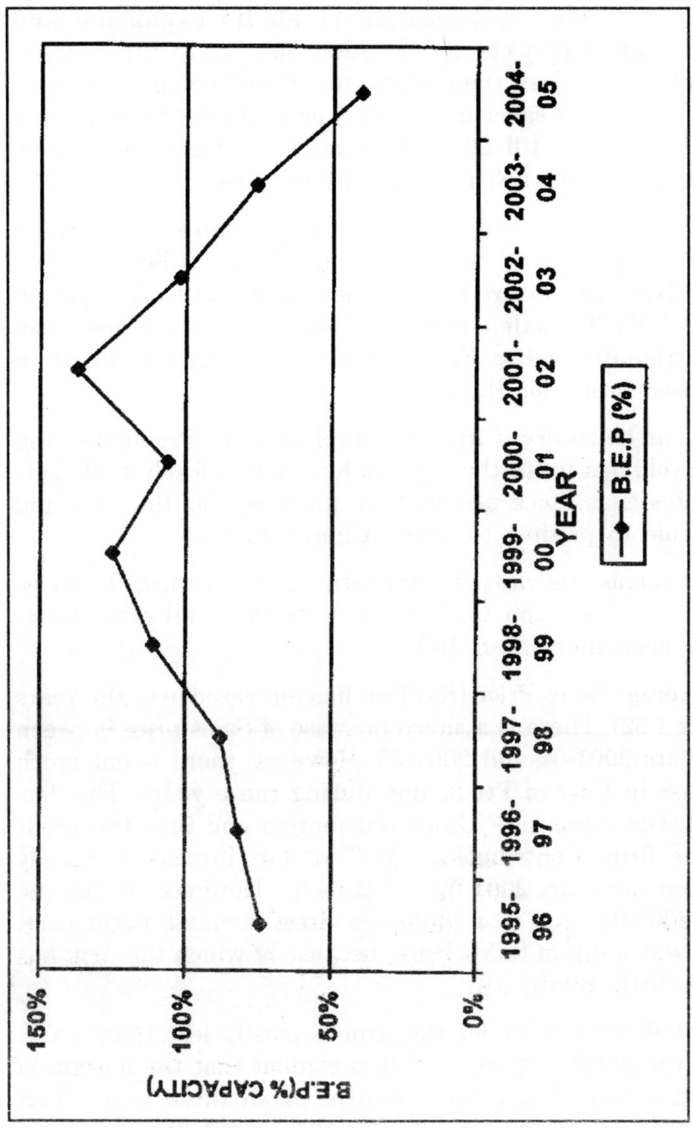

Chart 4.48: Break Even Point

Break Even Points between the years 1998-99 and 2002-03 have been more than 100% capacity of the firm (Chart 4.48). This is the period in which the firm was making losses. Firm registered a very high loss during the Financial year 2001-02. The fixed cost of the firm became very high after 1998-99 due to capitalization of all its expansion and modernization projects. At the same time since the capacity utilization was less than 100% and B.E.P being more than 100% due to poor sales price of steel products, the firm suffered successive losses till 2002-03. During this time, the margin of operation was also negative (Chart 4.49).

Net sales revenue as well as Net Expenditure has increased over the years. In all these years, the firm has been making profit. Net expenditure has been less than Net sales revenue. After 2001-02, sales revenue has increased more than proportionate to the Expenditure; which has resulted in increased profit for the firm.

It can be observed from the graph that the Production and Sales volumes in all these years have been closely tied. This indicates that Stock accretion is quite less for the firm and it is able to product to order (Charat 4.51).

So far as the capacity utilization is concerned, it can be seen from the graph that except 1999-00, in all other years it has been more than 100%.

Average Sales Price (Rs./Ton) has increased over the years (Chart 4.52). There is a sharp increase of Sales price between the years 2001-02 and 2004-05. However, there is not much increase in Cost of Production during these years. This has resulted in increasing Unit Contribution and thus the profit for the firm. Contribution (Rs./Ton) has increased sharply between the years 2001-02 and 2004-05. However, during the year 2001-02, due to a slump in Steel demand world over, there was a dip in Sales Price, because of which the firm has a very little profit.

Break-even point for the firm is mostly less than 100%. From the graph (Chart 4.53) it is evident that the margin of operation has always been positive in all these years. This indicates positive bottom line for the firm (Chart 4.54).

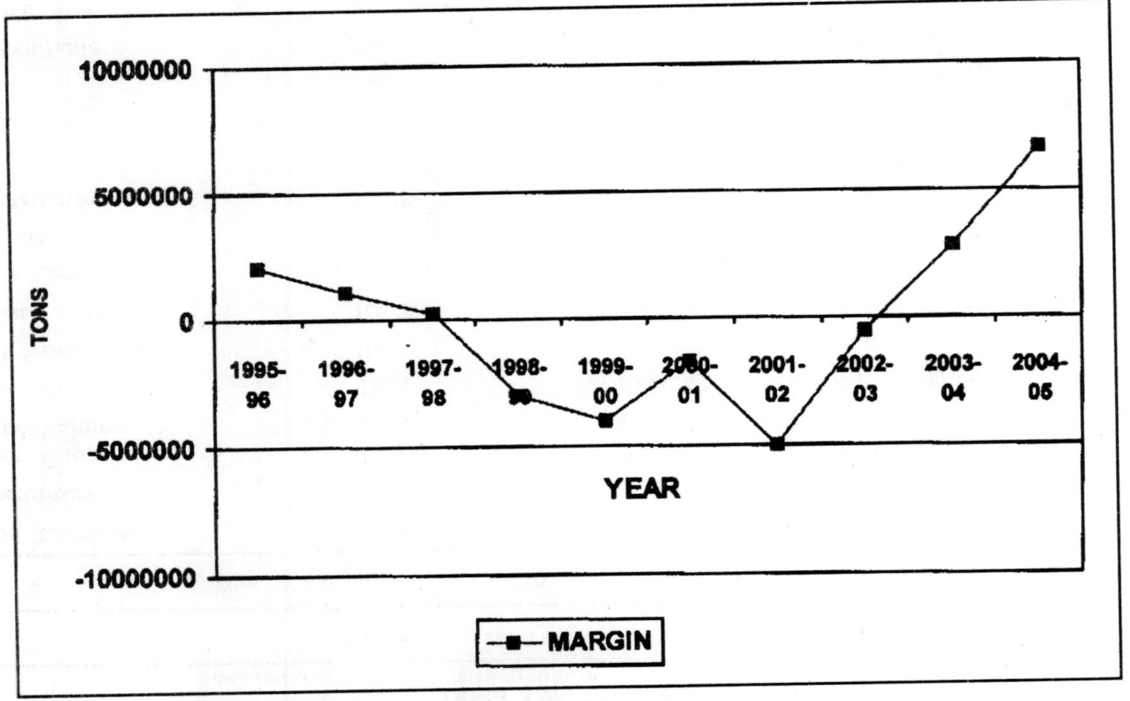

Chart 4.49: Margin Operation

TISCO

Table 4.25: TISCO

	Unit	2004-05	2003-04	2002-03	2001-02	2000-01
0	1	2	3	4	5	6
Net Sales Turnover	Rs./Crores		9365	7456	5662	5737
Net Expenditure	Rs./Crores		5269	5163	4487	4089
Production Capacity	Ton		3505000	3505000	3505000	3505000
Production Volume	Ton		4089255	4119495	3809235	3601503
Sales Volume	Ton		4035043	4150745	3738587	3674891
Unit Net Sales price	Rs./Ton		19367	15306	12547	13012
Unit Cost	Rs./Ton		12847	12241	11887	11340
- Variable Cost	Rs./Ton		7611	6752	6237	5688
- Fixed Cost	Rs./Ton		5236	5489	5650	5652
Unit Contribution	Rs./Ton		11756	8554	6310	7324
B.E.P.						
Percentage	%		52%	75%	97%	79%
Volume	Ton		1821418	2643586	3410809	2779285
Margin Available	Ton		2267837	1475909	398426	822218
Profit (PBT)	Rs./Crores		2666	1263	251	602

	Unit	1999-00	1998-99	1997-98	1996-97	1995-96
0	1	7	8	9	10	11
Net Sales Turnover	Rs./Crores	5111	4686	4849	4829	4544
Net Expenditure	Rs./Crores	3485	3372	3277	2790	2881
Production Capacity	Ton	3505000	2885000	2885000	2885000	2885000
Production Volume	Ton	3430407	3280768	3172121	2967074	2847310
Sales Volume	Ton	3432333	3125878	3068147	2939676	2729736
Unit Net Sales price	Rs./Ton	12240	11529	11751	11127	12314
Unit Cost	Rs./Ton	11215	10568	10607	9301	10325
- Variable Cost	Rs./Ton	5592	5983	6693	6560	6274
- Fixed Cost	Rs./Ton	5623	4585	3913	2741	4052
Unit Contribution	Rs./Ton	6648	5546	5058	4567	6040
B.E.P.						
Percentage	%	83%	94%	85%	62%	66%
Volume	Ton	2901560	2712279	2454196	1780712	1909889
Margin Available	Ton	528847	568489	717925	1186362	937421
Profit (PBT)	Rs./Crores	477	315	363	542	566

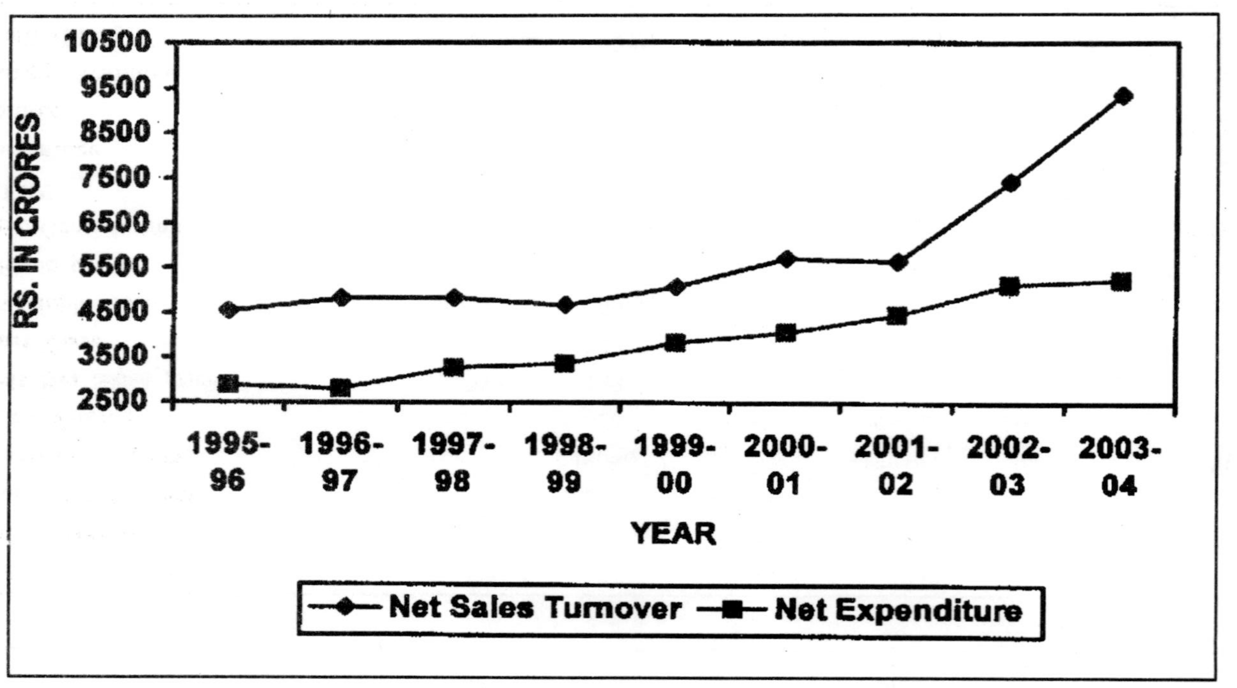

Chart 4.50: Sales Turnover and Expenditure

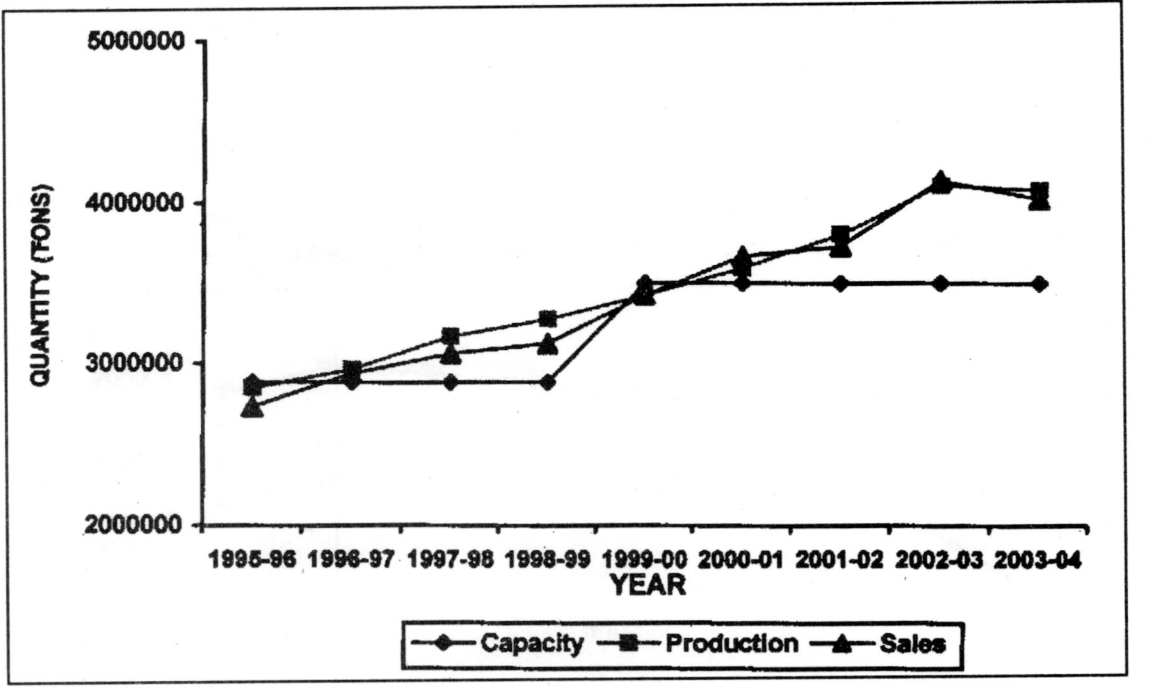

Chart 4.51: Capacity, Production and Sales

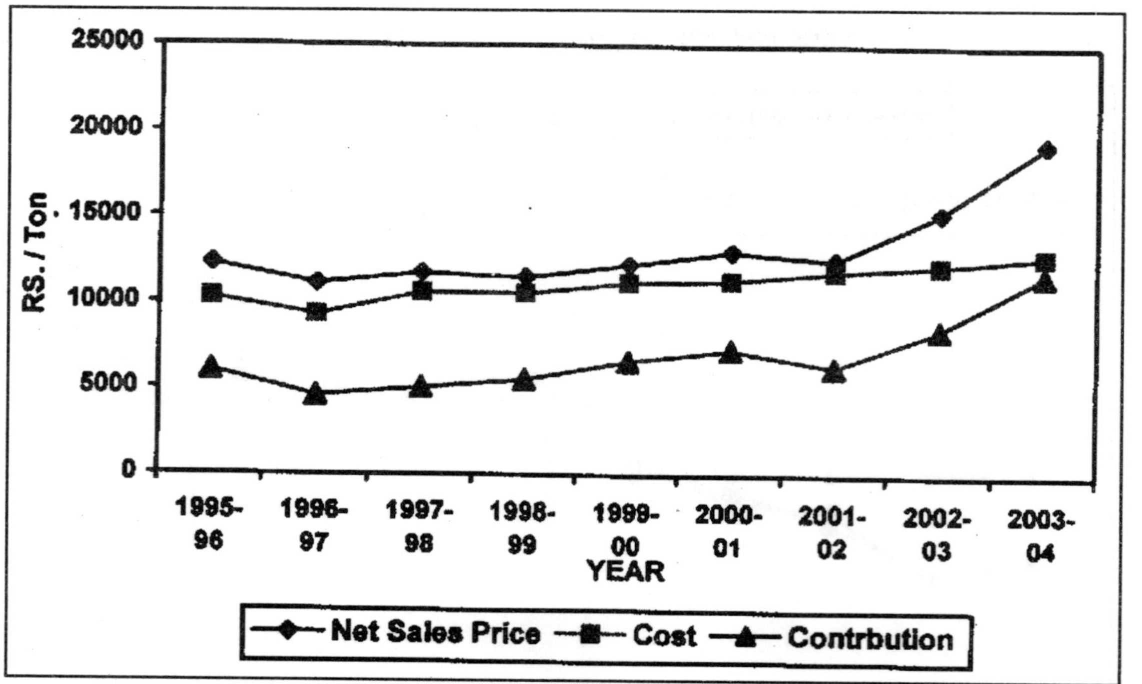

Chart 4.52: Average Sales Price, Cost and Contribution

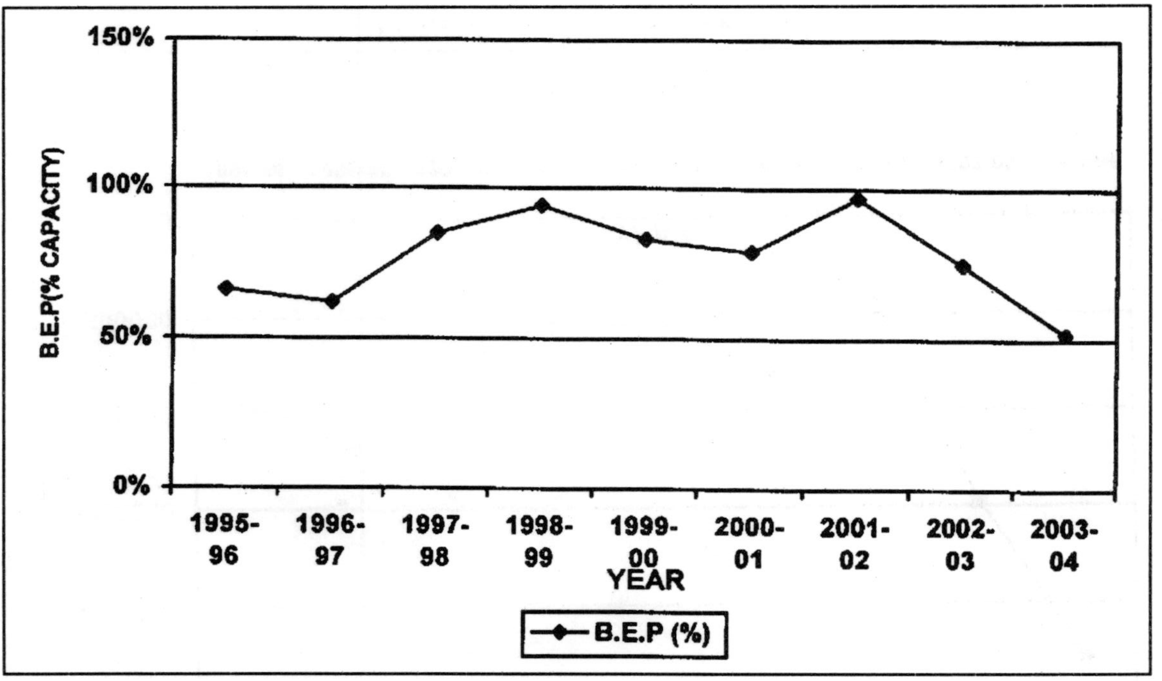

Chart 4.53: Break Even Point

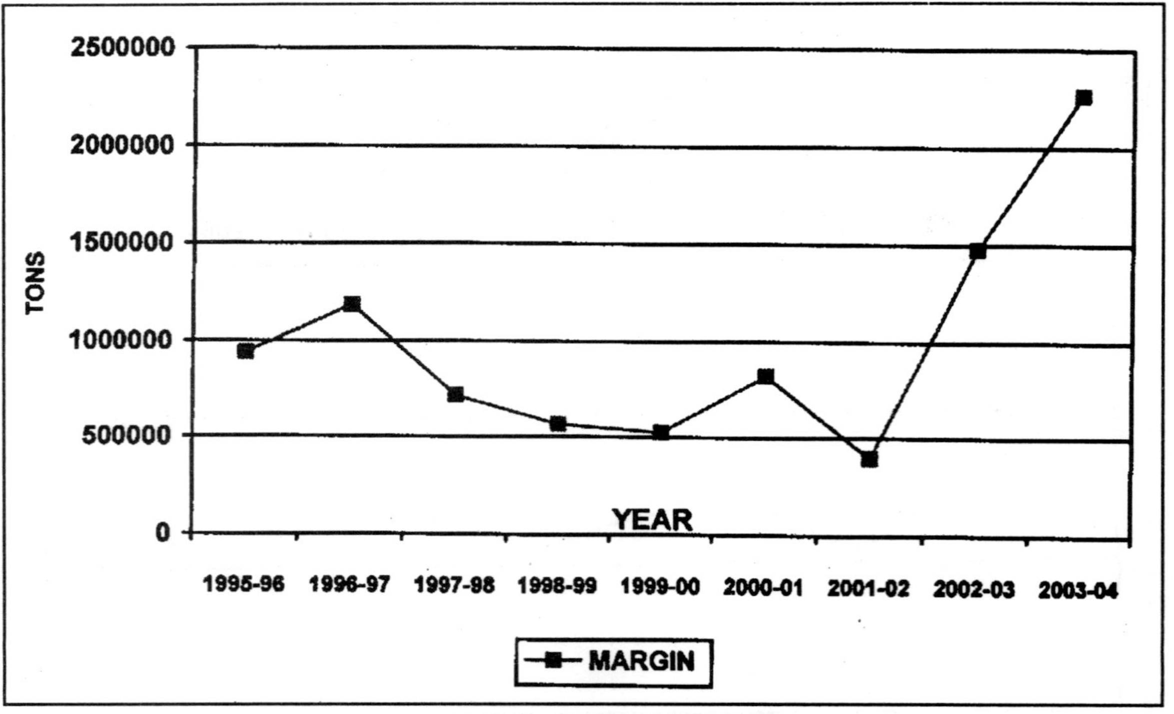

Chart 4.54: Margin of Operation

SENSITIVITY ANALYSIS FOR RSP (BASE: 2004-05)

Sensitivity analysis for RSP at various levels of Sales Price and input raw material prices with respect to 2004-05 has been made as follows (Table 4.26):

In case the sales price falls by 20% and raw material cost increases by 10% then the break even point will get shifted from the present level of 51% to 87%. However, if the sales prices falls by 20% and raw material cost also increased by 20%, the break-even point will shift from the present level of 51% to 100%.

Thus, it is evident that the firm needs to prepare itself to operate at 100% capacity in the future to maintain profit. Sales volume should also be closer to the production volume. Sales volume is an important criterion in achieving the B.E.P target. B.E.P production volume with less sales volume, will result in stock accretion of finished goods, which will result in financial loss for the firm. An aggressive marketing strategy is needed for long-term sustainability of profit for the firm.

Sales price may stabilize at a lower level in the future and the raw material expenditure may increase compared to 2004-05 due to increase in the imported coal prices, Ferro alloys prices etc. However the company is insulated from the increase in the input price of iron ore raw material due to sourcing of the material from the captive mines of SAIL. Thus resilience in the profitability strength is quite high for the company.

	15% Reduction in Sales Price and 30% increase in Raw material cost	20% Reduction in Sales Price and 30% increase in Raw material cost
Unit Net Sales price	21085	19604
Unit Cost	21341	21341
-Variable Cost	13189	13189
-Fixed Cost	8152	8152
Unit Contribution	7895	6415
B.E.P.		
- Percentage	95%	117%
- Volume	1593791	1961586

Table 4.26: Sensitivity Analysis for RSP (Base: 2004-05)

	No change	10% Reduction in Sales Price	20% Reduction in Sales Price	10% increase in Raw Material Cost	20% increase in Raw Material Cost
0	1	2	3	4	5
Unit Net Sales price	25526	22973	20421	25526	25526
Unit Cost	18859	18859	18859	19936	21013
-Variable Cost	10712	10712	10712	11787	12862
-Fixed Cost	8147	8147	8147	8149	8151
Unit Contribution	14814	12261	9709	13739	12664
B.E.P.					
- Percentage	51%	61%	78%	55%	59%
- Volume	848920	1025654	1295323	915594	993573

	10% Reduction in Sales Price and 10% increase in Raw material cost	20% Reduction in Sales Price and 20% increase in Raw material cost	20% Reduction in Sales Price and 10% increase in Raw material cost	10% Reduction in Sales Price and 20% increase in Raw material cost
0	6	7	8	9
Unit Net Sales price	22973	20421	20421	22973
Unit Cost	19936	21013	19936	21013
-Variable Cost	11787	12862	11787	12862
-Fixed Cost	8149	8151	8149	8151
Unit Contribution	11186	7559	8634	10111
B.E.P.				
-Percentage	67%	100%	87%	74%
-Volume	1124521	1664621	1456986	1244395

In the above table, it can be seen that if the average sales price falls by 15% and the raw material expenditure increases by 30% as compared to the levels in 2004-05, the company needs to achieve 95% of production and sales capacity to remain break even. However, if the sales price drops by 20%, then the break even point crosses 100% production capacity of the plant. The firm needs to take quick decisions in terms of increase in capacity and capacity utilization so as to create more wealth in the future.

CASH FLOW ANALYSIS

Introduction

It is mandatory for the companies filing reports with the SEBI (Securities and Exchange Board of India) to include a cash flow statement in their quarterly and annual reports. This is as per Accounting Standary-3 published by ICAI (Institute of Chartered Accountants of India).

The cash-flow statement does not consider the non-cash items such as Depreciation and tells how much actual money the company has generated and spent during a particular time frame. It is distinct form the Profit and Loss Account and balance sheet because it does not include the amount of future incoming and outgoing cash that has been recorded on credit. Therefore, cash is not the same as net income. Cash flow shows how the company has performed in managing inflows and outflows of cash. It also gives a clear picture of the company's ability to pay bills, creditors, and finance growth.

Many of the items in this statement are also found in both the Profit and Loss Account and balance sheet. But here, they're arranged to highlight the cash generated and spent. Cash flow is determined by looking at three components by which cash enters and leaves a company: operations, investing and financing,

Operations

For measuring the cash inflows and outflows caused by core business operations, the operations component of cash

STATEMENT OF CASH FLOW

Cash from Operations

- This is cash generated from day-to-day business operations.

Cash from Investing

- Cash used for investing in assets, as well as the proceeds from the sale of other businesses, equipment, or other long-term assets.

Cash from Financing

- Cash paid or received from issuing and borrowing of funds. This also includes dividend paid.

flow reflects how much cash in generated from a company's products or services. Generally, changes made in cash, accounts receivable, depreciation, inventory and accounts payable are reflected in cash from operations.

Cash flow is calculated by making certain adjustments to net income by adding or subtracting differences in revenue, expenses and credit transactions (appearing on the balance sheet and income statement) resulting from transactions that occur from one period to the next. These adjustments are made because non-cash items are calculated into net income (income statement) and total assets and liabilities (balance sheet). Because not all transactions involve actual cash items, many items have to be re-evaluated when calculating cash flow from operations.

For example, depreciation is not really a cash expense; it is an amount that is deducted from the total value of an asset that has previously been accounted for. That is why it is added back into net sales for calculating cash flow. The only time income from an asset is accounted for in CFS calculation is when the asset is sold.

Changes in accounts receivable on the balance sheet from one accounting period to he next must also be reflected in cash flow. If accounts receivable decrease, this implies that more cash has entered the company from customers paying off their credit accounts—the amount by which accounts receivable has decreased is then added to net sales. If accounts receivable from one accounting period to the next, the amount of the increase must be deducted from net sales because, although the amounts represented in AR are revenue, they are not cash.

An increase in inventory, on the other hand, signals that a company has spent more money to purchase more raw materials. If the inventory was paid with cash, the increase in the value of inventory is deducted from net sales. A decrease in inventory would be added to net sales. If inventory was purchased on credit, an increase in accounts payable would occur on the balance sheet, and the amount of the increase from one year to the other would be deducted from net sales.

The same logic holds true for taxes payable, salaries payable and prepaid insurance. If something has been paid off, then the difference in the value owed from one year to the next has to be subtracted from net income. If there is an amount that is still owed, then any differences will have to be added to net earnings.

Investing

Changes in equipment, assets or investments relate to cash from investing. Usually cash changes from investing are a "cash out" item, because cash is used to buy new equipment, buildings or short-term assets such as marketable securities. However, when a company divests of an asset, the transaction is considered "cash in" for calculating cash from investing.

Financing

Changes in debt, loans or dividends are accounted for in cash from financing. Changes in cash from financing are "cash in" when capital is raised, and they're "cash out" when dividends are paid. Thus, if a company issues a bond to the public, the company receives cash financing. However, when interest is paid to bondholders, the company is reduction its cash.

The cash flow statement enables tracking of cash inflows and outflows in the business and reveals the causes of cash flow shortfalls and surpluses. If cash flow from the operating activities is positive, then it indicates that the business is self-sufficient in funding its daily operational cash flows internally. If the number is negative, then it indicates that outside funds were needed to sustain the operations of the business.

Investing activities in business generally use cash to acquire new equipment and machinery. However there is also cash inflow while selling old fixed assets or hiving of a portion of the business. When a company needs cash to fund investing activities in a given year, it comes either from internal operating cash flow surplus or from financing activity increases or from cash reserves built up in prior years.

Financing activities represent the external sources of funds available to the business. Financing activities typically provides funds when a company has shortfalls in operating and/or investing activities. The reverse is also true when operating activities are a source of excess cash flow, and the overflow even after meeting cash flow from investing activities is used to reduce debt.

The increase/decrease in cash figure at the bottom of the cash flow statement represents the net result of operating, investing and financing activities. If a business ever runs out of cash, it can't survive, so this is a key number.

Cash flow statement is used not only to analyze sources and uses of cash from year to year but also from month to month if the accounting system is ready to produce monthly statements. The fluctuations in the cash flow can be understood from the statement.

Timely financial information is required to help manage businesses effectively. This is also required to predict cash requirement in the coming months.

CASH MANAGEMENT IN RSP

The source of cash in RSP is from allotment of fund by SAIL corporate office. As this makes RSP dependent so far as the sources of fund are concerned, therefore, cash management at RSP is done under some constraints. In addition, a small amount of cash is also generated in RSP through Secondary products sales.

The corporate office allocates funds to RSP on a daily basis. A limit is fixed by the corporate office above, which RSP cannot withdraw from its commercial banks. Banks deny for excess payments. Now whatever amount is allocated daily is according to the requirement. At the end of each day the balance remaining is carried forward to the authorized bank SBI, New Delhi of the corporate office. Theoretically the net balance for each day should be zero. But due to some logistics problem it does not happen so. The balance remains for one day and RSP gets some interest over it, which is calculated at the year-end.

For smoothening the cash flow functions SAIL/RSP has maintained some easy functions among its units. The *IUCA* (Inter Unit Current A/c) works in this regard. RSP need not go for payments to and receipts from its sister plants/central units. All such payments and receipts are being maintained in the IUCA and taken care by the corporate office. In reality, it is the single unit SAIL which is viewed to gain from profit/losses. As for example if RSP suffers from Loss, it cannot be said that it is under risk because it is the reserve under SAIL that matters.

The cash inflow and outflow of RSP can be summarized as under:

1. Inflow (Sources of funds):
   * Allocation from corporate office.
   * SAIL proceeds of secondary products.
   * Miscellaneous cash received at cash section centre.
   * Liquid credit at Rourkela and Kolkata.

2. Outflow (Application of Funds):

   * Payment of taxes and duties i.e. excise duty sales tax, income tax etc.
   * Payment of Inward and outward freight.
   * Payment of salary and wages.
   * Payment for power and fuels.
   * Payment for raw materials, spares and stores purchased directly by RSP
   * Other miscellaneous payments.

We know that when there are limited sources of funds, an efficient management should take steps in utilizing the funds properly.

CASH FLOW STATEMENT ANALYSIS OF RSP

It can be seen from Chart 4.55 that Cash flow form operating activities for the firm has been increasing over the years except during the years 2000-01 and 2001-02. It has witnessed a major upward jump of about 287% during the Financial Year 2003-04. Cash flows from Operating activities were negative during the years 1996-97, 1997-98 and 2001-02. The reasons for these can be analyzed from the behaviour of the mnajor elements as shown in Chart 4.56.

The reasons for increase in cash flows during 2003-04 were substantial reduction in the Loss, Decrease in inventory levels and increase in provisions, which has affected the Net Profit. During this year, the steel market revived after a long spell of slow down. Cash Flow from operating activities is the highest during the year 2004-05 due to very high profit for the firm (Chart 4.56).

During the Financial year 2000-01, although there was a reduction in net loss as compared to the previous year, reduction in inventory was very less, which has affected the cash flow.

The cash flows during the financial years 1996-97 and 1997-98 were negative due to losses suffered by the company

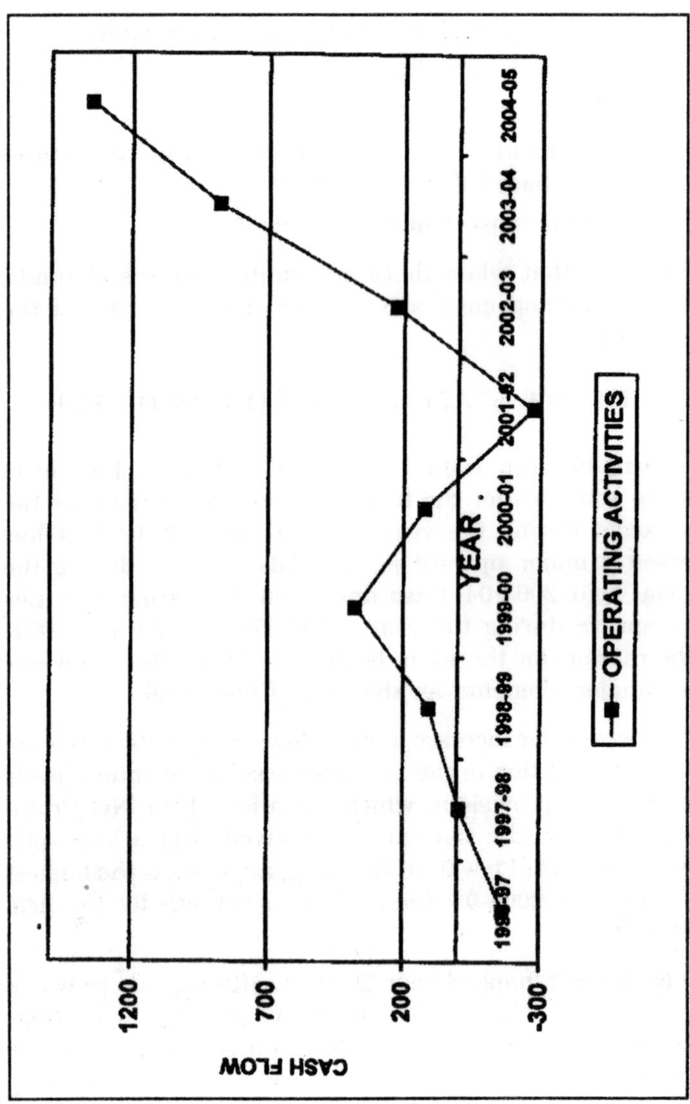

Chart 4.55: Cash Flow From Operating Activities

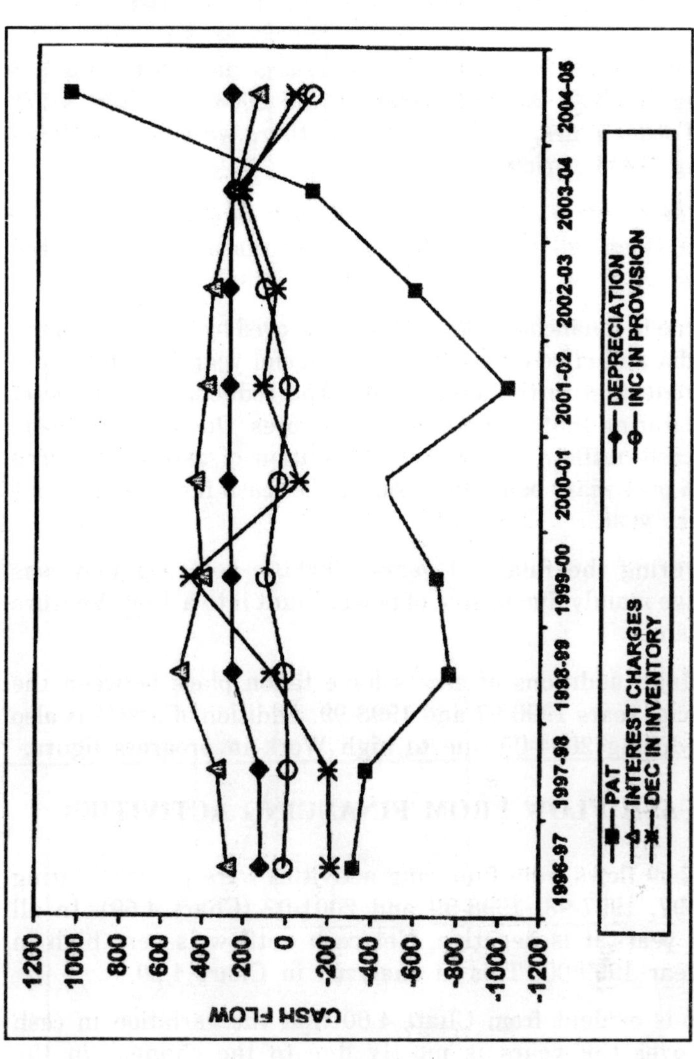

Chart 4.56: Major Elements

and increase in inventory levels by a substantial percentage. It was also negative in the year 2001-02 due to a substantial increase in the net loss of the firm during that period.

CASH FLOW FROM INVESTING ACTIVITIES

Cash flows from investing activities have been positive during 1999-00, 2000-01, 2001-02 and 2003-04 (Chart 4.57). In all other years, it is negative, i.e. there were cash outflows during these periods.

There was a steep increase in cash flow during 1999-00 and a steep fall during 2000-01. The reasons are analyzed below:

Due to Financial Restructuring approved by the Government of India and effected during the financial year 1999-00, there was reduction in the asset value. The reduction in the asset value during that year was Rs. 889 crores. Due to this reason, and cash outflow on account of addition of assets compared to the past years being too less, the net cash flow was positive in that year.

During the financial years 2000-01, net cash flow was positive mainly due to sale of power plant into a Joint Venture company.

Major additions of assets have taken place between the financial years 1996-97 and 1998-99. Addition of assets is also high during 2004-05 due to high Work in progress figure.

CASH FLOW FROM FINANCING ACTIVITIES

Cash flows from financing activities were positive during 1996-97, 1997-98, 1998-99 and 2001-02 (Chart 4.59). In all other years it is negative. Net cash outflow is very high in the year 1999-00. This is analyzed in Chart 4.60.

It is evident from Chart 4.60 that the variation in cash flow over the years is mostly due to the changes in the borrowings and IUCA balances of the firm.

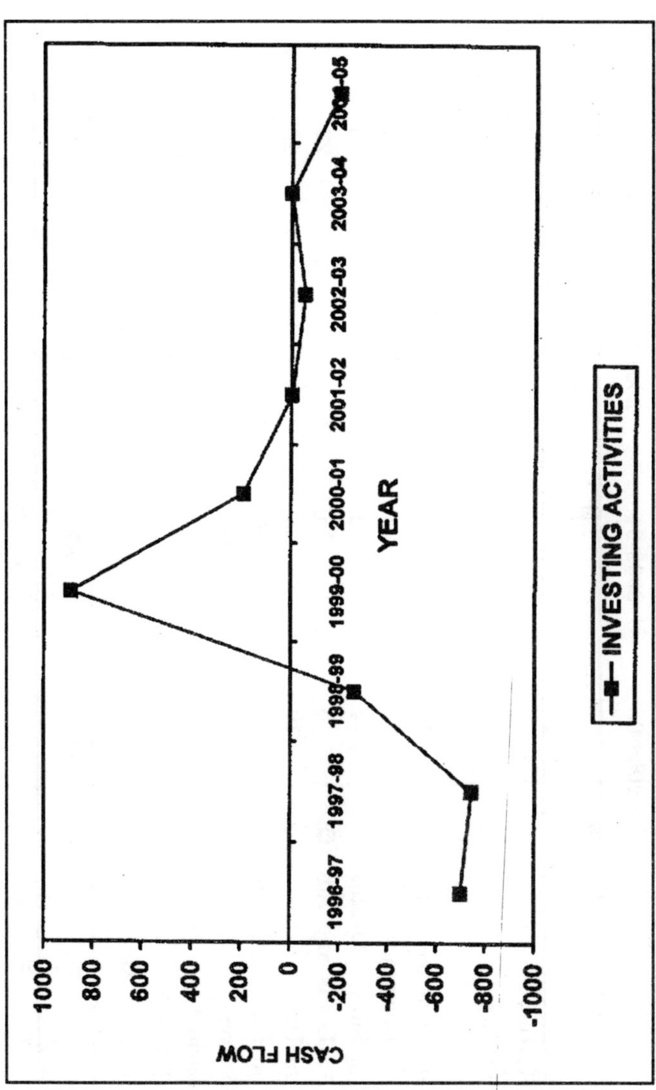

Chart 4.57: Cash Flow From Investing Activities

Table 4.27: Cash Flow Statement Analysis of RSP

(Rs. in Crores)

	2004-05	2003-04	2002-03	2001-02	2000-01
	1	2	3	4	5
Opg. Activities					
Profit After Tax	1045	-109	-593	-1036	-445
Depreciation	275.5	273.8	280.3	279	282
Interest and Finance Charges	151	256	365	390	444
Decrease in Inventory	-26	224	60	121	-58
Decrease in Sundry Debtor	-4	0	0	20	10
Decrease in Loans and Adv (Oth)	5	15	10	22	13
Decrease in Dre	10	26	9	-26	22
Decrease in Current Liabilities	20	-60	-9	-30	-33
Additional Prov	-112	260	113	-4	43
Interest Earned	-6	-7	-7	-9	-12
Dividend Earned	0	0	0	0	0
Profit on Sale of Assets	-9	-1	-1	0	-144
	1350	**878**	**227**	**-273**	**122**

Investing Activities					
Addition of Assets	-232	-11	-81	-30	-25
Sale of Assets	18	4	16	14	58
Sale of Houses	9	1	2	0	1
Sale of Power Plant	0	0	0	0	144
Sale of Investment	0	0	0	0	0
Interest Earned	6	8	8	10	12
Dividend Earned	0	0	0	0	0
	-199	**1**	**-56**	**-6**	**190**
Financing Activities					
Increase in Share Capital	0	0	0	0	0
Increase in RES/Surplus	0.0	0.0	0.0	0.0	0.0
Increase in Loan Amount + Increase in IUCA Balance	-990	-622	194	669	132
Dividend PMT	0	0	0	0	0
INT and Finance Charges	-151	-256	-365	-390	-444
	-1141	**-878**	**-272**	**278**	**-312**
Net Increase in Cash and Cash Equivalent	**9.30**	**-0.02**	**0.00**	**0.04**	**0.06**
Opening Balance	6.45	0.14	0.14	0.10	0.04
Closing Balance	15.75	0.12	0.14	0.14	0.10

Table 4.27 (concld.)

	1999-00	1998-99	1997-98	1996-97
	6	7	8	9
Opg. Activities				
Profit After Tax	-704	-765	-374.8	-316
Depreciation	265	256	127	120
Interest and Finance Charges	405	514	333	282
Decrease in Inventory	466	73	-200	-213
Decrease in Sundry Debtor	-8	-3	23	-21
Decrease in Loans and Adv (Oth)	28	-6	9	17
Decrease in DRE	-79	-2	-2	1
Decrease in Current Liabilities	-84	45	100	-33
Additional Prov	101	6	-9	9
Interest Earned	-12	-12	-13	-13
Dividend Earned	0	0	0	0
Profit on Sale of Assets	0	0	0	0
	378	**106**	**-7**	**-168**

Investing Activities				
Addition of Assets	-12	-278	-768	-723
Sale of Assets	889	2	10	11
Sale of Houses	0	0	0	0
Sale of Power Plant	0	0	0	0
Sale of Investment	0	0	0	0
Interest Earned	12	11	13	12
Dividend Earned	0	0	0	0
	890	**-265**	**-744**	**-700**
Financing Activities				
Increase in Share Capital	0	0	0	0
Increase in Res/Surplus	0.0	0.0	0.7	-13.5
Increase in Loan Amount + Inc in IUCA Balance	-863	672	1085	1161
Dividend PMT	0	0	0	0
Int and Finance Charges	-405	-514	-333	-282
	-1267	159	753	866
Net increase in cash and cash equivalent	-0.03	-0.99	1.00	-1.80
Opening Balance	0.07	1.06	0.06	1.86
Closing Balance	0.04	0.07	1.06	0.06

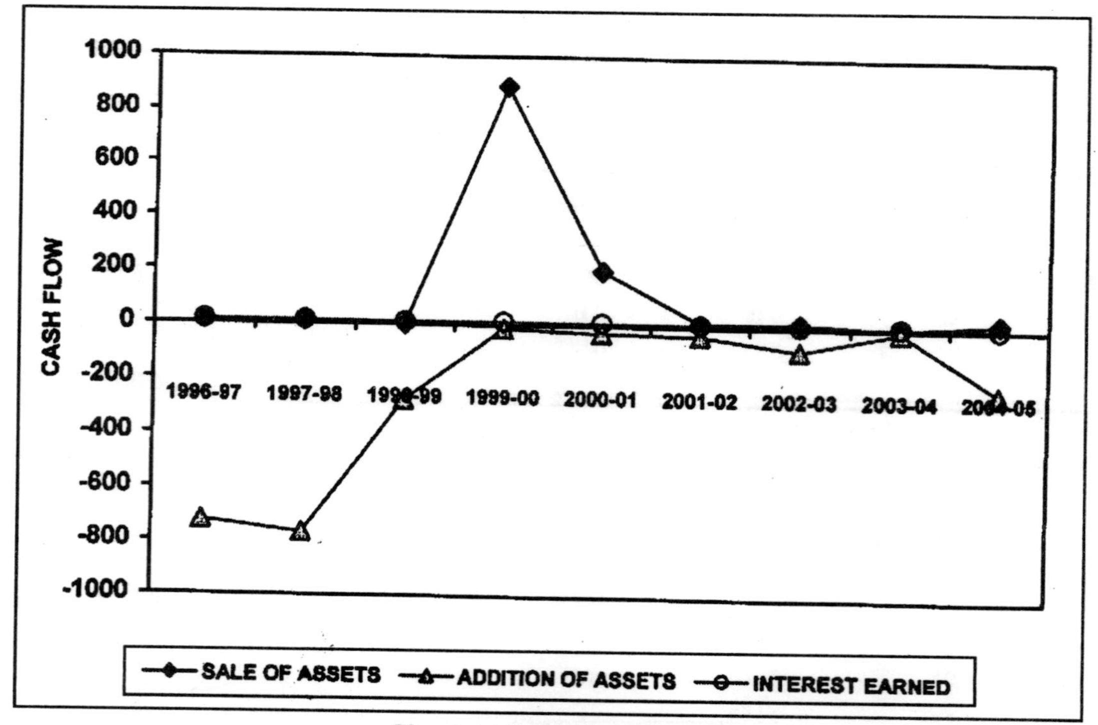

Chart 4.58: Major Elements

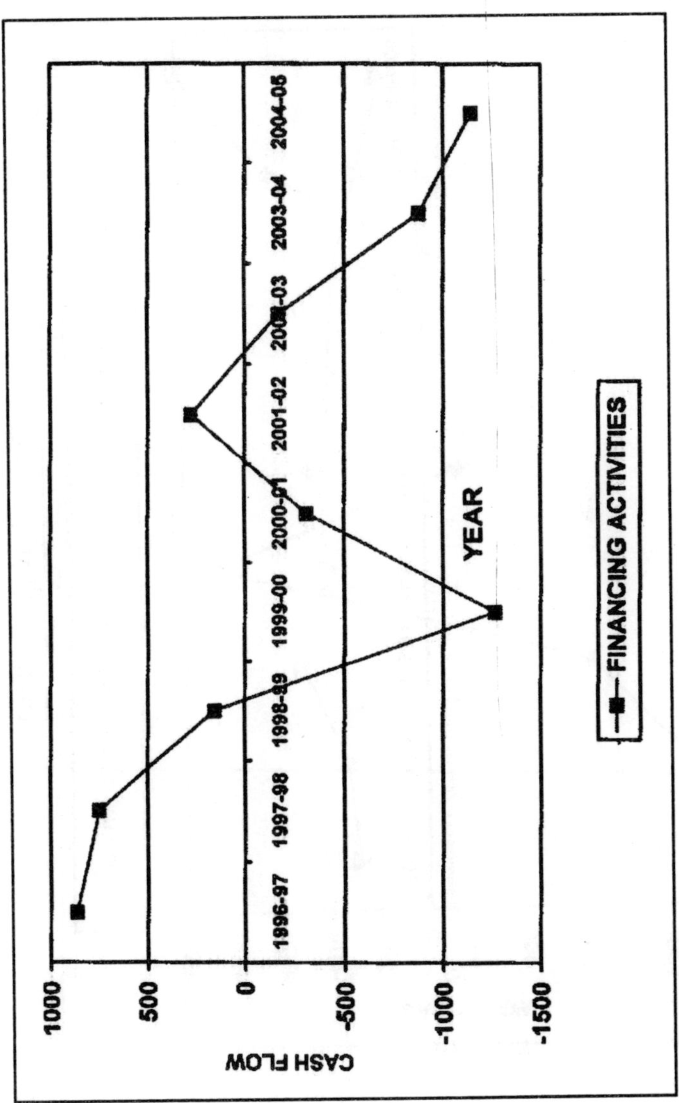

Chart 4.59: Cash Flow From Financing Activities

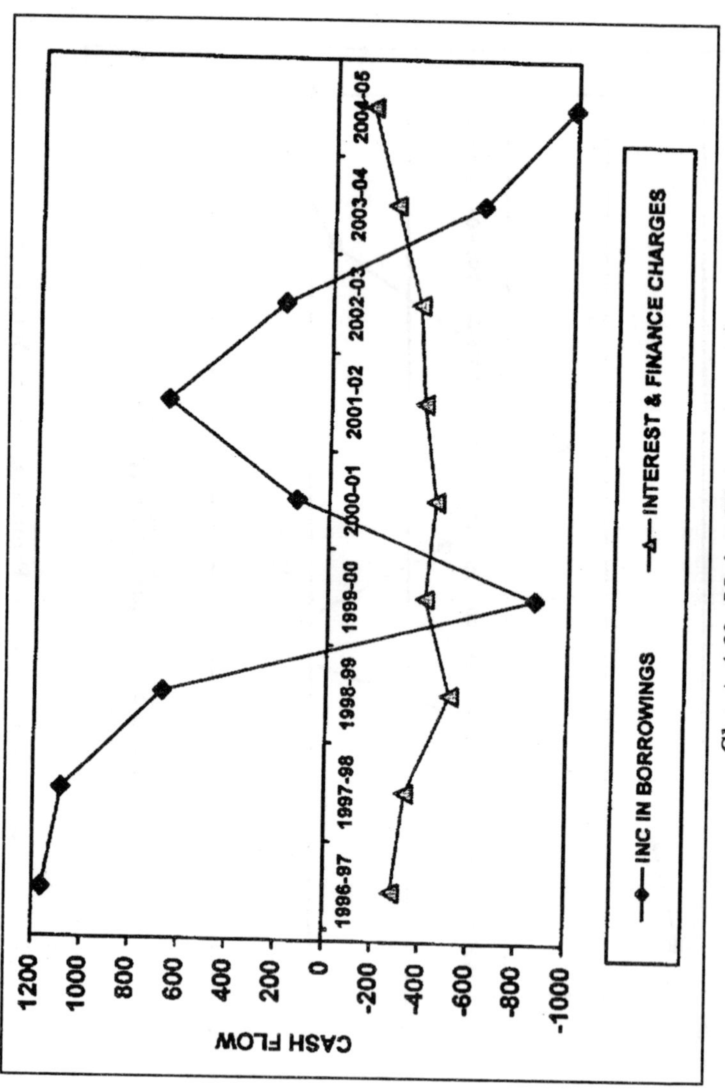

Chart 4.60: Major Elements

The RSP is one of the main plant units of SAIL. As per the Accounting policies of SAIL, the transactions of the plant units with other units and central units like Head Office, Central Marketing Organisation, Transport and Shipping Unit, Central Coal Supply Organisation, Raw Material Division etc. are done through Inter Unit Current Accounts (IUCA) appearing in the Balance Sheet both in the Asset and Liability sides. Majority of the loan amounts are transferred by the Head Office (SAIL) to RSP through IUCA. Sundry debtors balances also appear in the IUCA. It is not easy to segregate these items directly.

For the purpose of analysis, local borrowings appearing in the Balance-sheet of RSP as well as net IUCA amounts are clubbed together and kept under Financing activities head.

Reduction in the borrowings and IUCA was the highest during 1999-00. This was mainly due to the waiver of a major portion of SDF loan as a part of the Financial-restructuring scheme approved by Government of India for SAIL. Again borrowings increased by a bigger amount during the year 2001-02 due to huge loss suffered by the company. Considerable reductions in borrowings have taken place during the financial years 2003-04 and 2004-05 mainly due to an improved profit and cash situation of the firm.

It is seen from Chart 4.61 that the net cash flow and the closing balance appear to move in the same direction. These are negligible every year due to the nature of cash transactions done at the plant Unit levels of SAIL. Major chunk of closing balance of Cash is maintained in the Corporate Office (SAIL) books. This is described in details in the next page.

It is apparent from the graph that in the recent times, cash flow from operating activities is increasing and that from financing activities decreasing.

The cash flow statement is useful to analyze the following dimensions of business:

1) Financial Profitability,

2) Financial Flexibility,

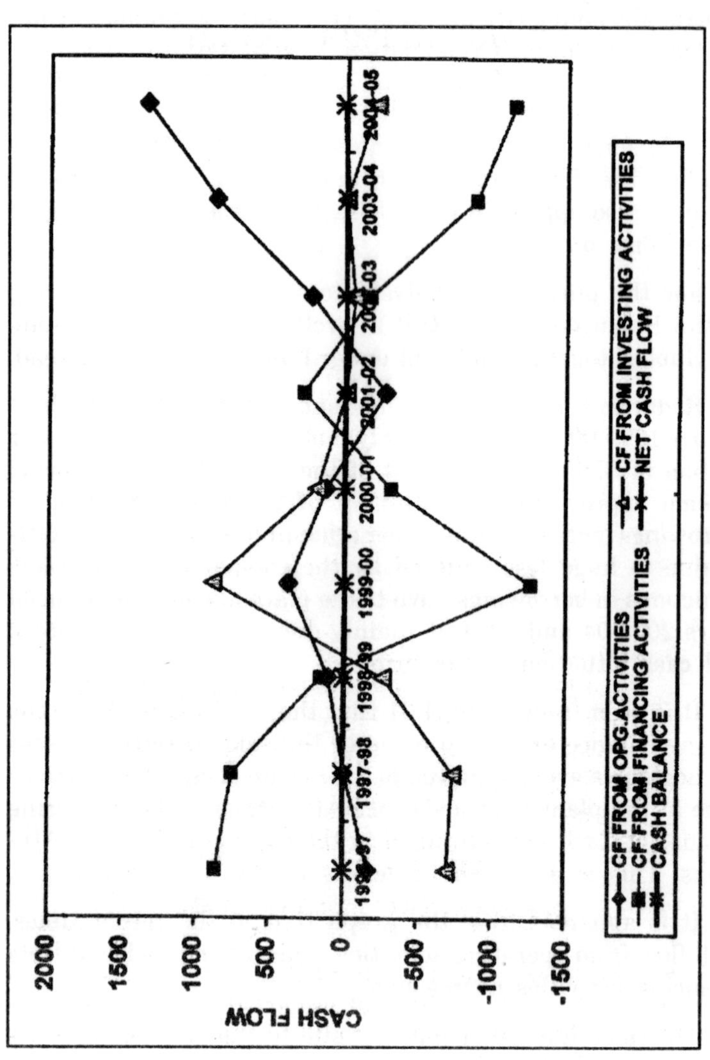

Chart 4.61: Summary of Cash Flow

3) Liquidity and
4) Risk.

FINANCIAL PROFITABILITY

- The operating activities have been the major sources of generation of cash for RSP. It indicates the strength of its Operations.
- Cash flows from operating activities were positive in all these years except in the years 1996-97, 1997-98 and 2001-02.
- In 1996-97 and 1997-98, the cash flows from operating activities were negative due to losses suffered by the company and increase in inventory levels by a substantial percentage. Whereas cash flow during the financial year 2001-02 was negative due to a substantial increase in the net loss of the firm during that year.
- In all other years except 2004-05, even if the company made losses, the cash flow from operations were positive due to considerable reduction in inventories.
- During the Financial year 2004-05, the Company has been able to bounce back to profitability by registering huge profit of Rs. 1045 crores in the upward steel market. Due to this, cash flow from operating activities has improved considerably during this time. There is an increase of cash flow of 287% during 2003-04 and 54% during 2004-05 as compared to the previous years.

FINANCIAL FLEXIBILITY

- The figures depict that RSP has added assets in all these years. Addition of assets was very high during the financial years 1996-97, 1997-98 and 1998-99. This was due to capitalization of major assets commissioned as a part of the modernization. During the years 1996-97 and 1997-98, both cash flows from operating as well as investing activities were negative. Company was suffering from losses. Cash flows from financing activities were positive, which had taken care of these. There was an increase in borrowings for the firm during this time. Flexibility of raising loan was possible due to the strong financial health of the parent company SAIL.

- However from 2003-04 on wards the scenario changed for RSP. Cash flow from operating activities was quite high to give flexibility for addition of assets and reduction in borrowings.

LIQUIDITY

- The company does not believe in keeping huge amount of idle cash.
- It transfers its idle cash to Corporate Office account at the end of the day's transaction as a matter of policy of its parent company, SAIL.
- The inventories, which might have blocked the liquidity flow, are found to have reduced.

FINANCIAL RISK

- Financial risk of the company is associated with that of its parent company SAIL, since RSP is an integral part of SAIL. Going by this, RSP doesn't have any Financial risk at present.
- On a stand-alone mode, the figures explain risk associated with the company. This was because:
  - The company made losses all these years in the last decade except in the year 2004-05, in which it made a huge profit. But, the company still has accumulated losses in the balance sheet.

However, the situation is comfortable at present, since there is reduction in the borrowings and IUCA balances during the years 2003-04/2004-05 due to better cash profit situation of the firm. This is contrary to the increase in loans and net

IUCA balances in all other previous years except 1999-00 in which the company got the benefit of the Financial restructuring, corroborating support extended by Corporate office to manage the operating and investing activities of the firm.

Recommendations

— The RSP needs to maintain the profit level of the financial year 2004-05 for 3 more years to be able to completely wipe out accumulated losses of the past years and become vibrant. To achieve this it needs to operate at 100% capacity utilization and adopt a strong marketing strategy to sell them too.

CASH MANAGEMENT IN SAIL

Cash management in SAIL comprises of managing cash for all its units. Management of cash takes place at the corporate level.

Centralized Banking System

Today in most multinational, corporate, cash management is organized centrally. Typically, the major goal is to concentrate overall group liquidity as much as is possible and reasonable. In a broader sense, cash management comprises of all incoming and outgoing payments in the most efficient way. To achieve this, organizations need, on the one hand, instruments like bank policy and cash pooling, and on the other hand, software intelligence. In reality the right mix of organizational and software intelligence probably leads to the best result. The necessary links between banks, treasury software and accounting system can be realized via interfaces.

Advantages include, reduction in error, capacity to handle larger volumes of transactions, anywhere banking through centralized operations. It is a step further towards centralizing the infrastructure for setting up critical network architecture for bringing the entire core banking operation under the single umbrella.

Centralized banking system in SAIL

The SAIL has cash credit clean (CCC) account with SBI, New Delhi; to send instructions to the concerned upcoming branches and up country branches regarding opening/closing/ amending the operation of the amount with the stipulated condition. No daily revolving cash credit limit or monthly limit is fixed for the CC account. Operational remittance statements are being sent by the plant/units after certification from bank to facilitate reconciliation at corporate level. Corporate office allocates funds by fixing limits for cash drawl for different units. Individual plant units are working strictly within the allocated limits. As a result individual plant units have very little roles to play in the centralized cash management system of SAIL. However, each plant units have bigger role to play for management of cash at plant levels to manage with the scarce resource.

SAIL has been very well managing its funds from and to its various units. By 6 pm of each day SAIL analyzes funds and calculates the balance. If it has surplus balance then quotations from different banks are invited and the surplus amount for each day is deposited as a fixed for 1 week or more in that bank which quotes the highest internet.

For a better functioning, SAIL has maintained the provision for IUCA (Inter Unit Current Account). As all the plants come under SAIL, any transaction between the plants is not subjected to payments and receipts tangibly. As any transaction under SAIL means money first, unless the money is paid no transactions are carried forward. If all the plants under SAIL go on for money receipt and payments among each other, it would mean making the job more complex.

Therefore, any purchase of raw materials among the sister plants, purchase of some secondary etc. are not subjected to any further receipts and payments of cash. All this is taken care by the corporate office itself. These transactions are made through IUCA codes for accounting purpose.

Table 4.28: Cash Flow Analysis of SAIL

(Rs. in Crores)

	2004-05	2003-04	2002-03	2001-02	2000-01
0	1	2	3	4	5
Opg. Activities					
Profit after tax	6817	2512	-304	-1707	-729
Depreciation	1192	1175	1146	1156	1150
Interest and Finance Charges	605	899	1334	1562	1752
Decrease in Inventory	-1139	663	297	477	104
Decrease in Sundry Debtor	-358	110	-271	298	130
Decrease in Loans and Adv	-464	-184	-94	139‘	-51
Decrease in Dre	84	158	41	-206	128
Decrease in Current Liabilities	373	-69	-180	-184	-1
Additional Prov	1796	1690	740	141	645
Interest Earned	-263	-75	-89	-105	-100
Dividend Earned	-13	-8	-3	-6	0
Profit on Sale of Assets	-11	-41	-144	-662	-287
	8618	6830	2475	904	2740

	2004-05	2003-04	2002-03	2001-02	2000-01
0	1	2	3	4	5
Investing Activities					
Addition of Assets	-561	-333	-241	-352	-335
Sale of assets	97	37	18	40	30
Sale of Houses	11	41	160	191	0
Sale of Power Plant					
Sale of Investment	-64	0	-5	-103	-59
Interest Earned	207	79	92	186	89
Dividend Earned	13	8	3	6	0
	-297	-168	27	639	117
Financing Activities					
Increase in Share Capital	0	0	0	0	0
Increase in Res./Surplus	0	22.6	-0.2	-0.2	0.6
Increase in Loan Amount	-2912	-4281	-1050	-231	-832
Dividend PMT	-701				

INT and Finance Charges	-605	-899	-1334	-1562	-1752
	-4225	-5158	-2384	-1794	-2583
Net Increase in Cash and Cash	**4096.30**	**1504.25**	**118.79**	**-251.06**	**274.75**
Opening Balance	2035.82	512.91	416.37	667.43	392.68
Closing Balance	6132.12	2017.16	535.16	416.37	667.43

Table 4.28: (contd.)

	1999-00	1998-99	1997-98	1996-97
0	6	7	8	9
Opg. Activities				
Profit After Tax	-1720	-1574	133	515
Depreciation	1134	1218	745	637
Interest and Finance Charges	1789	2017	1554	1179
Decrease in Inventory	2172	768	-1031	-1102
Decrease in Sundry Debtor	104	-34	129	-32
Decrease in Loans and Adv		-148	-218	66
Decrease in DRE	-397	-34	402	-300
Decrease in Current Liabilities	-531	82	215	-146
Additional Prov.	474	16	-160	-203
Interest Earned	-613	-298	-240	-247
Dividend Earned	0	0	0	0
Profit on Sale of Assets	0	-1	-4	0
	4122	**2013**	**1524**	**367**

Investing Activities				
Addition of Assets	-197	-1226	-2428	-2478
Sale of Assets		-267	47	60
Sale of Houses	0	1	4	0
Sale of Power Plant	0	6	23	21
Sale of Investment	10	167	0	-55
Interest Earned	1189	80	120	56
Dividend Earned	0	0	0	0
	3614	**-1239**	**-2235**	**-2396**
Financing Activities				
Increase in Share Capital	0	0	0	0
Increase in Res./Surplus	-3.6	4.22	0.0	-41.5
Increase in Loan amount		1003	2593	2848
Dividend PMT				
INT and Finance Charges	-1789	-2017	-1554	-1179
	-7727	**-1011**	**1040**	**1627**
Net Increase in Cash and Cash Equivalent	**8.78**	**-236.98**	**329.18**	**-402.60**
Opening Balance	383.90	620.88	291.70	694.3
Closing Balance	392.68	383.90	620.88	291.70

CASH FLOW FROM OPERATING ACTIVITIES

It can be seen from Chart 4.62 that Cash flow from operating activities for the firm has been increasing over the years except during 2000-01 and 2001-02. It has witnessed a major upward jump of about 180% during the Financial Year 2003-04. The reasons for these can be analyzed from the behaviour of the major elements as shown in Chart 4.63.

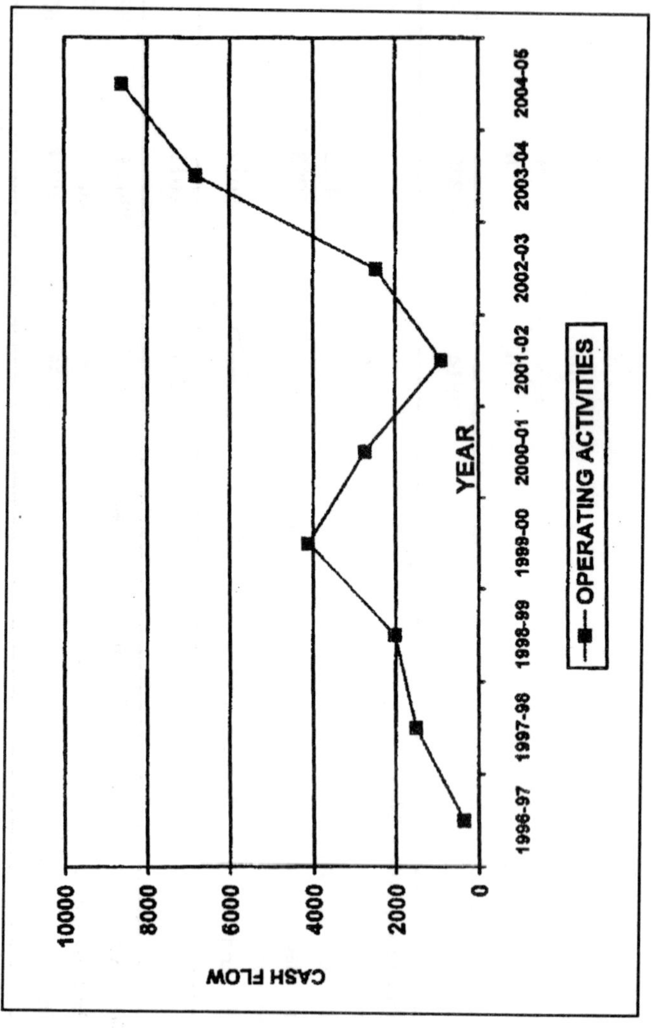

Chart 4.62: Cash flow From Operating Activities

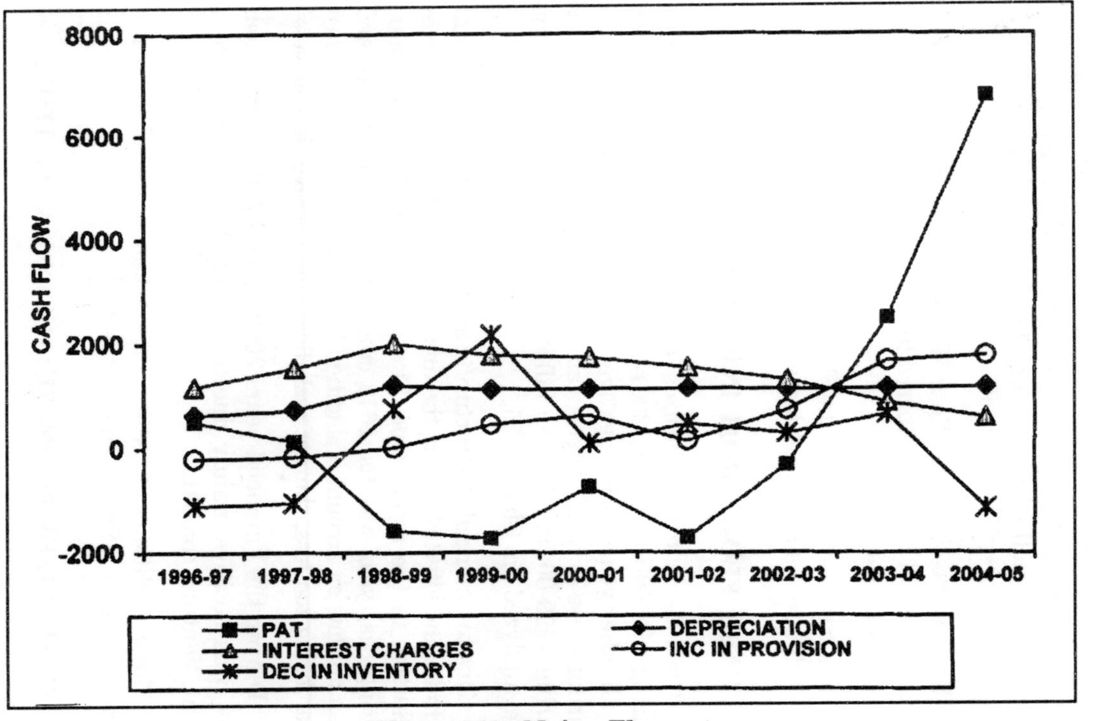

Chart 4.63: Major Elements

The reasons for increase in cash flows during 2003-04 were substantial improvement in Profit after Tax, Decrease in inventory levels and increase in provisions, which has affected the Net Profit. During this year, the steel market revived after a long spell of slow down. The firm registered positive net profit after five years of losses.

During the Financial Year 2000-01, although there was a reduction in net loss as compared to the previous year, reduction in inventory was very less, which has affected the cash flow.

The cash flow during the financial year 2001-02 was still lower due to a substantial increase in the net loss of the firm.

CASH FLOW FROM INVESTING ACTIVITIES

Cash flows from investing activities have been positive during 1999-00, 2000-01, 2001-02 and 2002-03 (Chart 4.64). In all other years, it is negative, i.e. there were cash outflows during these periods. There was a steep increase in cash flow during 1999-00 and a steep fall during 2000-01. The reasons are analyzed in Chart 4.65.

Due to Financial Restructuring approved by the Government of India and effected during the financial year 1999-00, there was reduction in the asset value. The reduction in the asset value during that year was Rs. 2612 crores. Due to this reason, and cash outflow on account of addition of assets compared to the last year being too less, the net cash flow was positive in that year.

During the Financial years 2000-01 and 2001-02, net cash flow was positive mainly due to sale of Power plants into a Joint Venture company.

Major additions of assets have taken place between the financial years 1996-97 and 1998-99.

CASH FLOW FROM FINANCING ACTIVITIES

Cash flow from financing activities was positive during 1996-97 and 1997-98. In all other years it is negative. Net cash outflow is very high in the year 1999-00 (Chart 4.66). This is analyzed in Chart 4.67.

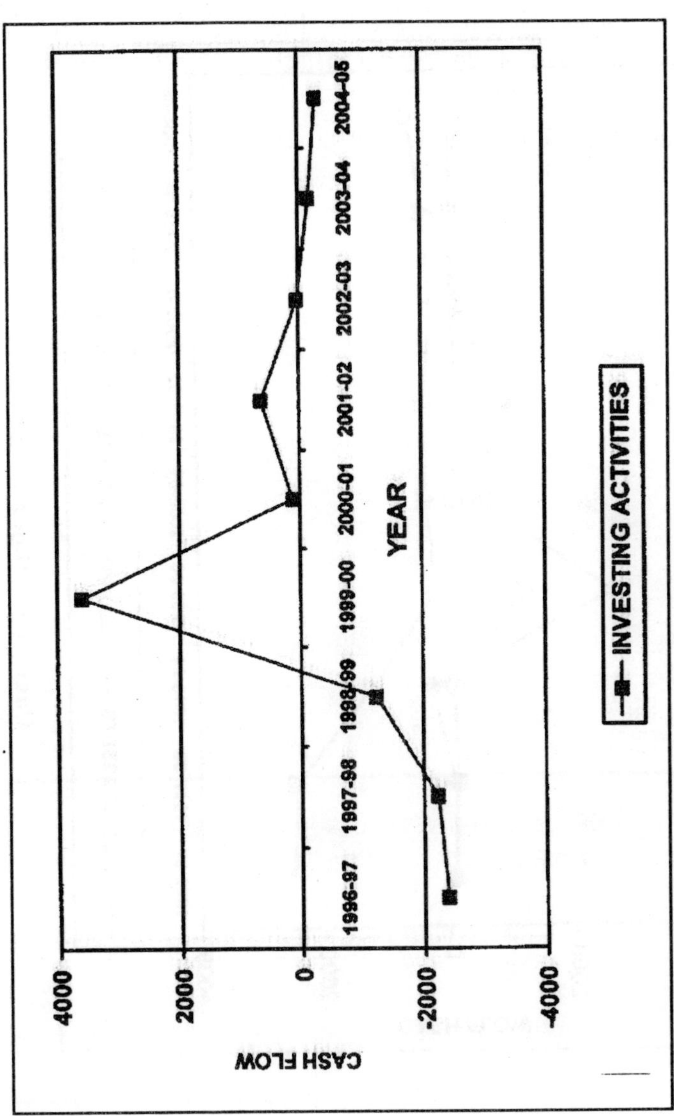

Cahrt 4.64: Cash Flow From Investing Activities

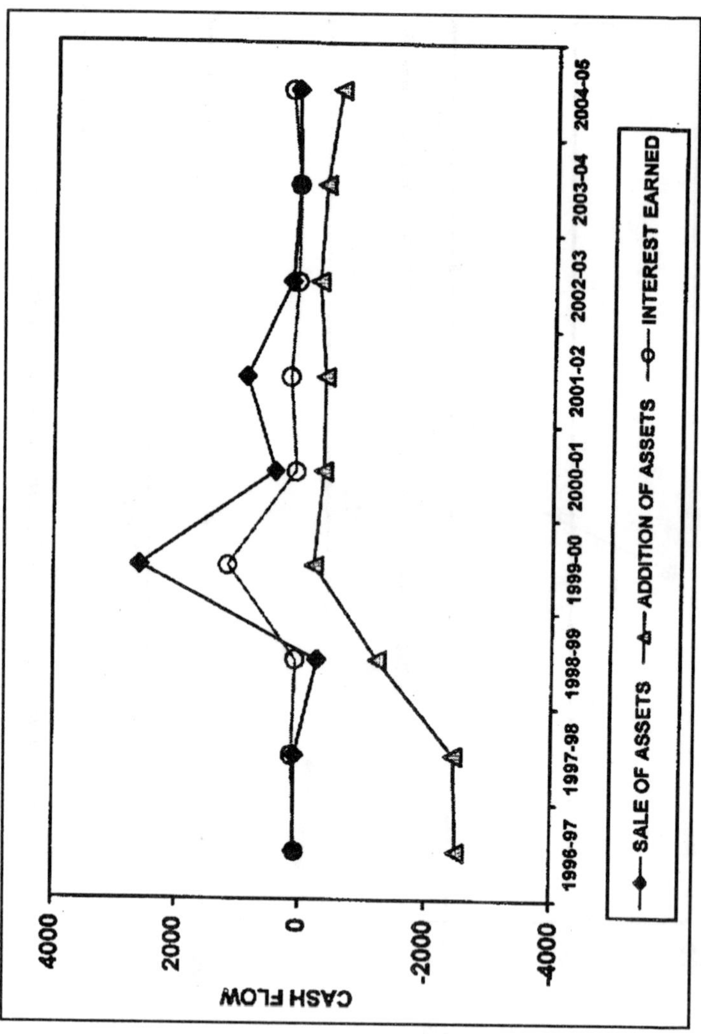

Chart 4.65: Major Elements

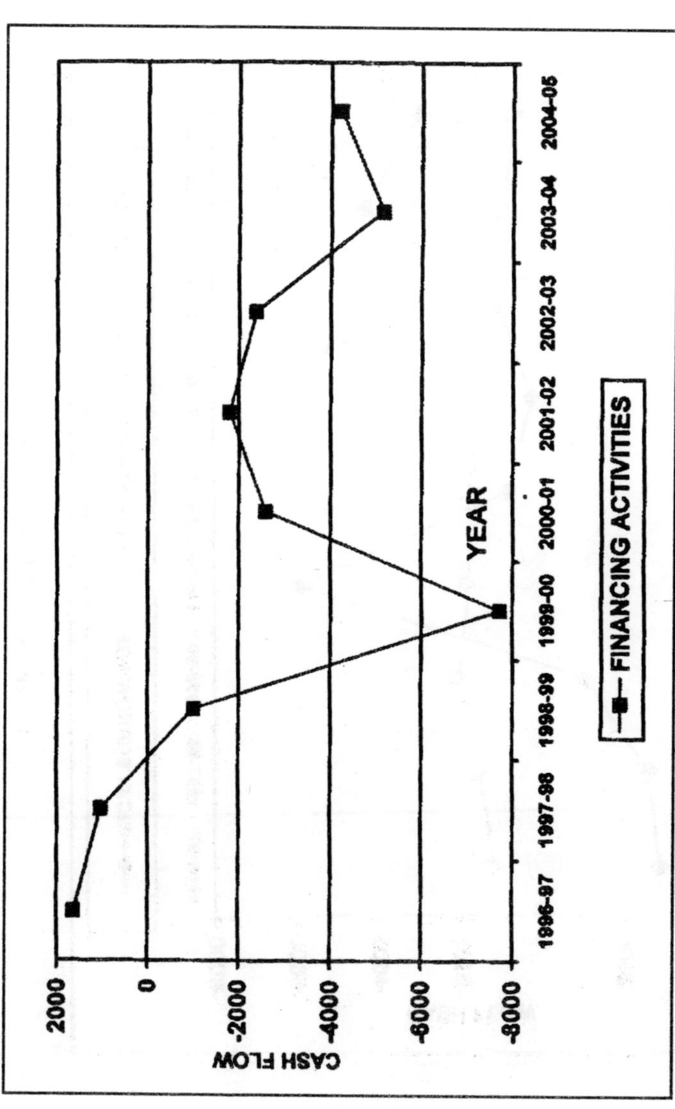

Chart 4.66: Cash Flow From Financing Activities

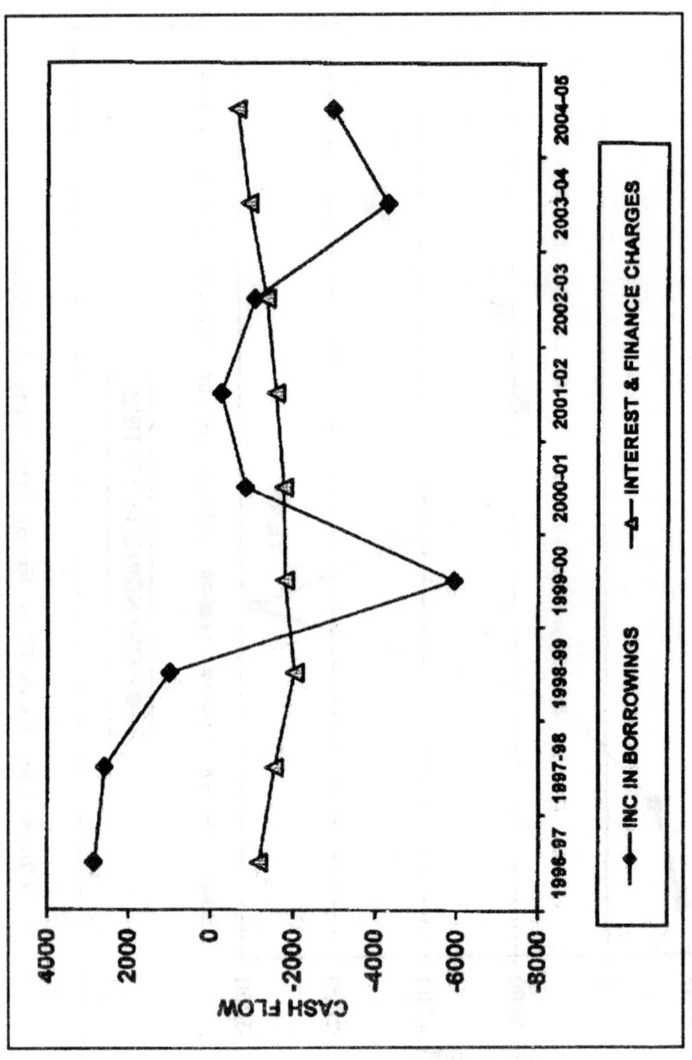

Chart 4.67: Major Elements

It is evident from Chart 4.67 that the variation in cash flow over the years is mostly due to the changes in the borrowings of the firm. Reduction in the borrowings was the highest during 1999-00. This was mainly due to the waiver of a major portion of SDF loan as a part of the Financial-restructuring programme approved by Government of India for SAIL. In the succeeding years after this, there have been net reductions of borrowings of the firm. Considerable reductions in borrowings have taken place during the financial years 2003-04 and 2004-05 mainly due to an improved profit situation of the firm.

It is seen from Chart 4.68 that the net cash flow and the closing balance appear to move in the same direction. Closing balances of Cash and Bank balance has been very high during the financial years 2003-04 and 2004-05. This is mostly due to a substantial increase in cash flow from operating activities.

The cash flow statement is useful to analyze the following dimensions of Business:

1) Financial Profitability,
2) Financial Flexibility,
3) Liquidity and
4) Risk.

FINANCIAL PROFITABILITY

- The operating activities have been the major sources of generation of cash for SAIL. It indicates the strength of its operations. Economies of scale and market presence are the two most important criteria contributing to this.
- Even if the company made considerable losses form 1998-99 to 2002-03, it could manage positive cash flows from operations. In all these years there has been a decrease in the inventory. During the year 1999-00, the company registered a huge loss of Rs. 1720 crores. However, the cash flow form operating activities was

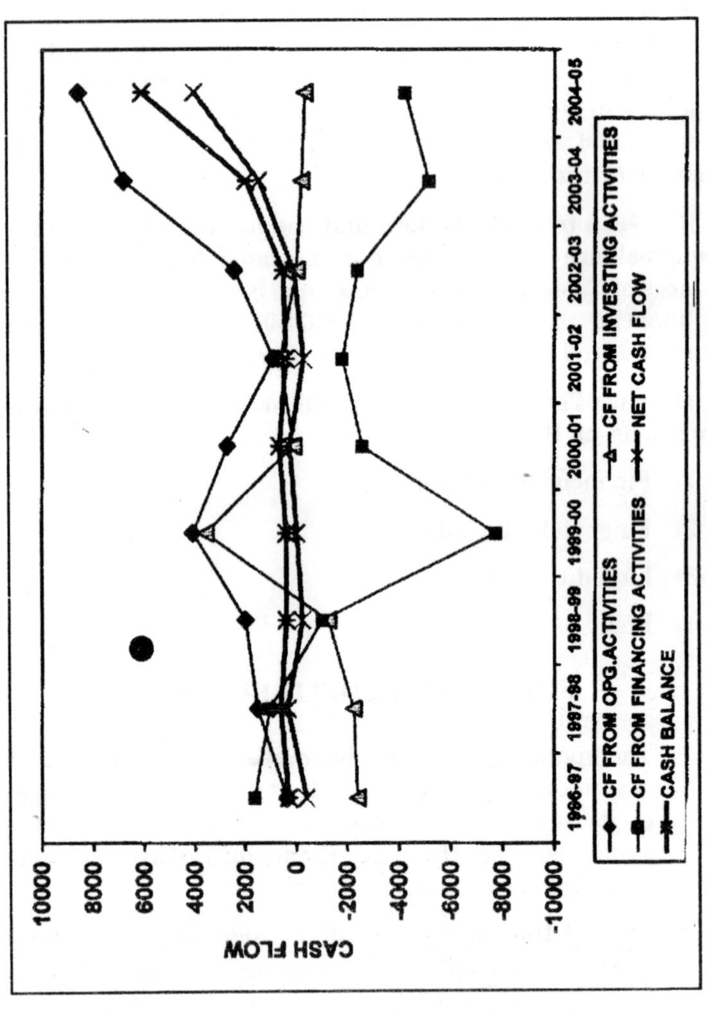

Chart 4.68: Summary of Cash flow

Rs. 4122 crores due to a substantial decrease in the inventory to the extent of Rs. 2172 crores and the reduction in loans and advances given to the subsidiaries on account of the relief under the Financial restructuring programme approved by the Govt. of India.

- During the Financial years 2003-04 and 2004-05, the Company has been able to bounce back to profitability by registering high profits in the upward steel market. Due to this, cash flows from operating activities have gone up considerably. There is an increase of cash flow by 176% during 2003-04 and 26% during 2004-05 as compared to the previous years.
- Net Cash from operating activities have been increasing in the previous years from 2001-02 to 2003-04. it had reduced by 67% from 2000-01 to 2001-02 showing decreasing profitability trend but it managed to show a positive upward profitability trend after that as it has seen constant increase; 174% from 2001-02 to 2002-03 and 176% from 2002-03 to 2003-04.
- The holding of inventories has gradually decreased between 1998-99 and 2003-04, which has given comfort to the cash position of the firm.
- The company has suffered heavy losses in the previous years between 1999-00 and 2002-03. However, it has bounced back with considerable profits during 2003-04 and 2004-05, which has wiped out all the previous losses of the firm.

FINANCIAL FLEXIBILITY

- The figures depict that SAIL has added assets in all these years. Addition of assets was very high during the financial years 1996-97, 1997-98 and 1998-99. This was due to capitalization of major assets commissioned as a part of the modernization across all the SAIL Units. During the years 1996-97 and 1997-98 there was enough Financial Flexibility to manage with negative Cash Flow from investing activities. This was due to the fact that the company was making profits year after year and because of having good reserves and financial strength of the company, it had taken fresh loans to supplement the investment activities in asset formation.

- Net Cash Flows from investing activities are negative in all these years except in the financial years between 1999-00 and 2002-03, during which it was positive. There was very little Financial Flexibility during these years owing to losses suffered by the Company faced with a steel market recession globally. The firm has managed to get positive cash flow from sale of houses during 2001-02 and 2002-03, sale of power plants to JV companies during 2000-01 and 2001-02. The company also got relief as a part of Financial restructuring from Government of India during 1999-00.

LIQUIDITY

- The company does not believe in keeping huge amount of idle cash.
- The company has also utilized its cash in the repayment of borrowing which has substantially reduced the burden of interest and finance charges after 1998-99.
- The company maintains sufficient cash balance as a precautionary measure to manage day-to-day requirement.
- However, it can be seen that cash balance, as on 31st March, 2005 is a whopping Rs. 6132 crores. This increase in cash balance is due to a substantial increase in the profit of the company. This amount of liquidity with the company will act as strength to take dynamic business decisions in the future.

- The inventories, which might have blocked the liquidity flow, are found to be reduced.

FINANCIAL RISK

- After 1998-99, there has been a steady decrease in the total borrowings of the company. The reduction has been speedier in the financial years 2002-03, 2003-04 and 2004-05.
- The reductions in the total borrowings in these years have been made possible through repayment/ prepayment of loans and swapping of costlier loans with cheaper loans.
- The company enjoyed the confidence of the investors through timely repayment of loans. This has taken away the risk of insolvency from the minds of the investors.
- However, during the financial years 2000-01 and 2001-02, due to accumulated losses of the company, Debt: Net wroth ratio increased beyond the norm 2:1, even though reduction of borrowings was there. With the company making profit from Qtr-IV of the financial year 2002-03 onwards, the accumulated losses got wiped out slowly and the company got positive reserves. Net worth improved and the Debt: Net worth ratio improved to much below 1. At this point it appears that the financial strength of the company is very good and there is no risk of insolvency.
- The efforts taken by the company in reducing the borrowings steadily between 1998-99 till date have paved the way for a risk free financial position.

ANALYSIS OF CASH AND BANK BALANCE HELD BY SAIL

From the year 2000-01 to 2001-02 the amount of cash got reduced by 37.6%. However, it has shown an increasing trend since then. In the year 2003-04 and 2004-05, SAIL had a huge amount of cash and bank balance. The main reason for the huge amount of cash in 2003-04 is better realization of sales and huge profit. SAIL has not kept much cash to its account and has gone for repayment of borrowings in the previous years. However, the repayment of borrowings has been done in large amount in the years 2002-03, 2003-04 and 2004-05, as there have been better profits. In addition to this, it has also gone for "debt-swapping" in the past. It has paid off high interest bearing loans and has given stress on low interest bearing debt instruments. Moreover, due to repayment of loans there have been lesser interest and finance charges paid, leading to generation of cash. Selling of inventories has also led to better sales realization and generation of cash.

Now, the motive for holding cash in SAIL is mainly transactions and precautions motive.

Thus, the following possibilities may arise:

- SAIL may go for up gradation of technology.
- It may modernize the old assets.
- It can also plan for huge investments in some profitable and related diversified projects in the future.
- It may explore new markets to diversify its export base.
- It can plan for some capital expenditure. The plan for capital expenditure covers up gradation/modernization of some existing assets as well as installation of some new facilities like development of iron ore mines, installation of blast furnace etc.
- It can also maintain cash for meeting short-term solvency on accounts of outstanding loan repayment on maturity.

CASH FLOW ANALYSIS IN TISCO

Table 4.29: Cash Flow Analysis in TISCO (Rs. in crores)

	2003-04	2002-03	2001-02	2000-01
0	1	2	3	4
Opg. Activities				
Profit After Tax	1746	1012	205	553
Depreciation	625	555	525	492
Interest and Finance Charges	141	342	403	412
Decrease in Inventory	-96	-24	-100	23
Decrease in Sundry Debtor	376	149	269	-134
Decrease in Loans and Adv (Others)			0	0
Decrease in DRE	-37	-46	38	4
Decrease in Current Liabilities	268	128	-55	208
Additional Provisions	12	64	1	-16
Interest Earned	-21	-39	-31	-36
Dividend Earned	-98	-19	-50	-44
Profit on Sale of Assets/Invest.	-33	-26	-51	-8
	2882	**2098**	**1154**	**1455**
Investing Activities				
Addition of Assets	-960	-451	-535	-605
Sale of Assets	53	40	32	8
Sale of Houses			0	0
Sale of Power Plant/Unit			0	0
Sale of Investment	-968	-432	-81	-79
Interest Earned	25	31	34	35
Dividend Earned	98	23	50	44
	-1753	**-790**	**-500**	**-598**

(contd.)

0	1	2	3	4
Financing Activities				
Increase in Share Capital	0.41	21	-138	-6
Increase in Res/Surplus				
Increase in Loan Amount	-852	-687	36	-235
Dividend PMT	-295	-146	-186	-159
INT and Finance Charges	-105	-341	-386	-412
	-1252	-1154	-674	-812
Net Increase in Cash and Cash Equivalent	**-122.38**	**153.92**	**-20.03**	**45.85**
Opening Balance	373.12	219.20	239.23	193.38
Closing Balance	250.74	373.12	219.20	239.23

	1999-00	**1998-99**	**1997-98**	**1996-97**
0	5	6	7	8
Opg. Activities				
Profit After Tax	423	282	322	469
Depreciation	427	382	343	327
Interest and Finance Charges	388	360	323	389
Decrease in Inventory	72	42	-18	52
Decrease in Sundry Debtor	-19	8	-9	-230
Decrease in Loans &Adv (Others)	0	0	0	0
Decrease in DRE	-8	-17	32	-16
Decrease in Current Liabilities	37	20	-12	-10
Additional Provisions	-10	-8	-21	13
Interest Earned	-33	-71	-92	-136
Dividend Earned	-31	-26	-27	-25
Profit on Sale of Assets/Invest.	-152	-140	-25	-8
	1093	833	817	824

(contd.)

0	5	6	7	8
Investing Activities				
Addition of Assets	-1148	-1149	-1119	-756
Sale of Assets	27	30	14	305
Sale of Houses	0	0	0	0
Sale of Power Plant/Unit	471	0	0	0
Sale of Investment	-235	235	326	-414
Interest Earned	44	65	102	137
Dividend Earned	31	26	27	25
	-809	**-793**	**-651**	**-703**
Financing Activities				
Increase in Share Capital	150	5	4	1
Increase in Res/Surplus				
Increase in Loan Amount	-32	360	496	242
Dividend PMT	-155	-147	-166	-157
INT and Finance Charges	-390	-351	-323	-393
	-427	**-133**	**11**	**-307**
Net Increase in Cash and Cash Equivalent	**-142.81**	**-93.22**	**178.03**	**-185.71**
Opening Balance	336.19	429.41	251.38	437.09
Closing Balance	193.38	336.19	429.41	251.38

CASH FLOW FROM OPERATING ACTIVITIES

It can be seen from Chart 4.69 that cash flow from operating activities for the firm has been increasing over the years except during 2001-02. It has witnessed a major upward jump of about 82% during the Financial Year 2002-03. The reasons for these can be analyzed from the behaviour of the major elements as shown in Chart 4.70.

The reasons for increase in cash flows during 2002-03 and 2003-04 were substantial improvement in Profit after Tax and

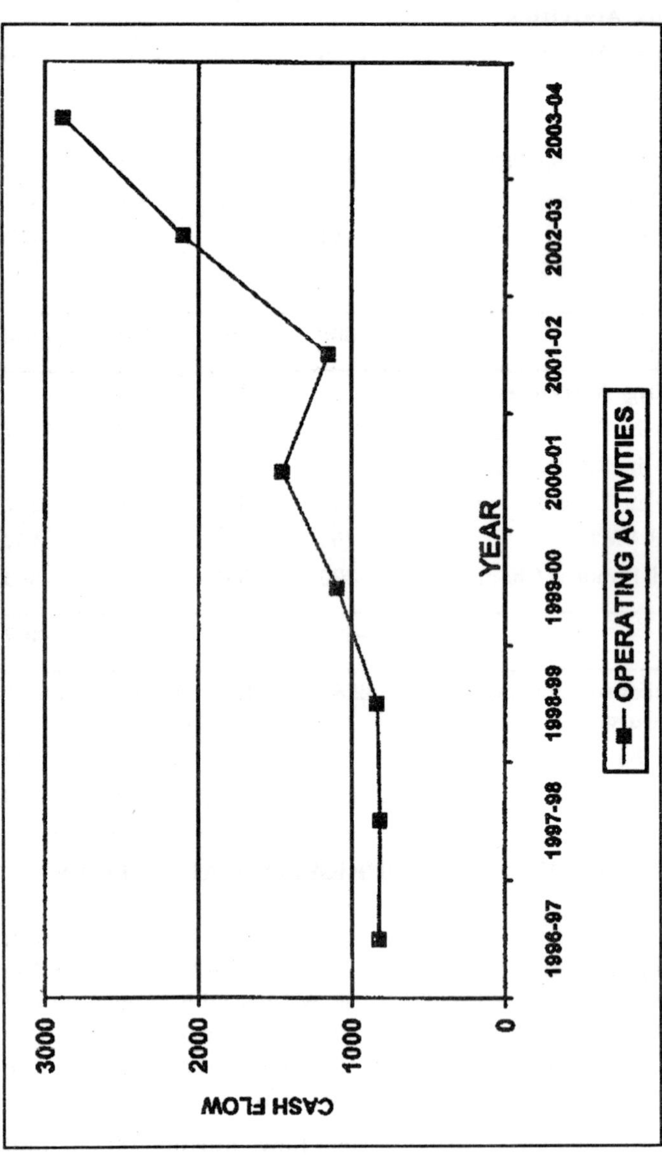

Cahrt 4.69: Cash Flow From Operating Activities

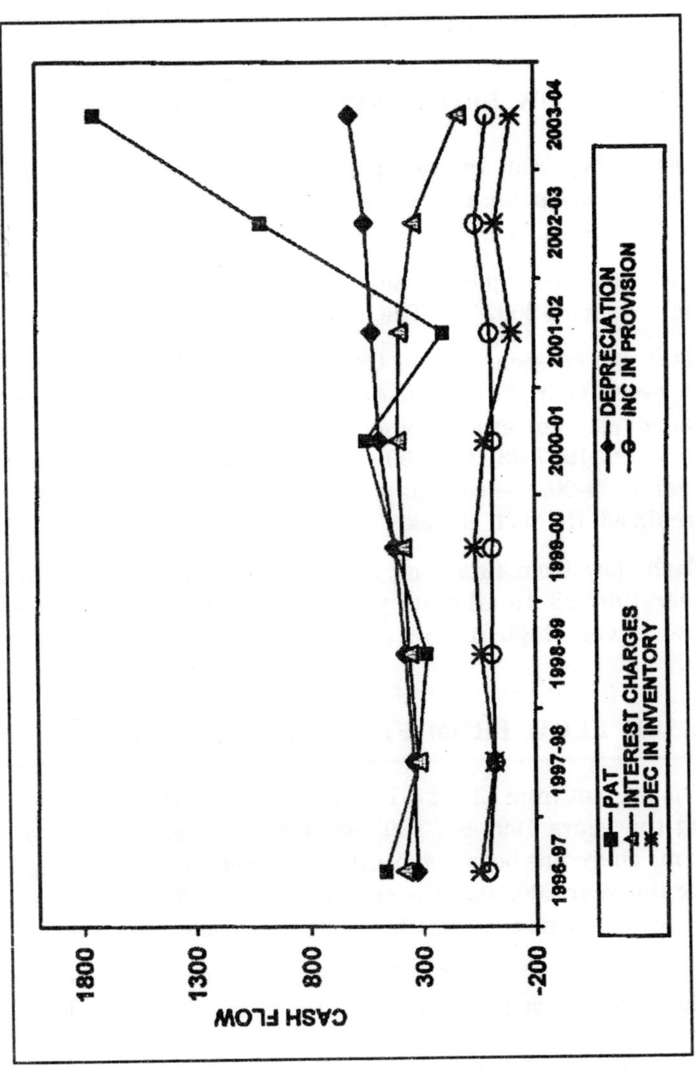

Chart 4.70: Major Elements

increase in provisions, which has affected the Net Profit. During these years, the steel market revived after a long period of slow down. The firm registered huge net profits.

Cash flow during the financial year 2001-02 was quite low due to a substantial reduction in the net profit of the firm.

CASH FLOW FROM INVESTING ACTIVITIES

Cash flows from Investing activities have been negative in all these years, i.e. there were cash outflows during these periods (Chart 4.71).

There was a steep increase of about 122% in cash out flow during the year 2002-03. The reasons are analysed below.

As it can be seen from in Chart 4.72, the firm has added assets every year. This indicates that the company is doing capital investment gradually every year. This was very high in the years 1997-98, 1998-99, 1999-00 and 2003-04. During the year 1999-00, the company has sold a portion of its assets and realized Rs. 471 crores.

Cash flow from financing activities was positive only in the year 1997-98. In all other years it was negative. Net cash outflow is very high in the year 2003-04. This is analyzed below.

CASH FLOW FROM FINANCING ACTIVITIES

It is evident from Chart 4.74 that the borrowings increased during the years 1996-97, 1997-98, 1998-99 and 2001-02 for the firm. There has been a substantial reduction in borrowings during the year 2002-03. The company has paid dividends all these years because of which there were cash outflows.

It is seen from Chart 4.75 that net cash flow and the closing balance appear to move in the same direction. Even if there was a huge increase in cash flow from operating activities during the financial years 2002-03 and 2003-04, there was not much increase in the closing balance of cash and bank balances.

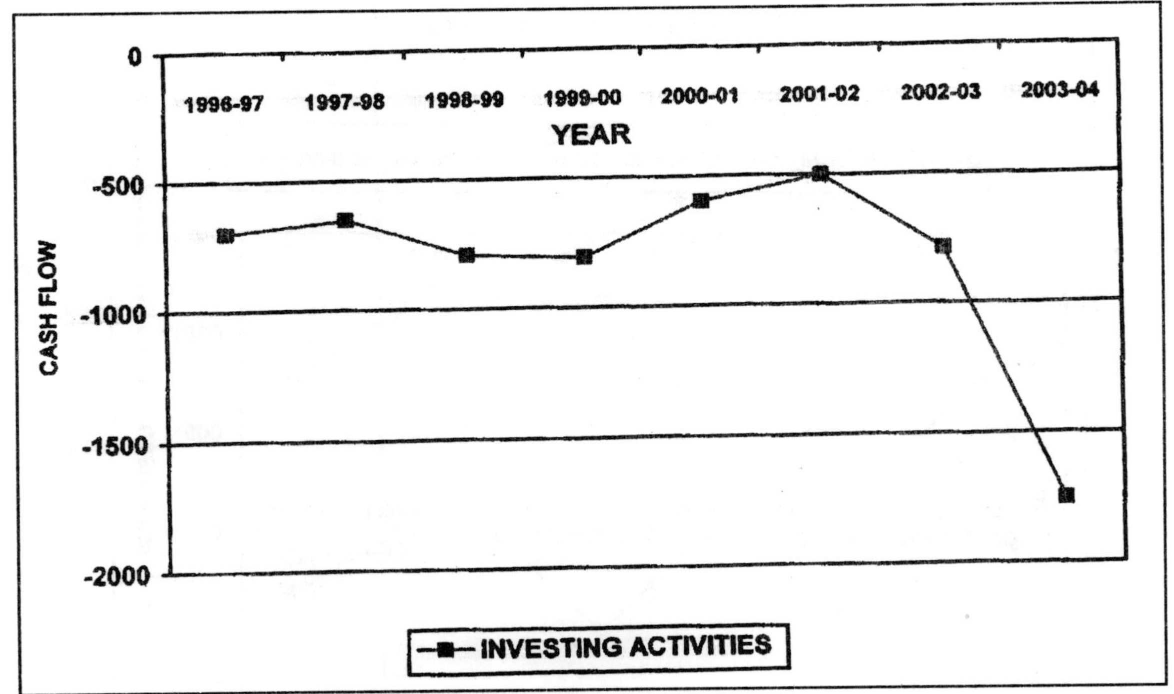

Chart 4.71: Cash Flow From Investing Activities

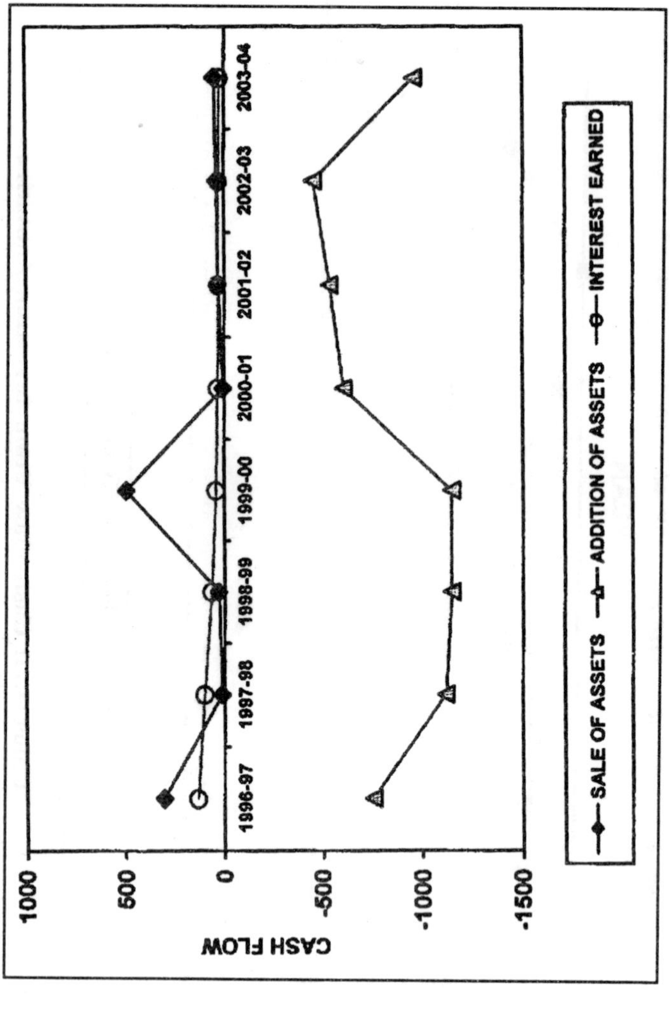

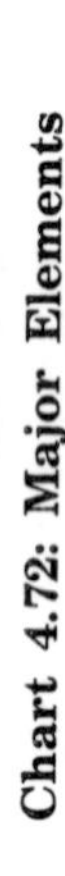

Chart 4.72: Major Elements

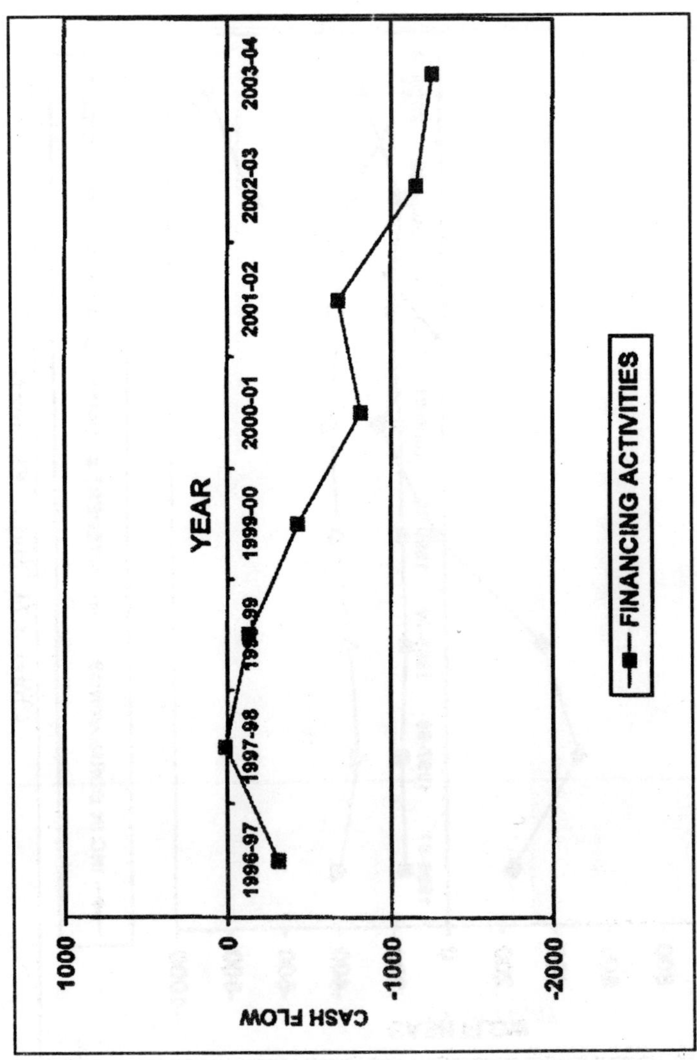

Chart 4.73: Cash Flow From Financing Activities

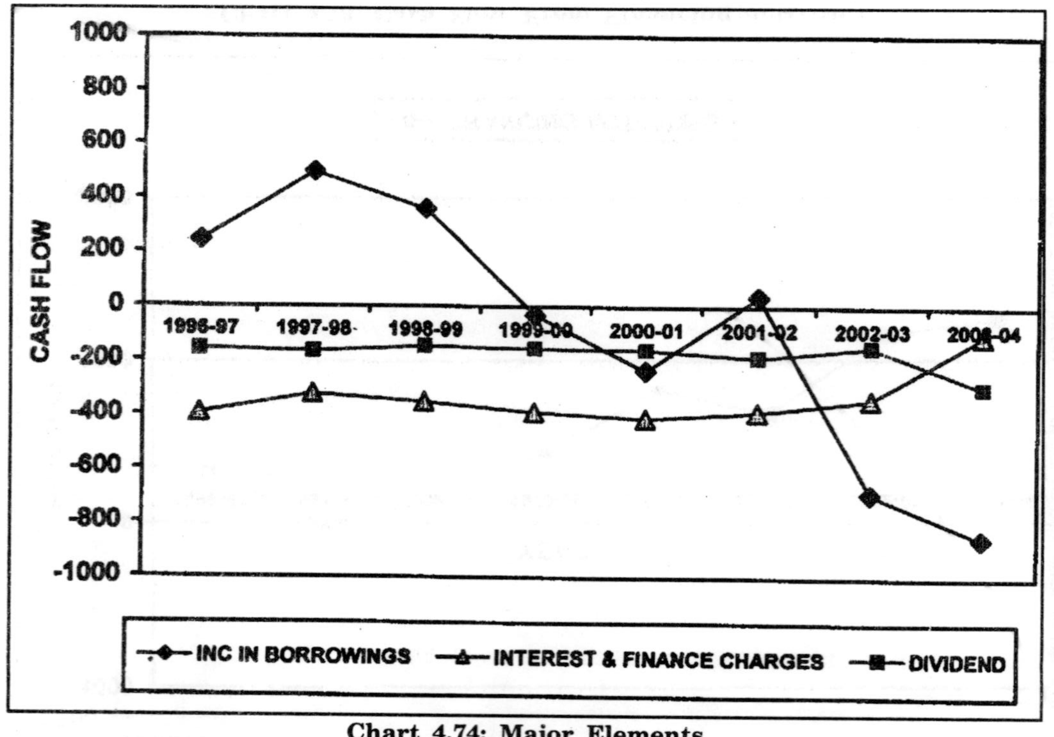

Chart 4.74: Major Elements

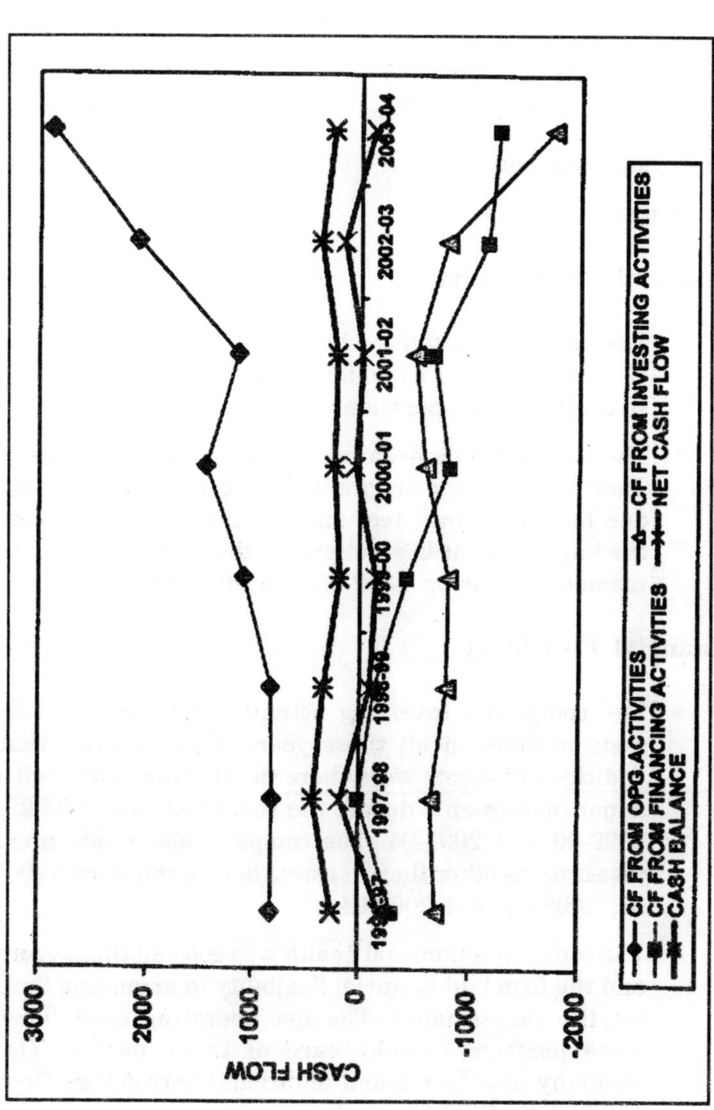

Chart-4.75: Summary of Cash Flow

This was because, the firm spent more on investing and financing activities during those years.

The cash flow statement is also useful to analyze the following dimensions of Business:

1) Financial Profitability,

2) Financial Flexibility,

3) Liquidity and

4) Risk.

Financial Profitability

- The operating activities have been the major sources of generation of cash for TISCO. It indicates the strength of its operations.
- The company has been making profit all these years. There was a drop in profit during the year 2001-02 due to a declining steel market. But after that, with the improvement in steel prices, the company's profits zoomed up during 2002-03 and 2003-04.

Financial Flexibility

- The company's investing activities have resulted in cash outflows in all these years. Figures show that additions of assets were there in all these years, with major investments during the years 1997-98, 1998-99, 1999-00 and 2003-04. The company also made huge investments other than in assets during the years 1996-97, 2002-03 and 2003-04.
- The company's financial health was good all these years and the firm had financial flexibility in arranging fund for the investments. The net operating cash flows were positive to take care of these partly. The company also had taken additional borrowings from 1996-97 to 1998-99.

Liquidity

- The company does not believe in keeping huge amount of idle cash.
- It has utilized its cash in the repayment of borrowings from 1999-00 onwards, which has substantially reduced the burden of interest and finance charges.
- It has also invested its idle cash in investments other than assets.
- The company maintains sufficient cash balance as a precautionary measure to manage day-to-day requirements.

Financial Risk

- After 1998-99, there has been a steady decrease in the total borrowings of the company, except during the year 2001-02. The reduction has been speedier during the financial years 2002-03, 2003-04.
- The company enjoyed the confidence of the investors through timely repayment of loans. This has taken away the risk of insolvency from the minds of the investors.
- Since the company has been making profits year after year and a steady reduction in borrowings as well as increase in asset base in noticed, there is no financial risk associated with company.
- The efforts taken by the company in reducing the borrowings steadily between 1998-99 till date have paved the way for a risk free financial position.

ANALYSIS OF CASH AND BANK BALANCE HELD BY TISCO

The motive for holding cash in TISCO is mainly for transactions and precautions.

Comparative Analysis

It can be seen from the comparative graphs (Chaert 4.76a and 4.76b) that, the cash flows in case of RSP and SAIL have not been smooth like that of TISCO. Investment plans are quite smooth and gradual in case of TISCO, but it is not so incase of SAIL and RSP. Smooth investment plans don't affect cash flows from operating activities severely. This is one of the main reasons behind huge fluctuations in profit and loss figures of SAIL and RSP. However, in the last few years, the efforts behind reduction in borrowings and inventory levels have reduced the interest and finance charges considerably in case of SAIL and RSP. RSP and SAIL need to achieve more than 100% capacity utilization so as to increase cash flow from operating activities in future. RSP also needs to curtail its fixed cost component further to keep its cash flows from operations and PAT sustainable in future.

Financial Ratio Analysis

Raito analysis is a powerful tool of financial anlaysis. It is the method of calculating and analyzing the financial strengths and weaknesses of a company from its financial statements, i.e. Balance sheet and Profit and Loss account. These ratios can be compared with other companies in the same sector for understanding the strengths and weaknesses. After analysis, the company can take corrective actions to get over the weaknesses. The historical trends of these ratios indicate a company's financial condition, its operations and attractiveness for investment.

Types of Financial Ratios

The type of financial ratio analysis of a company depends on the perspective of the analyst. The stakeholders of a company are generally interested to know more about the company. They can be the owners, investors, creditors, management etc.

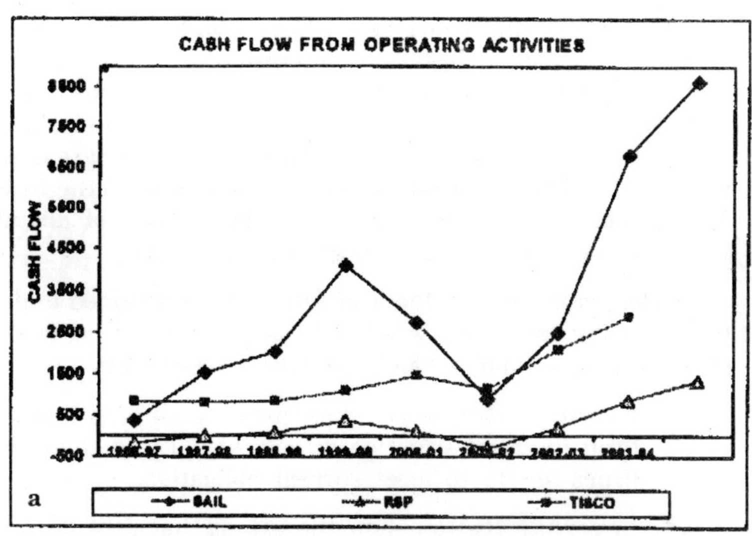

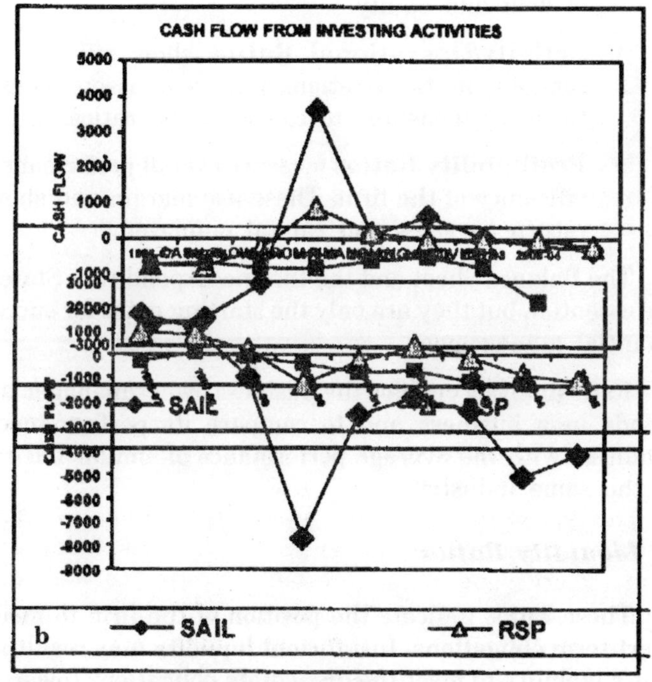

Chart 4.76a-b: Cash flow from operating activities

Owners are interested in the profitability and financial position of the firm. Investors are interested in the profitability; market capitalization, price to earnings ratios. Short-term creditors are interested in the liquidity position and short-term solvency of the firm. While, long-term creditors are more interested in long-term solvency and profitability of the firm. Management is interested to protect the interest of all the stakeholders and see the firm growing profitably.

Based on these, the financial ratios can be grouped under the following categories which tell us about different facets of a company's finances and operations. These are,

- **Liquidity Ratios** give a picture of a company's short-term financial situation or solvency. These show the firm's ability to meet current obligations.
- **Leverage Ratios** show the extent that debt is used in a company's capital structure. These show the mix of debt and equity.
- **Activity/Operational Ratios** show efficiency of a company in its operations and use of assets. These use turnover measures to calculate the ratios.
- **Profitability Ratios** measure overall performance and efficiency of the firm. These use margin and show the return on sales and capital employed.

The Balance Sheet and the Income/Expenditure Statement are essential, but they are only the starting point for successful financial management.

Ratio analysis enables the business owner/manager to spot trends in a business and to compare its performance and condition with the average performance of similar businesses in the same industry.

1) Liquidity Ratios

These ratios indicate the position of the firm to meet the short-term obligations. Insufficient liquidity may result in the firm's inability to meet the immediate obligations towards the creditors. This may result in poor credit worthiness, loss of creditors' confidence in the business and even legal problems. A very high degree of liquidity is also bad for the firm. Idle assets earn nothing. Thus it is very important for the firm to strike a proper balance between these two. These ratios include the *Current Ratio, Quick Raito, and Working Capital.*

a) Current Ratios

The Current Ratio is one of the best-known measures of financial strength of a firm. It is calculated by dividing current assets with current liabilities as shown below:

Current Ratio = Total Current Assets/Total Current Liabilities

The current ratio is the measure of short-term solvency of the company. Current assets include cash and those assets, which can be converted to cash within one year like inventory, marketable securities, sundry debtors etc. Current liabilities include items, which are required to be paid within one year like sundry creditors, short term financing from Banks (Working Capital), accrued expenses, income tax liability etc.

A generally acceptable current ratio is 2 to 1. But whether or not a specific ratio is satisfactory depends on the nature of the business and the characteristics of its current assets and liabilities. The minimum acceptable current ratio is 1:1, but that relationship is usually playing it too close for comfort. It represents a margin of safety for the creditors of the firm.

If the business's current ratio is too low, the following options can be exercised to raise it:

- By paying off some debts.
- By increasing current assets from loans or other borrowings with a maturity of more than one year.
- By converting non-current assets into current assets.
- By increasing current assets from new equity contributions.
- By putting profits back into the business.

Current ratio only indicates quantity of liquidity and not the quality. Quick ratios as illustrated below show the quality of liquidity of the firm.

b) Quick Ratios

The Quick Ratio is also known as the "acid-test" ratio and is one of the best measures of liquidity. It is calculated as shown below:

Quick Ratio = (Cash and Bank Balance + Government Securities + Receivables) / Total Current Liabilities

The difference between current ratio and quick ratio is that quick ratio does not include inventory in the numerator. It only uses the items of the current assets, which are more liquid than the inventory like cash, receivables, and government securities. Out of these, cash and government securities are the most liquid current assets.

This ratio indicates the immediate liquidity position of the firm to meet any eventuality.

Inventory is less liquid because it depends on selling of the products in the market and getting the realization out of it. Sales again depend on the market situation and booking of matching order.

The Quick Ratio is a much more exact measure than the Current Ratio. By excluding inventories, it concentrates on the really liquid assets, with value that is fairly certain.

An acid test of 1:1 is considered satisfactory unless the majority of the "quick assets" are in accounts receivable, and the pattern of accounts receivable collection lags behind the schedule for paying current liabilities.

c) Net Working Capital Raito

Working Capital is more a measure of cash flow than a ratio. The result of this calculation must be a positive number. It is calculated as shown below:

Net Working Capital = Total Current Assets – Total Current Liabilities excluding short-term borrowings.

Bankers look at Net Working Capital over time to determine a company's ability to face financial crises. Loans are often tied to minimum working capital requirements.

Net working capital ratio is calculated as follows:

Net working capital ration = Net working capital/Net assets

This ratio should be more than 1: 1, which indicates creditors confidence in dealing with the Business Organization.

2) Leverage Ratio

This indicates the composition of capital structure in the business and the risk factor associated with it. Capital structure includes owner's capital, reserve and surpluses, creditors money like short-term borrowings/long-term borrowings/public and corporate deposits through debt instruments.

If the rate of return from the business is higher than the cost of debt, then the shareholders of the firm will be happy if the debt portion is higher in the capital. This will give them more return on a small equity base. However, if the earning potential of the firm is less, it will be risky for the firm to have more exposure to borrowings. The creditors look at this ratio and the earning potential of the firm before lending money. The credit rating of the firm is also in some sense dependent on this ratio. This is one of the most important ratios, which decided the overall financial flexibility of the firm to take on short-term and long-term challenges in the business. An optimum mix of debt and equity is important for the firm.

This composition can be expressed with the help of the following ratios:

a) Debt Ratio:

Debt Ratio = Total Debt / (Total Debt + Net worth = Capital employed)

Net Worth = Equity capital + reserves and surpluses including P and L Debit balance due to unabsorbed losses of the firm.

b) Debt-Equity Ratio:

Debt-Equity Ratio = Total Debt / Net worth

c) Debt / Worth Ratio:

This Debt/Worth Ratio indicates the extent to which the business is reliant on debt financing (creditor money versus owner's equity):

Debt/Worth Ratio = Total Liabilities / Net Worth

These ratios are known as "Leverage ratios", "Gearing ratios". These show the short-term and long-term solvency of the firm.

Generally, the higher is this ratio, the more risky a creditor will perceive its exposure in the business, making it correspondingly harder to obtain credit.

Among all of these, the most popular ratio is Debt-Equity ratio. It is quite simple, easy to understand and interpret.

The maximum limit of Debt-Equity ratio generally accepted is 2 : 1. However, it varies from sector to sector. A sector where more amount of credit sales takes place, the norm will be higher and for a sector having almost nil credit sales like services sector, the standard will be quite low.

A comfortable ratio will be less than 1:1 Lower Debt-Equity ratio gives financial flexibility for the management to take dynamic decisions like business expansion, diversification etc.

Management Ratios

Other important ratios, often referred to as Management Ratios, are also derived from Balance Sheet and Statement of Income information. These are explained below.

3) Activity Ratio

The following ratios fall under the activity ratio.

a) Inventory Turnover Ratio

This ratio indicates inventory management and sales performance of the firm. It also indicates efficiency of the firm in terms of production and sales performance. The Inventory Turnover Raito is calculates as follows:

Inventory Turnover Ration = Net Sales / Inventory

The more times inventory can be turned in a given operating cycle, the greater is the profit. This ratio shows how quickly the inventory is converted into receivable/cash. A high ratio indicates a better inventory management, less blockage of fund, synchronized production/sales efforts and above all a better profitability for the firm. However, a low inventory turnover ratio indicates high levels of inventory, poor production discipline, poor sales performance, possibility of non-moving stock in the inventory and more over a dent on the profitability of the firm. A low ratio adds pressure on the working capital requirement of the business unit.

b) Accounts Receivable Turnover Ratio

This ratio indicates how well accounts receivable are being collected. If receivables are not collected reasonably in accordance with their terms, management should rethink its collection policy. If receivable are excessively slow in being converted to cash, liquidity could be severely impaired. Getting the Accounts Receivable Turnover Ratio is a two step process and is calculated as follows:

Accounts Receivable Turnover = Sales / Accounts Receivable.

c) Return on Assets Ratio

This measures how efficiently profits are being generated from the assets employed in the business when compared with the ratios of firms in a similar business. A low ratio in comparison with industry averages indicates an inefficient use of business assets. The Return on Assets Ratio is calculated as follows:

Return on Assets = Net Profit Before Tax /Total Assets.

4) Profitability Ratio

Profit is the most important thing in a business unit. The concern of Management is to produce sufficient profit at eh end of the financial year. This is the main output of the management during the year. Enough profit year after year gives financial strength and support to take proper decision for the growth of the Organization. Profitability ratios are calculated to measure operating efficiency of the firm.

Profitability ratios are calculated in relation to:

- Sales Turnover and
- Investment.

Some of the profitability ratios are described below:

a)Gros s Margin Ratio

The Gross Margin Ratio is calculated as follows:

Gross Margin Ratio = Gross Profit / Net Sales

Gross Profit = Net Sales – Cost of Goods Sold

This ratio shows the operational margin trend of the company over the period.

b) Net Profit Margin Ratio

The Net Profit Margin Ratio is calculated as follows:

Net Profit Margin Ratio = Net Profit Before Tax / Net Sales

This ratio shows the net margin trend of the company over the years.

The management should interpret the performance of the firm using both the above two ratios. While the Gross margin ratio shows the operational efficiency of the company, the net margin ratio shows the total performance. Net margin ratio for a firm may be low; still the gross margin ratio could be high. This means that because of high burden of depreciation (due to addition of assets during that year) and interest, the net margin ratio has been low, even when the operational efficiency of the firm is high. This generally happens during huge capitalization of new production facilities in the firm. This symptom indicates that there is no reason for panic in the short-term. However, if both Gross margin as well as net margin ratio is lower, then it indicates serious problems in the operations of the company and the management needs to take corrective measures to come out of this situation in the short-term.

c) Return on Investment (ROI) Ratio

The Return on Investment is perhaps the most important ratio of all. It is the percentage of return on funds invested in the business by its owners. In short, this ratio tells the owner whether or not all the effort put into the business has been worthwhile. If the ROI is less than the rate of return on an alternative, risk-free investment such as a bank savings account, the owner may be wiser to sell the company, put the money in such a savings instrument, and avoid the daily struggles of small business management. The ROI is calculated as follows:

Return on Investment = Net Profit before Tax / (Net Worth + Debt = Capital Employed)

Return on Equity is another ratio, which the shareholders of the company look at keenly. This indicates the efficiency at which their capital is utilized in the company. This is calculated as follows:

Return on Equity = Net Profit after Tax / Net Worth.

These Liquidity, Leverage, Profitability, and Management Ratios allows the business owner to identify trends in a business and to compare its progress with the performance of others through data published by various sources. The owner may thus determine the business's relative strengths and weaknesses.

Important Financial ratios are analyzed for SAIL, RSP and TISCO and a comparison is made below. Even if analysis is made for most of the possible ratios in case of RSP, these cannot be read in isolation. RSP being an integral part of SAIL, it is directly influenced by the performance of its parent company. In fact the interpretation of various of SAIL is useful to assess financial health of RSP too. Similarly, if RSP's financial ratios are improved, those of SAIL will also improve. Thus from management's perspective, it is all the more important to analyze the ratios of RSP and take corrective measures where ever necessary to improve these.

Analysis of Ratios: SAIL

The detailed calculation of the various ratios are tabulated in table 4.30:

Table 4.30: Calculation of the Various Ratios

	1995-96	1996-97	1997-98	1998-99	1999-00
0	1	2	3	4	5
Liquidity Ratio					
Current Asset	9600	10640	12027	11399	8259
Current Liability	4404	4378	4532	4599	5027
Current Ratio	**2.18**	**2.43**	**2.65**	**2.48**	**1.64**
Inventory	5431	6533	7563	6795	4623
Current Asset-Inventory	4169	4107	4464	4603	3636
Quick Ratio	**0.95**	**0.94**	**0.98**	**1.00**	**0.72**
Leverage Ratio					
Total Debt	14574	17421	20015	21018	15083
Net Worth	7937	7998	8489	6886	4765
Debt-Equity Ratio	1.84	2.18	2.36	3.05	3.17

0	1	2	3	4	5
Activity Ratio					
Sales	14710	14131	14665	14994	16250
Inventory Turnover Ratio	2.7	2.2	1.9	2.2	3.5
Profitability Ratio					
Sales	14710	14131	14665	14994	16250
Gross Margin	2712	2404	2447	1617	1203
Gross Margin Ratio	**0.18**	**0.17**	**0.17**	**0.11**	**0.07**
Net Profit Before Tax	1319	588	149	-1618	-1720
Net Profit Ratio	**0.09**	**0.04**	**0.01-0.11**		**-0.11**
Capital Employed	21950	24993	27787	27415	20580
Return on Investment	6%	2%	1%	-6%	-8%

	2000-01	2001-02	2002-03	2003-04	2004-05
0	6	7	8	9	10
Liquidity Ratio					
Current Asset	8362	7107	7305	8037	14187
Current Liability	5274	4857	4772	5974	6608
Current Ratio	**1.59**	**1.46**	**1.53**	**1.35**	**2.15**
Inventory	4519	4042	3744	3081	4221
Current Asset-Inventory	3843	3065	3560	4955	9966
Quick Ratio	**0.73**	**0.63**	**0.75**	**0.83**	**1.51**
Leverage Ratio					
Total Debt	14250	14019	12928	8689	5770
Net Worth	4164	2252	1989	4659	10011
Debt-Equity Ratio	**3.42**	**6.23**	**6.50**	**1.86**	**0.58**
Activity Ratio					
Sales	16233	15502	19207	24178	31800
Inventory Turnover Ratio	**3.6**	**3.8**	**5.1**	**7.8**	**7.5**

(contd.)

0	6	7	8	9	10
Profitability Ratio					
Sales	16233	15502	19207	24178	31800
Gross Margin	2713	111	2176	402	11163
Gross Margin Ratio	**0.13**	**0.07**	**0.11**	**0.19**	**0.35**
Net Profit Before Tax	-729	-1707	-304	2628	9365
Net Profit Ratio	**-0.04**	**-0.11**	**-0.020.11**		**0.29**
Capital Employed	19486	17611	16920	15995	20430
Return on Investment	**-4%**	**-10%**	**-2%**	**17%**	**46%**

The different ratios are analyzed below graphically in Chart 4.77.

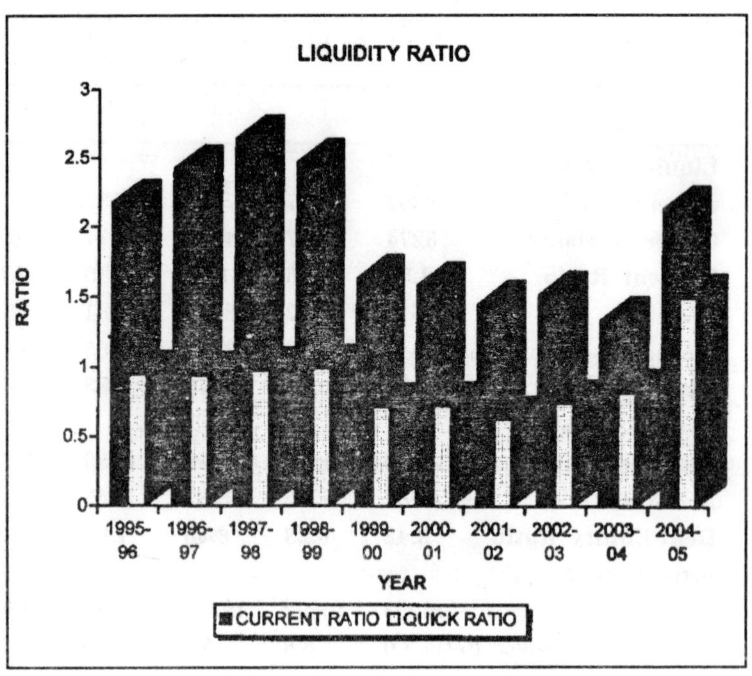

Chart-4.77: Liquidity Ratio

It is evident from the Chart 4.77 that the company maintained very comfortable current ratio of more than 2:1 between the financial years 1995-96 and 1998-99 and again in 2004-05, which is considered comfortable for smooth operations of the business. During this time the acid test ratio is also close to 1:1, which is quite favorable for the firm.

Between the years 1999-00 and 2003-04, the current ratio slipped below 2:1, but still was almost close to 1.5:1. This indicates that there was not much of short-term risk for the on-going business operations of the firm.

The position became again stronger during the year 2004-05 with overall improvement in the business. This is also indicated by a stronger quick ratio of 1.51:1 during that period.

Debt-Equity ratio indicates the financial flexibility of the company to take dynamic decisions. The graph (Chart 4.78) shows that the ratio kept on increasing between the years 1995-96 and 2000-01. After 1995-96 the ratio went up beyond 2:1 and was quite high during the years 2001-02 and 2002-03. During this time the ratio crossed even 6:1. Troubled by a slump in steel market, situation was grim during these two years.

Continuous efforts by the firm in repayment of long term borrowings and prudent loan management through loan swaps during these trying times for the company have helped a lot of in easing the situation. Along with this, the revival of world steel market form 2003-04 onwards has suddenly brought down this critical ratio from a high of 6.5 to 1.86 as on 31st March, 2004 and 0.58 as on 31st March, 2005. This speaks of a great makeover effort by the firm. Its economy of scale and prudent financial management has helped it in this direction.

It is evident from Chart 4.79 that there is a sign of improvement in the ratio from the year 1999-00 on wards. During the difficult times, i.e. from 2000-01 to 2003-03 there was a concerted effort to reduce the inventory, which is quite visible in the improvement in the ratio during that period. There was no let up in this effort after that. During the financial years 2003-04 and 2004-05 the ratio crossed 7 with

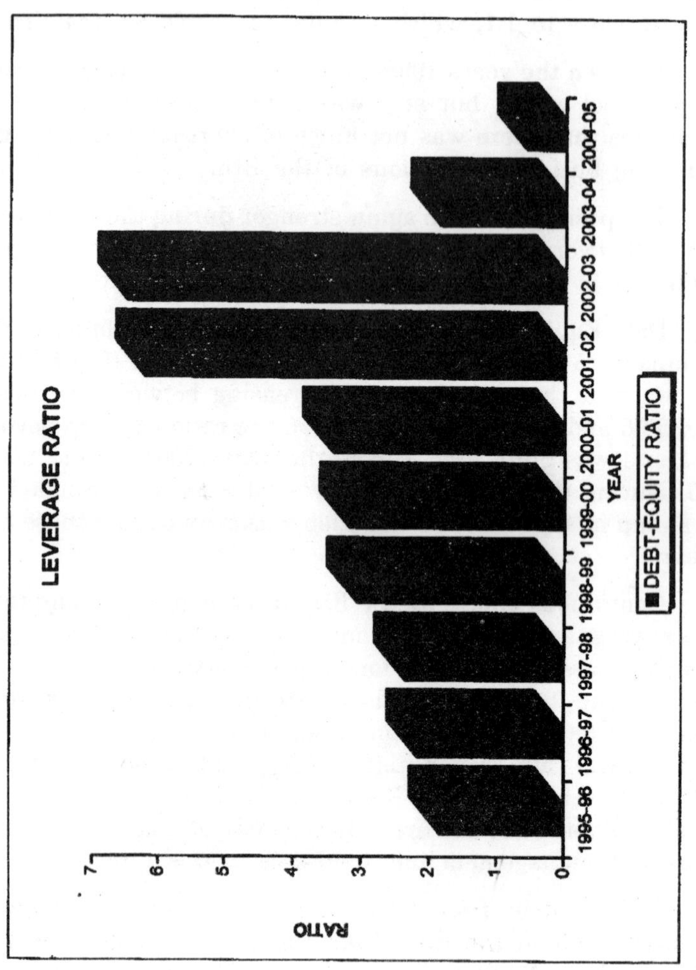

Chart 4.78: Leverage Ratio

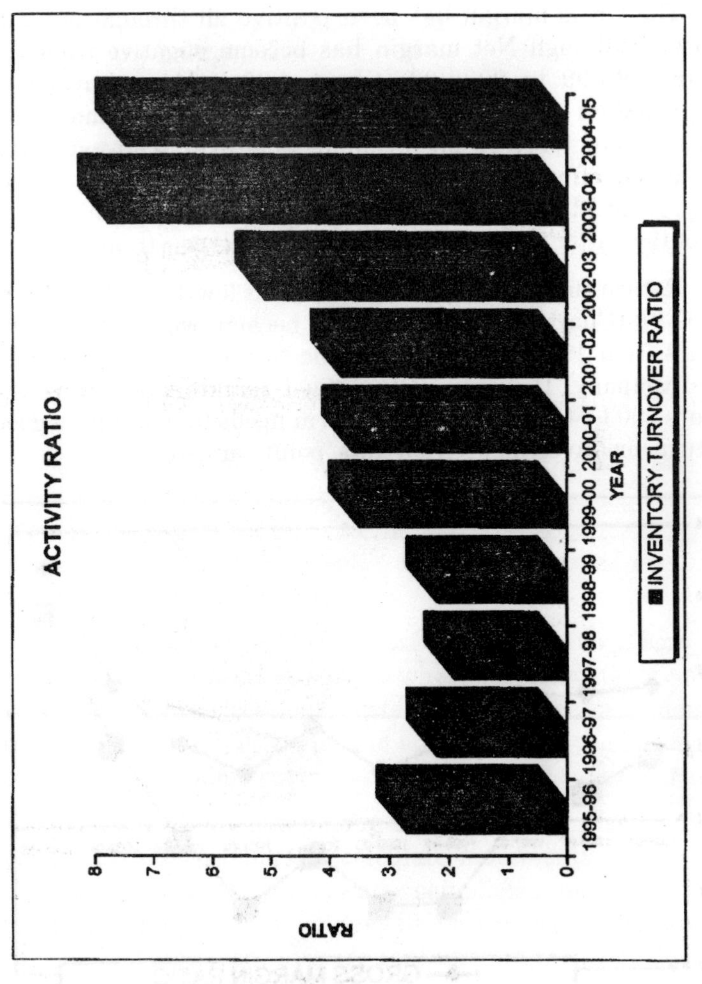

Chart 4.79: Activity Ratio

proper inventory management and drastic improvement in sales turnover of the firm, which is quite a healthy number for the firm.

Profitability Ratio

The Gross margin has been positive all through out this period, although Net margin has become negative from the year 1998-99 to 2002-03 (Chart 4.80a). Huge burden of Depreciation and interest as well as a poor steel market is responsible for this situation of the firm. However, the sustained efforts of he firm in cost reduction drive and an improving steel market have brought it out of this crisis situation after 2002-03 and made it emerge stronger.

Return on Investment figures were low from 1995-96 to 1997-98 (Chart 4.80b). Ratio even became worse during the years from 1998-99 to 2002-03 due to the losses suffered by the company. However, it improved remarkably during the years 2003-04 and 2004-04. The firm needs to maintain a good return on investment from this point onwards.

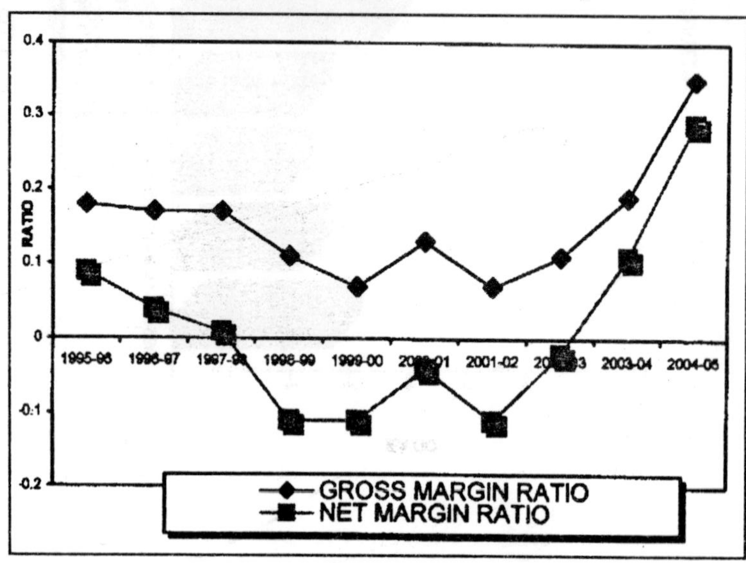

Chart-4.80a: Profitability Ratio

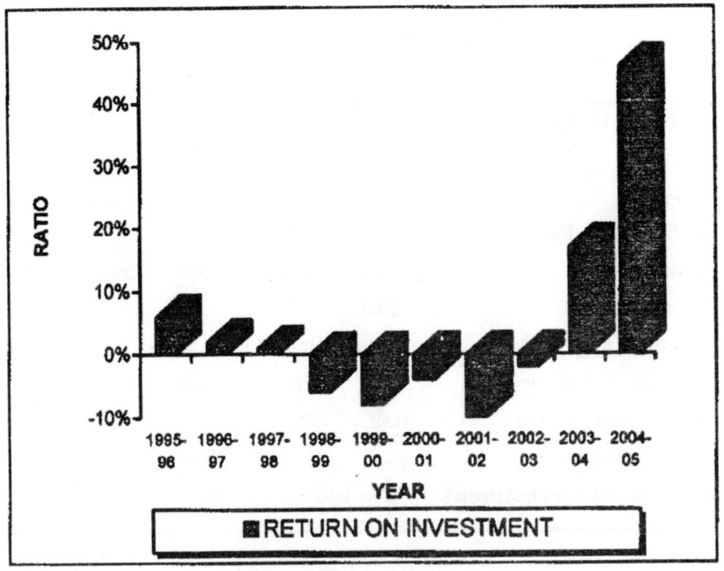

Table 4.31: Analysis of Ratios: RSP

	1995-96	1996-97	1997-98	1998-99	1999-00
0	1	2	3	4	5
Liquidity Ratio					
Current Asset	1293	1509	1678	1613	1127
Current Liability	375	375	434	447	545
Current Ratio	**3.454.033.873.612.07**				
Inventory	939	1147	1335	1245	793
Current Asset-Inventory	355	362	343	368	334
Quick Ratio	**0.950.970.790.820.61**				
Leverage Ratio					
Total Debt	2100	2496	2700	3244	1519
Net Worth	750	456	110	-687	-1470
Debt-Equity Ratio	**2.8**	**5.5**	**24.5**	**-4.7**	**-1.0**

(contd.)

0	1	2	3	4	5
Activity Ratio					
Sales	2420	2298	2202	2437	2701
Inventory Turnover Ratio	2.6	2.0	1.6	2.0	3.4
Profitability Ratio					
Sales	2420	2298	2202	2437	2701
Gross Margin	240	91	86	4	-33
Gross Margin Ratio	**0.100.040.040.00**				**-0.01**
Net Profit Before Tax	-55	-310	-374	-765	-704
Net Profit Ratio	**-0.02**	**-0.14**	**-0.17**	**-0.31**	**-0.26**
Capital Employed	2567	3122	3866	6171	4990
Return on Investment	-2%-10%		-10%	-12%	-14%

	2000-01	2001-02	2002-03	2003-04	2004-05
0	6	7	8	9	10
Liquidity Ratio					
Current Asset	1211	997	924	686	727
Current Liability	583	488	508	648	451
Current Ratio	**2.08**	**2.041.821.061.61**			
Inventory	859	740	691	467	500
Current Asset-Inventory	352	258	233	219	227
Quick Ratio	**0.60**	**0.530.460.340.50**			
Leverage Ratio					
Total Debt	1582	1349	1495	1577	900
Net Worth	-1893	-2954.68	-3538	-3621	-2567
Debt-Equity Ratio	**-0.8**	**-0.5**	**-0.4**	**-0.4**	**-0.4**
Activity Ratio					
Sales	2565	2310	3145	3813	4674
Inventory Turnover Ratio	**3.0**	**3.1**	**4.6**	**8.2**	**9.3**
Profitability Ratio					

(contd.)

0	6	7	8	9	10
Sales	2565	2310	3145	3813	4674
Gross Margin	281	-367	53	421	1472
Gross Margin Ratio	0.11	-0.16	0.02	0.11	0.31
Net Profit Before Tax	-445	-1036	-593	-109	1045
Net Profit Ratio	-0.17	-0.45	-0.19	-0.03	0.22
Capital Employed	4842	4484	4176	3774	3889
Return on Investment	-9%-23%		-14%-3%		27%

It is evident from Chart 4.81 that the company maintained very comfortable current ratio of more than 2:1 between the financial years 1995-96 and 2001-02, which is considered comfortable for smooth operations of the business.

The quick ratio of RSP is not very indicative of the real situation. This is because of the fact that cash balance of RSP is transferred to the Corporate Office (SAIL) at the end of the each day and necessary accounting entries are passed through IUCA (Inter Unit Current Account) Codes. Thus this ratio needs to be interpreted along with that of SAIL. Going by this it can be concluded that the acid test ratios from 1995-96 to 1998-99 and from 2003-04 to 2004-05 were quite comfortable for the business operations of the firm.

Debt-Equity ratio was worse from 1996-97 on wards till now. From the year 1998-99 till date the net wroth of the firm is negative and so also the ratio. Even though the firm made huge profit of Rs. 1045 crores during the financial year 2004-05, the accumulated losses are not yet fully wiped out. The firm needs to maintain profit every year to improve its ratio in the coming years.

However, since RSP is an integral part of SAIL, the risk perceived on the business is linked to the ratio of SAIL, which indicates that it was bad from 1998-99 to 2002-03 and improved fast after 2002-03.

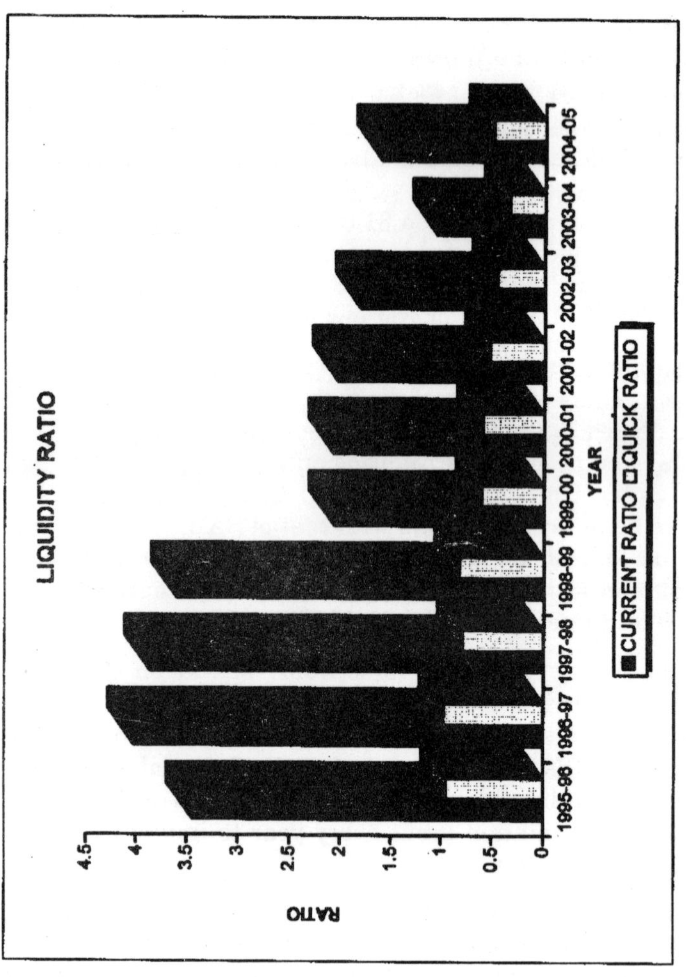

Chart 4.81: Liquidity Ratio

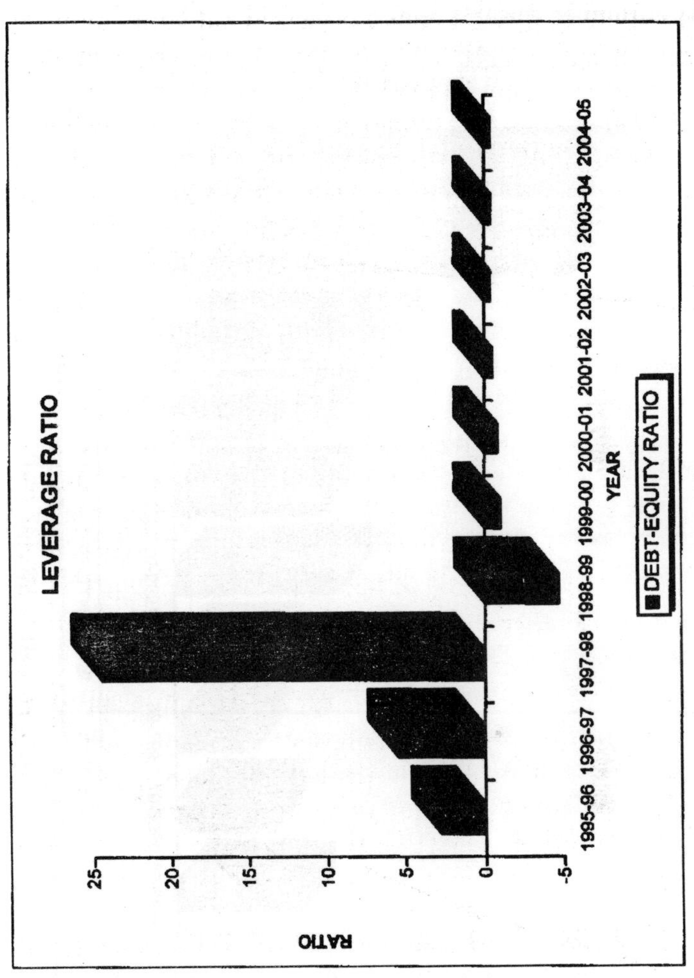

Chart 4.82: Leverage Ratio

It is evident from Chart 4.83 that there is a sign of improvement in the ratio from the year 2002-03 onwards. During the financial years 2003-04 and 2004-05, the ratio crossed 7 with proper inventory management and drastic improvement in sales turnover of the firm, which is quite a healthy number for the firm.

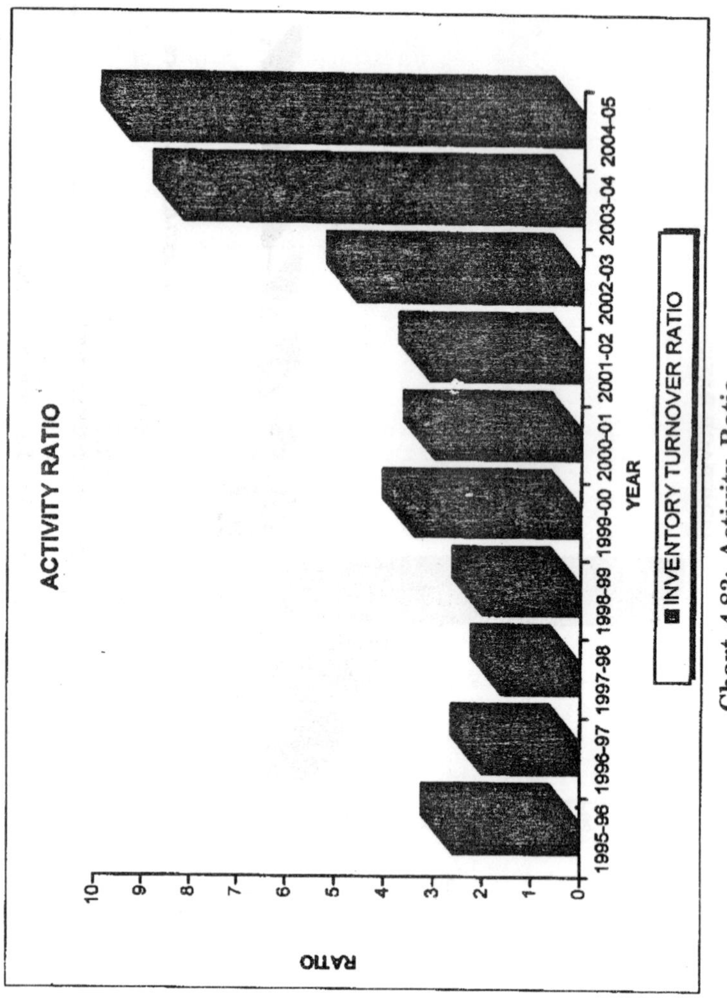

Chart 4.83: Activity Ratio

Profitability Ratio

Gross margin has been positive all through out this period except in the years 1999-00 and 2001-02 (Chart 4.84a). Net margin has been negative from the year 1995-96 to 2003-04. Huge burden of Depreciation and interest as well as a poor steel market created this situation for the firm. However, the sustained efforts of the firm in cost reduction drive and an improved steel market have brought it out of this crisis situation after 2002-03 and made it emerge stronger.

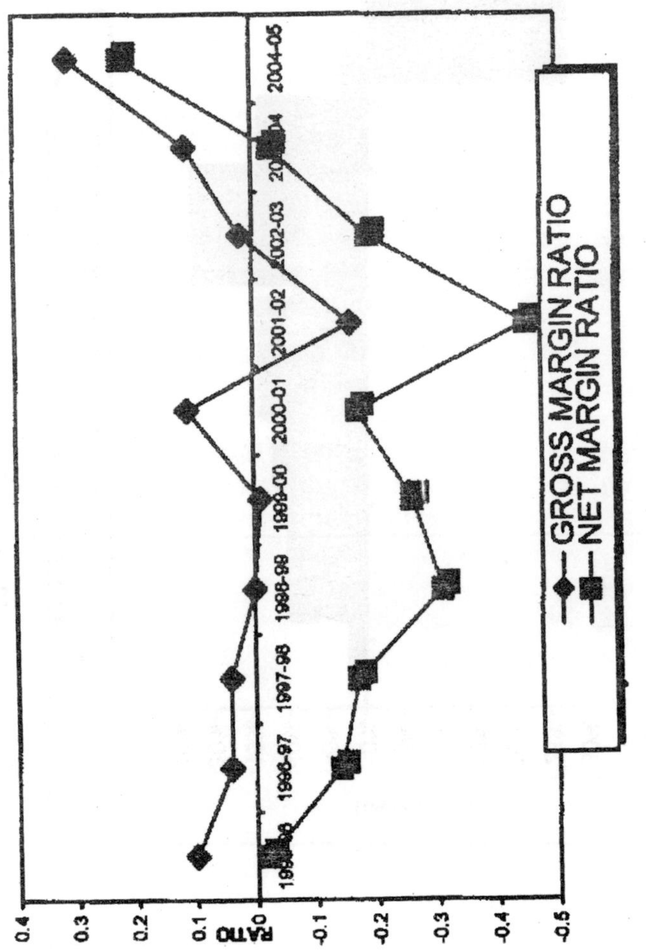

Chart 4.84a: Profitability Ratio

Return on Investment figures were negative from 1995-96 to 2003-04, due to the losses suffered by the firm during that period. However, the ratios improved remarkably during the years 2003-04 and became 27% during the year 2004-05. The firm needs to maintain a good return on investment from this point onwards (Chart 4.84b).

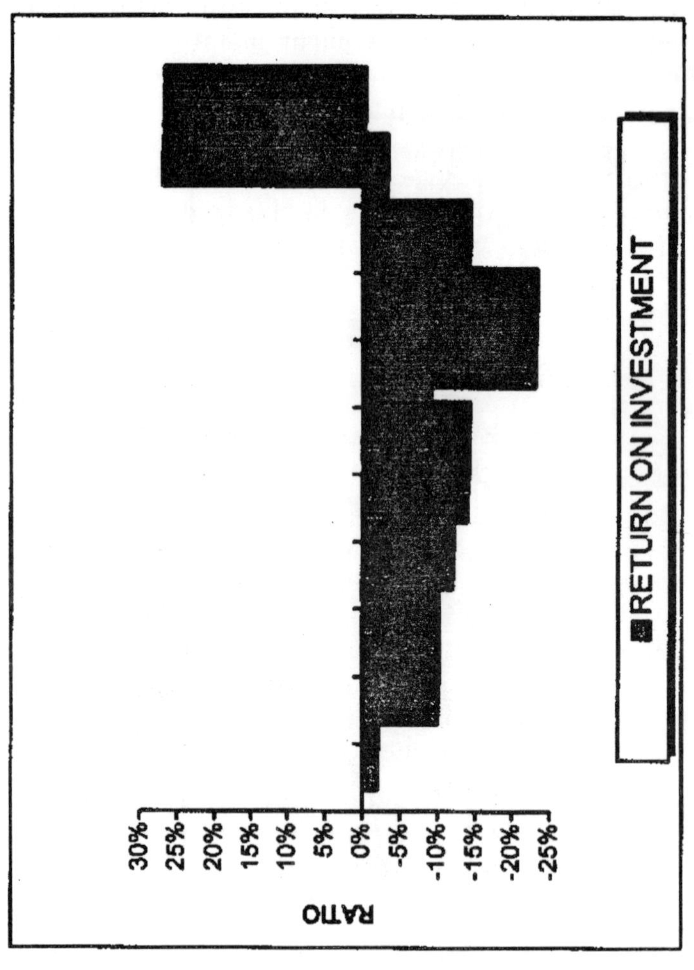

Chart 4.84b: Return on Investment

ANALYSIS OF RATIOS: TISCO

Table 4.32: TISCO

	1995-96	1996-97	1997-98	1998-99	1999-00
0	1	2	3	4	5
Liquidity Ratio					
Current Asset	3237	3451	3420	3230	3025
Current Liability	1521	1666	1716	1804	1828
Current Ratio	**2.132.071.991.791.65**				
Inventory	1092	1040	1058	1017	945
Current Asset-Inventory	2145	2411	2362	2214	2080
Quick Ratio	**1.411.451.381.231.14**				
Leverage Ratio					
Total Debt	3842	4083	4579	4938	4907
Net Worth	3574	3696	4049	4131	4517
Debt-Equity Ratio	1.1	1.1	1.1	1.2	1.1
Activity Ratio					
Sales	5854	6351	6433.49	6275	6891
Inventory Turnover Ratio	5.4	6.1	6.1	6.2	7.3
Profitability Ratio					
Sales	5854	6351	6433.49	6275	6891
Gross Margin	1143	1143	966	999	1263
Gross Margin Ratio	0.20	0.18	0.15	0.16	0.18
Net Profit Before Tax	566	542	363	315	477
Net Profit Ratio	0.10	0.09	0.06	0.05	0.07
Capital Employed	7417	7778	8628	9070	9424
Return on Investment	8%	7%	4%	3%	5%

	2000-01	2001-02	2002-03	2003-04	2004-05
0	6	7	8	9	10
Liquidity Ratio					
Current Asset	3226	3095	3648	4083	
Current Liability	2087	2007	2691	3999	

(*contd.*)

0	6	7	8	9	10
Current Ratio	**1.551.541.361.02**				
Inventory	922	1022	1153	1249	
Current Asset-Inventory	2304	2074	2495	2834	
Quick Ratio	**1.101.030.930.71**				
Leverage Ratio					
Total Debt	4672	4708	4226	3373	
Net Worth	4851	3446	3186	4360	
Debt-Equity Ratio	**1.0**	**1.4**	**1.3**	**0.8**	**0.3**
Activity Ratio					
Sales	7759	7607	9793	11921	15877
Inventory Turnover Ratio	8.4	7.4	8.5	9.5	
Profitability Ratio					
Sales	7759	7607	9793	11921	15877
Gross Margin	1471	1146	2123	3413	6103
Gross Margin Ratio	0.19	0.15	0.22	0.29	0.38
Net Profit Before Tax	602	251	1263	2666	5297
Net Profit Ratio	0.08	0.03	0.13	0.22	0.33
Capital Employed	9523	9545	9696	10136	
Return on Investment	6%	3%	13%	26%	42%

It is evident from Chart 4.85 that there is a steady decline in the current as well as quick ratios for the firm from 1995-96 on wards. The current ratio was close to 2:1 till the years 1997-98 and the quick ratio was close to 1 till the year 2002-03.

The reason behind fall in the ratio over these years is due to more than proportionate increase in current liabilities as compared to the current assets. Even if the ratio appears to be low, there is no short-term risk associated with the company, because all other ratios as analyzed in the next pages are quite healthy. It can be concluded from the above that the firm has adopted a very aggressive working capital management policy for the company.

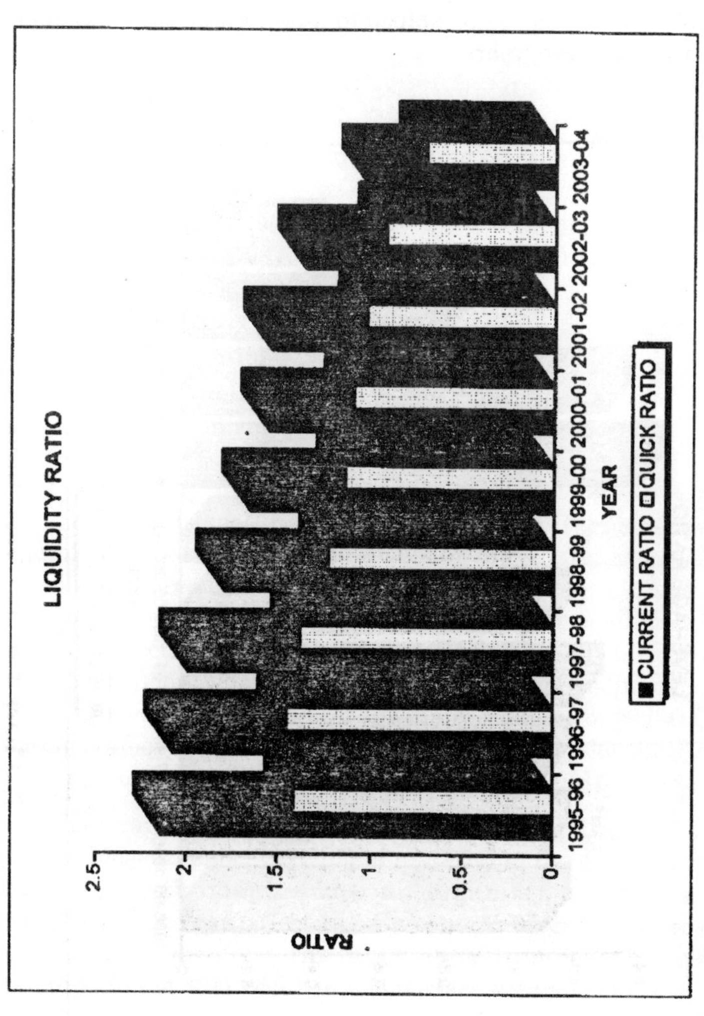

Chart 4.85: Liquidity Ratio

Debt-Equity ratio indicates the financial flexibility of the company to take dynamic decisions. The graph below (Chart 4.86) shows that the ratio is quite comfortable for TISCO. It has been less that during the years 2003-04 and 2004-05. Prudent financial management and decision regarding capital investment in stages has helped in maintaining the ratio under control all these years.

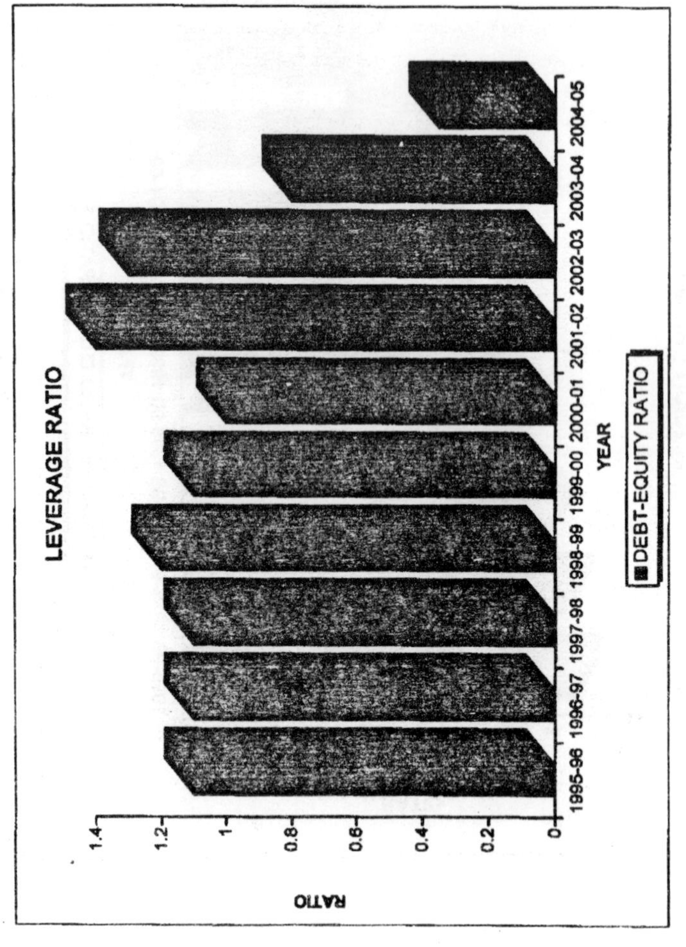

Chart 4.86: Leverage Ratio

It is evident from Chart 4.87 that the ratio has been very good over these years. It was little low during the financial year 2001-02 due to poor steel demand during that year. Overall, inventory turnover ratio is very good for the firm. The ratio has been more than 7 since the year 1999-00 and reached to an all time high of 9.5 during 2003-04.

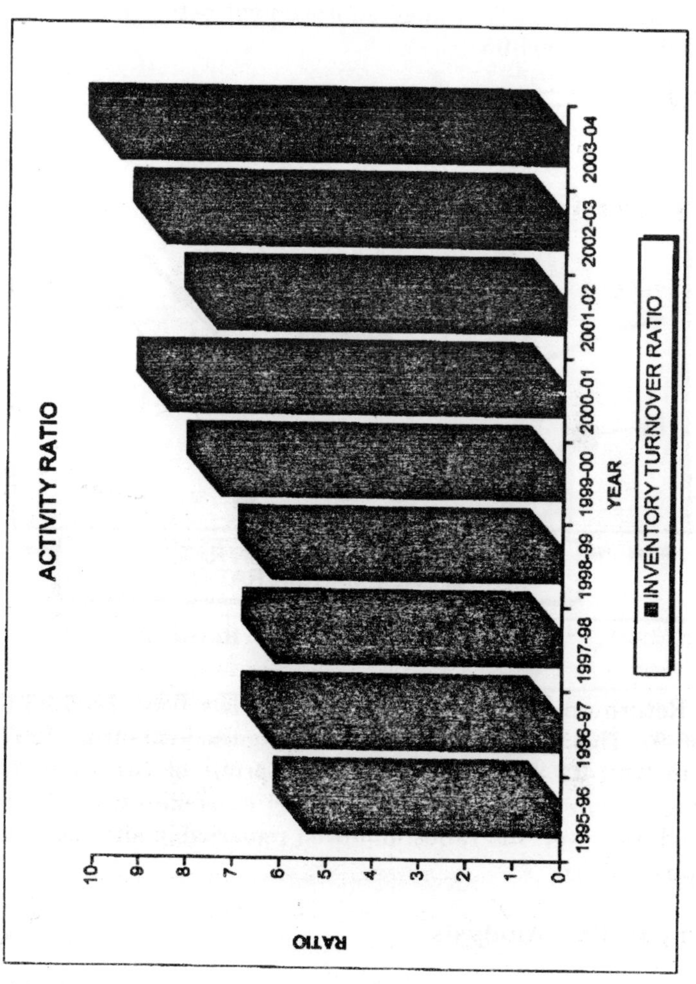

Chart 4.87: Activity Ratio

Profitability Ratio

The Gross margin as well as net margin ratios are quite strong all these years for the firm. It can also be observed from the graph that both these ratios have followed the same trend during this period. With an improved steel market the ratios have witnessed a huge improvement between the years 2002-03 and 2004-05.

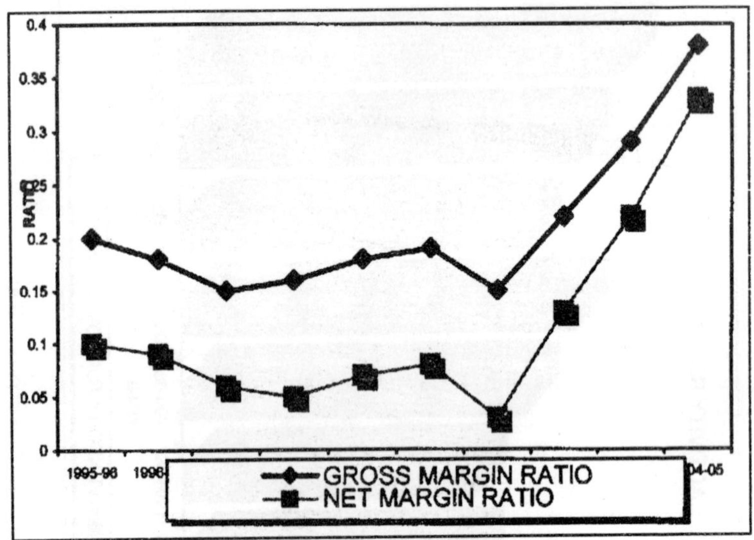

Chart 4.88a: Profitability Ratio

Return on Investment figures were low from 1995-96 to 1996-97. This even became worse during the years from 1997-98 to 2001-02 due to very less net profit of the company owing to slow down in the world steel economics during that period. However, the ratios improved remarkably after 2001-02 (Chart 4.88b).

Comparative Analysis

The current ratio of RSP is higher than those of SAIL and TISCO. While TISCO has maintained low ratio, the ratio of SAIL is quite comfortable from business point of

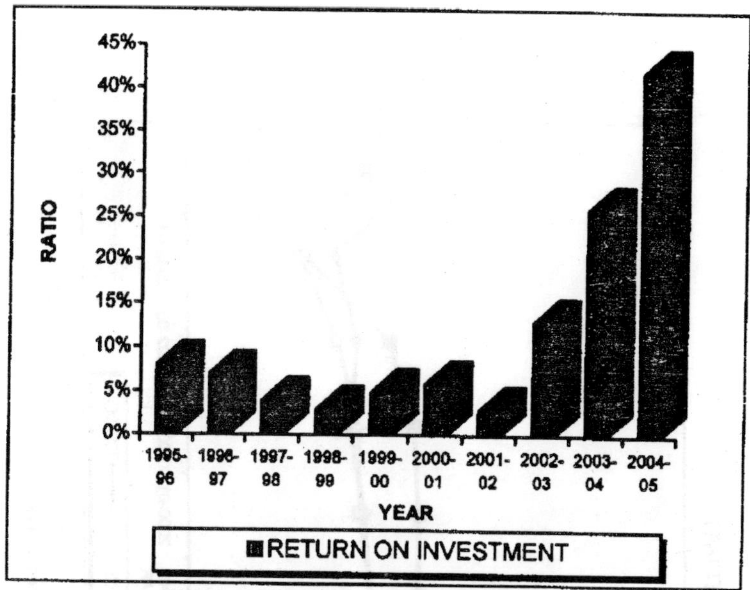

Chart 4.88b: Return of Investment

view. RSP's ratio is generally on the higher side. It needs to improve working capital management to bring down this ratio (Chart 4.49).

Debt-Equity ratio of TISCO has been quite comfortable over the years. In case of SAIL, the ratio kept on increasing till the years 2002-03 to a very unmanageable level, after which it started improving remarkably (Chart 4.90). As on 31st March, 2005, the ratio for SAIL was 0.58, which is very comfortable for the firm to take strategic decisions in the future. Since, RSP is one of the main Units of SAIL, the leverage ratio of SAIL applies on RSP also for taking any major decision for the plant unit, which requires Board approval. However going by the ratio of RSP alone, it had negative ratios after 1998-99 due to losses suffered by it. However in the recent times, since the company started making profit, the ratio has started improving.

From Chart 4.91 it is seen that the inventory turnover ratios of RSP and SAIL moved almost in the same line.

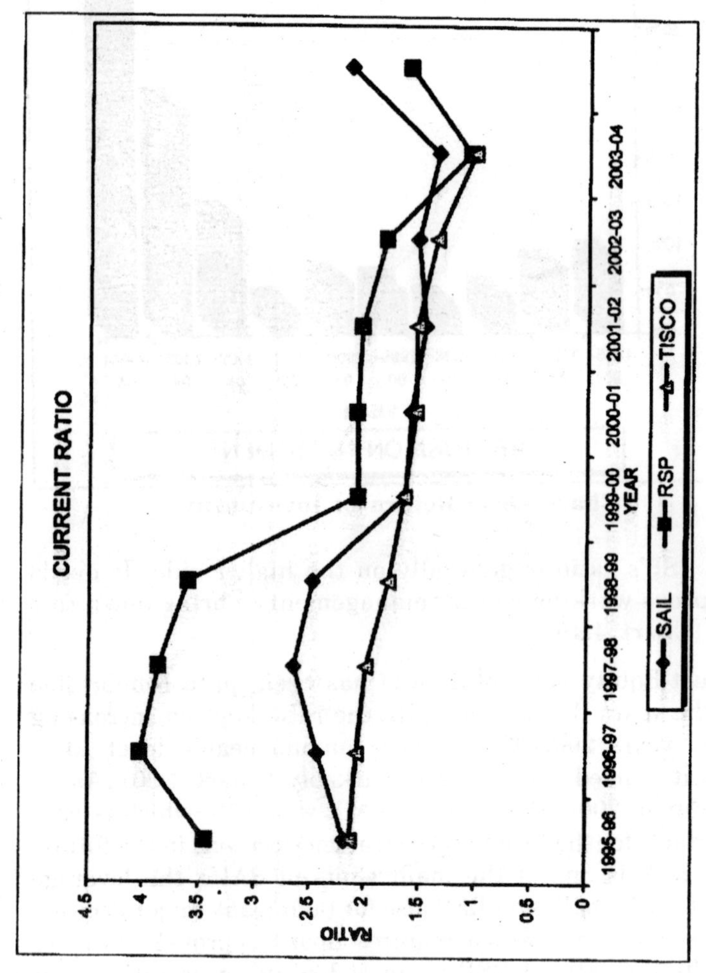

Chart-4.89: Current Ratio

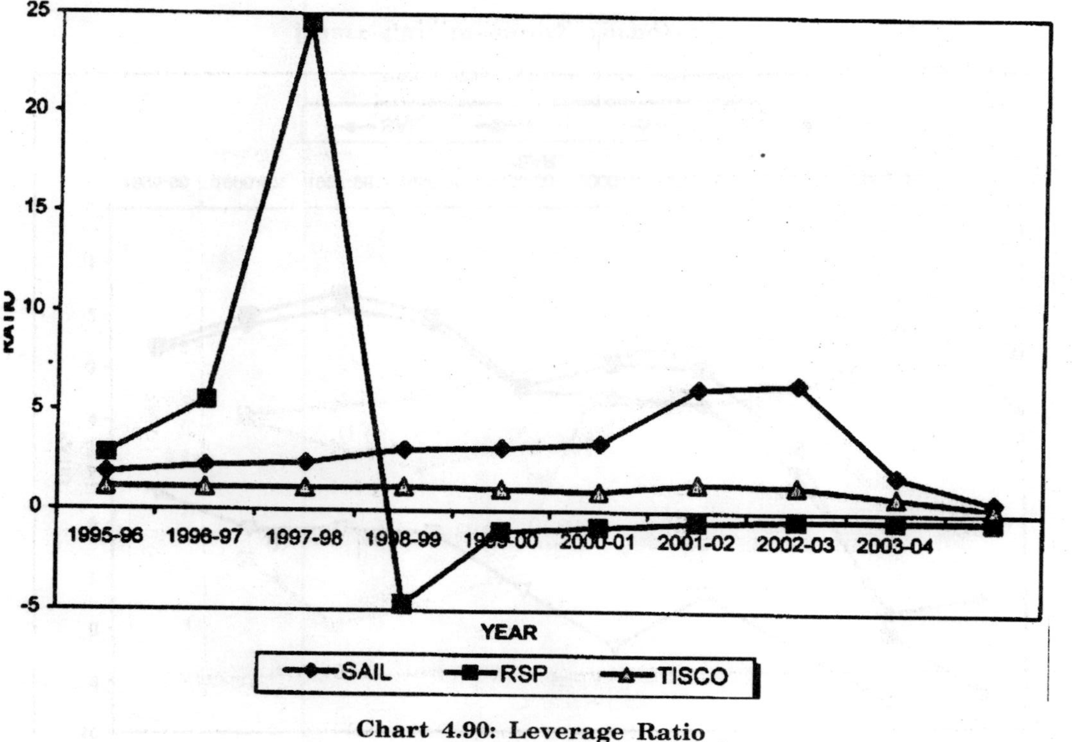

Chart 4.90: Leverage Ratio

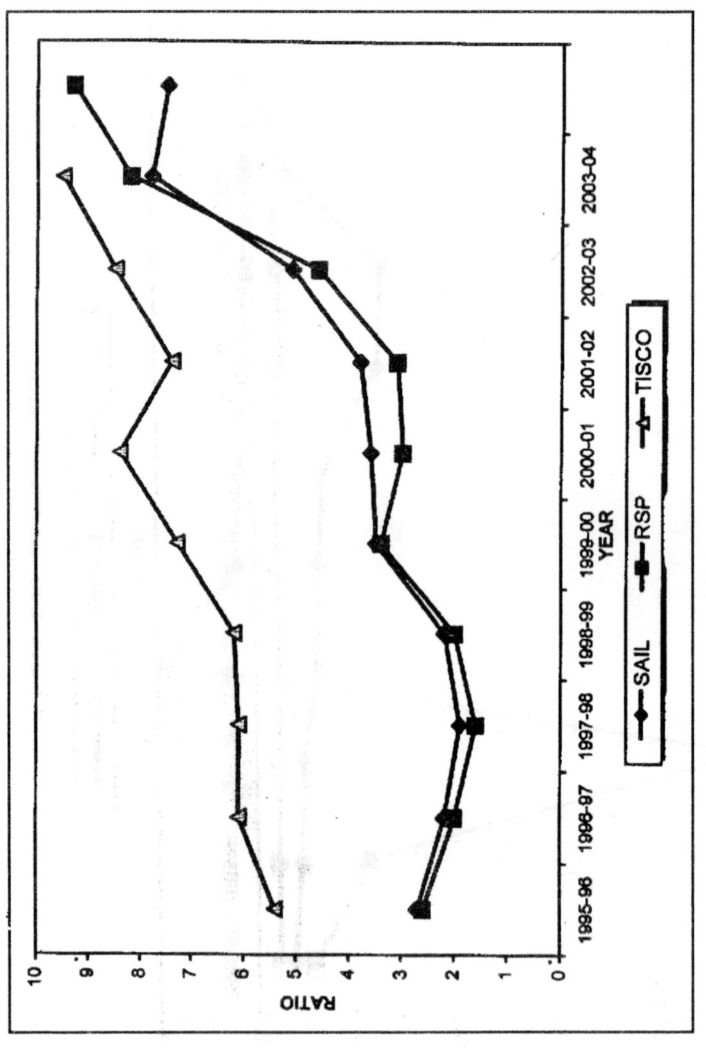

Chart 4.91: Inventory Turnover Ratio

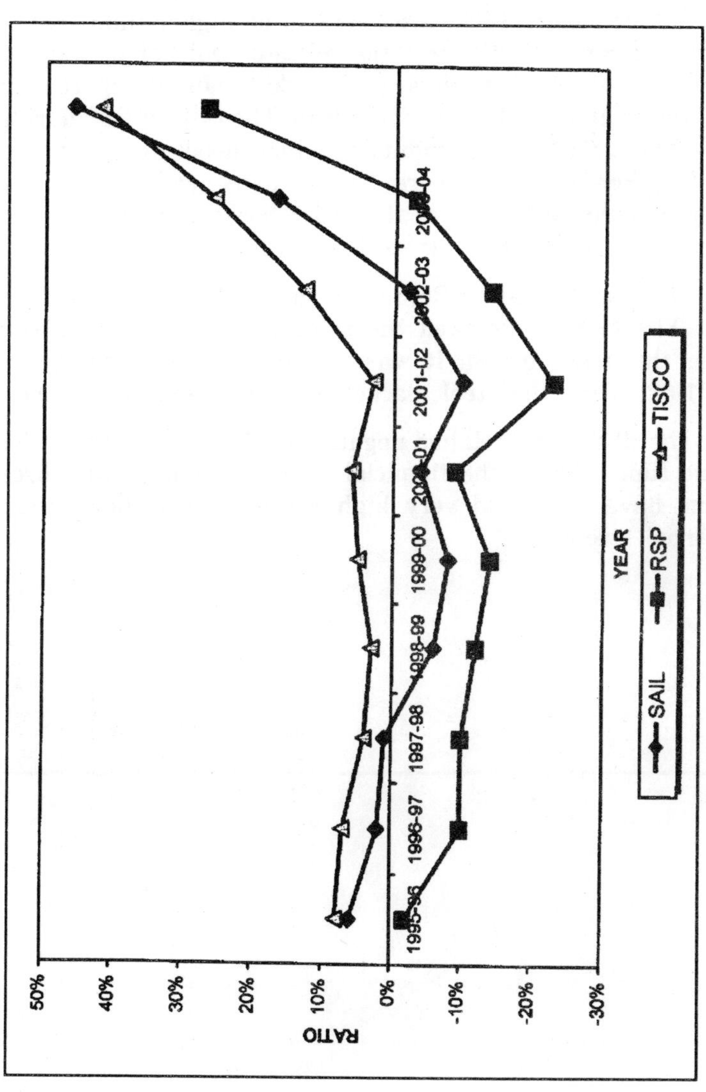

Chart 4.92: Return on Investment

However, during the year 2004-05, the ratio for RSP has been more than that of its parent company SAIL. This is a very good sign for RSP.

The ratios of TISCO are found to be higher than that of RSP and SAIL. A higher ratio indicates quicker conversion from inventory to sales, thus lower working capital requirement and improving profitability of the firm. The ratio of RSP during the year 2004-05 is a landmark, which needs to be crossed by it in the subsequent years. The company needs to integrate its production activities to the order booking so as to avoid generation of non-moving stock in finished products.

The rise and fall of Return on Investment for SAIL, RSP and TISCO have followed the same pattern, which is seen from the above graph. It was the lowest during the years 2001-02, when the steel market was in a very bad shape.

The RSP and SAIL had negative return on investment for some time. During the financial year 2004-05, all the three firms have witnessed very high ratios, which shows their internal strength.

5

Summary of the Findings, Conclusions and Suggestions

INTRODUCTION

In this chapter, an attempt has been made to present the summary of the discussions made in different chapters and sub chapters of the study in a concise form. This chapter is broadly divided into two parts. The first part covers summary of findings, while the second part covers suggestions based upon the analysis in the study. The anlaysis and discussions made are based on the data collected from secondary sources published by RSP, SAIL, TISCO and various other institutions, books, periodicals and Newspapers. The practical utility and further extension of the study are also mentioned towards the end of this chapter keeping in view the extent of research work done in the script.

SUMMARY OF FINDINGS

Steel Industry - An Appraisal

In this chapter, an appraisal of global steel scenario and India steel scenario has been carried out. The future predictions based on logic are also outlined.

Global Steel Scenario

Steel Economy has a direct correlation with GDP growth rate of the Economy of a country. The global economy witnessed a gradual recovery from late 2003 onwards. The growth in China has become one of the major factors currently driving the world economy. Indian GDP is also expected to grow at 7 to 8% in the coming years. Global Steel industry is growing at a rapid pace from 780 Mt in 2001 to 906 MT of finished steel consumption in 2004. If it goes like this, within 2 years this will touch one billion mark. However, steel is still in its relative infancy. Growth in the sector is on the cards. Part of the growth will be met by improving upon the unutilized capacity and partly through creation of new capacities to meet the demand supply gap.

Steel sector passed through a recession between the years 2001 and 2002. Since mid 2002-03, steel prices have seen serial hikes almost on a monthly basis. This has given a big relief to the steel producers. The steel prices will stabilize at a level soon.

Asia's total production of crude steel during 2003 is estimated at 436.8 million tons, out of a global production of 969.3 million tons with a percentage share of 45%. This percentage has further increased to 46.5% in 2004. China recorded an annual growth of 21.2% in 2003 and 22.5% in 2004 reaching 272.5 million ton crude steel production. India recorded a growth of 10.3% in 2003 and 2.5% in 2004. Overall growth in the Asian region during 2003 and 2004 were 11.6% and 12.3% respectively against world growth of 7.6% and 9% respectively. Growth in the Asian region has been the highest in the world. The reasons are cheaper availability of raw material, cheaper manpower, availability of steel making technology, open market conditions, growing economy. Steel producing giants are in Asian region and growth rate especially in China and India are more than the world average.

Following are the indications of movement of steel economy in the future time horizon:

- **Between 2005 and 2008**, there will be a slow down in steel demand and the growth will be at the rate of 5 to 6% pa. There will also be major addition of new steel capacities through capital investment route. There will be a strong pressure on the prices of steel products. Competition will continue and prices of steel products may fall.
- **After 2008:** To reduce the effect of price competition steel consolidation may take place among the major steel producers through merger and acquisition route. There will be pressure on steel prices and marginal steel producers may either close down their businesses or merge with a bigger entity. Technology and capacity will play a vital role to meet customers demand in terms of quality and cost.

Indian Steel Scenario

With the onset of liberalization in India, the steel industry will become competitive. The growth of the steel sector is intricately linked with the growth of the Indian economy too. India though is able to compensate for the domestic demand of steel but it needs to look for more lucrative markets through exports and make itself a force in the steel sector. The Indian steel industry has performed very well in recent years. At present, total (crude) steel making capacity is over 34 million tones and India is the 9th largest producer of steel in the world. The peak rate of customs duty has been reduced sharply during the last 5 years. Customs duty on several raw materials used by the steel sector like non-coking coal, metcoke and nickel has also been reduced to five per cent.

The New Industrial Policy has opened up the iron and steel sector for private investment by removing it from the list of industries reserved for public sector and exempting it from compulsory licensing. While the existing units are being modernized/expanded, a large number of new/greenfield steel plants are setting up plants in different parts of the country based on modern, cost effective technologies. The National

Steel Policy has set an ambitious target of 60 MT of steel production by 2010 and to 100 MT by 2018. India looks at attaining top three slots in terms of steel production in the world. What is worrying is the per capita consumption of steel in the country. This needs to change substantially in future with the growth of economy. To support India's vision; primary steel producer shave lined up major capacity expansion. Electric arc furnace (EAF) based steel producers are also gearing up to meet the spiraling projected demand. In fact, EAF producers are expected to have a higher share of 50 per cent in total steel production by 2020, as against the current 35 per cent.

As India aspires to more than treble its steel capacity over the next 15 years. Sustenance of this burgeoning capacity is becoming the core issue. The main obstacle to the steel industry's growth could be raw material availability, metallurgical coal/coke and scrap in particular.

A BRIEF PROFILE OF RSP

Rourkela Steel Plant (RSP) is a part of the group company Steel Authority of India ltd. (SAIL). RSP's functioning is influenced by the decisions of SAIL.

SAIL and Rourkela Steel Plant

Steel Authority of India Ltd. is the largest producer of steel in the country. It is a fully integrated iron and steel maker producing both basic and special steels for construction, engineering, power, railways, automotive, defense industries and for exports too. Its crude steel production capacity is 13 Million Tons. It has ranked 16th in the world in terms of crude steel production during 2004. Its products range from Long products to Flat products to special grade and alloy steel to stainless steel. Long products include bars, structures, channels, rails, railway wheels and axles, rods, joints etc. Flat products include Hot rolled coil (HR Coil), Plate, Cold rolled coil/sheet (CR Coil/Sheet), Galvanized-Plain and corrugated Coil/Sheet (GP/GC) etc. Special Products like Electrolytic Tin Plate (ETP), Cold rolled grain non-oriented (CRNO), ERW

(Electric resistance welded) pipe, SW (Spiral welded) pipe etc., are also produced by the company.

The SAIL produces iron and steel at four integrated steel plants and three special steel plants. The integrated steel plants are situated close to the raw material sources in the East and central region of the country. The integrated steel plants are Rourkela Steel Plant (RSP), Bhilai Steel Plant (BSP), Bokaro Steel Ltd. (BSL) and Durgapur Steel Plant (DSP). Ranked among the top ten companies in the country, it achieved highest ever turnover of Rs. 31800 crores and net profit of Rs. 6817 crores during the financial year 2004-05, which is a landmark by itself. It has its captive iron ore mines meeting the total requirement of raw materials in its integrated steel plants at present. It has a wide marketing network connecting around 35 stock yards through out the country managed by its marketing arm CMO (Central marketing Organisation) and the exports are managed through its International Trade Division (ITD).

The SAIL is geared up to double its capacity by the years 2012. Long term Plan of SAIL envisages increasing its domestic market share from a level of around 26% to around 27%. For realistic achievement and investments in stages, the plan has been split into two stages - Stage -1 pertaining to the period up to 2006-07 and Stage-2 up to 2011-12. Crude steel production by SAIL is planned to reach a level of 18.7 MTPA by 2012, leading to saleable steel production of 17.38 MTPA. On the raw material front SAIL will take up the certain steps including development of captive mines to meet the increased requirement in the future. The capital expenditure envisaged will be financed mainly through internal accruals, and will be supplemented by market borrowing if the need arises. Company's debt-equity ratio will be maintained at, a level of 1:1.

Rourkela Steel Plant

Rourkela Steel Plant (RSP) is an integrated steel plant in the family of SAIL with a capacity of 2 Million Tonnes of Hotmetal Production. It was the first plant to be commissioned in the public sector after Government of India decided to set up three plants in the Second Five-year Plan. After modernization, the capacities have been enhanced to 2 MT of Hot Metal, 1.9 MT of Continuous Cash Slabs and 1.671 Mt of Saleable steel.

Rourkela Steel Plant produces a wide variety of special purpose steels, the use of its plates in ship building and high pressure vessels, Silicon Steel in the electrical industries, Corrugated Galvanized Sheets for roofing including industrial roofing, pipes in the oil and gas sectors, Tin plates in packaging industry and special plates in the defense of the nation are well known. Its steel production is totally through continuous cast route of steel, which is considered to be a cost effective process. RSP has also implemented ISO 9001 in almost all the major shops under it.

Rourkela Steel Plant functions under the aegis of SAIL. The unit is generally headed by a Managing Director, who is also a part of the Board of the Directors of the Navaratna Steel behemoth, SAIL. Among the Direct reporting Officers to the M.D are ED (Works), GM (Projects), ED (Personnel, Ed (Material Management), GM (Finance and Accounts) etc. They look after the key functions of the company.

Being an integral part of SAIL, RSP depends on the central units of SAIL for its day-to-day activities. Even though the MD of RSP is empowered to take independent decisions for day-to-day operations of the plant, there are some areas like transfer prices, allocation of coal during crisis, operation/non operation of certain facilities depending on the market conditions etc., where the decisions are enforced by the Corporate office on the plants.

Rourkela Steel Plant made major improvements in the areas of steel quality, packaging, delivery and customer satisfaction thereby vastly enhancing the acceptability of its products in the highly competitive steel market. In around two and a half years, it has achieved one of the most dramatic turnarounds in Corporate Indian History. The Steel plant, which was on the threshold of oblivion a few years ago, is now firmly on the net profit mode. While RSP's turnaround started on a modest note in the year 2003-04, it gradually picked up speed and registered highest ever net profit of Rs. 1045 crores in the financial year 2004-05.

Over the last four years, a series of communication exercises, workshops and interaction sessions have been conducted involving employees' participation in large and small groups. Of all the HR interventions initiated in the plant the one that has created the greatest impact is the "The Mass Contact Exercise" (MCE).

ROURKELA STEEL PLANT – AN ANALYTICAL STUDY

An analysis of strength and weaknesses of RSP is carried out, which gives an idea about its positioning *vis-à-vis* its competitors in the market place. It shows that RSP has advantage of sourcing iron ore from the captive sources which provides as shield against price rises, continuous casting route of steel making, special steel production facilities. But its concerns are quality, low capacity and high manpower. It may address these issues in future so as to remain viable in the market. A detailed financial analysis is also undertaken in the study for RSP. Prior to this, the behaviours of sales price and input prices affecting the profitability of the company are analysed.

Sales price analysis shows that net sales price for various products were depressed during the financial year 2001-02, after which it started improving. The maximum jump of 34% in the sales price took place during the financial year 2004-05 in which the company recorded the highest ever turnover of Rs. 4674 crores and profit of Rs. 1045 crores. However, a temporary down ward pressure on the sales price front is seen during May 2005 to Jul 2005. During this time, there has been a reduction of about 10 to 15% in the sales prices of the base items like HR coil, CR Coil/sheet, GP/GC and about 5 to 10% in case of plates as compared to 2004-05 prices.

Out of all the raw materials consumed by RSP, Coal, Ferro alloys, Aluminum, Copper, Boiler coal are purchased from external agencies. Coal is a major raw material, which accounts for about 20% of the total expenditure of the company. The input purchase rates of these items between 2000-01 and 2004-04 show an increase. Stiff increase is there in case of coal.

The raw material Iron ore is generated by the captive mines of the group company SAIL and is transferred for consumption on cost of generation basis. Thus it is insulated from the variations in the market price. This shows that input prices of the items generated captively are almost stable for RSP, even if there is a price rise in the market.

Financial Analysis

RSP's financial performance is dependent upon the decisions taken by itself and the competitors in the market. The major integrated steel plants in the country are Stele Authority of India Ltd. (SAIL), TISCO, Rastriya Ispat Nigam Ltd. (RINL), which together cater to around 60% of the total steel requirement in the country at present. Therefore Financial analysis of RSP is required to be done along with that of the major players in the country so as to judge the performance of the company and be able to benchmark the key parameters for future achievement. As a part of this research, three companies namely RSP, SAIL and TISCO are considered to carry out the financial anlaysis. SAIL is the biggest public sector steel company in the country, RSP is one of the main steel plants of SAIL and TISCO is the biggest private sector steel company in the country at present. Performance of RSP is compared with those of SAIL and TISCO and suggestions for future improvement are worked out. Different models have been used in the course of financial analysis. Analysis of working capital, financial statements, break even, cash flow, ratios are done as a part of this study.

Most of the financial trends of RSP can be best understood from the financial analysis in conjunction with those of its parent company SAIL. Certain financial analysis like working capital, Cash/Funds flow of RSP is inconclusive without considering those of SAIL too. This is because of the fact that balance sheet entries in RSP like sundry debtors (to the extent of prime sales through Central Marketing organization of SAIL), sundry creditors of raw materials, borrowings are operated through IUCA (Inter-unit Current Accounts) transactions.

Working Capital Analysis

Companies need cash to meet expenses for day-to-day activities. They have to pay wages, pay for raw materials, pay bills etc. Money available to them to do this is known as the firms' working capital. The main sources of working capital are the current assets as these are the short-term assets that the firm can use to generate ash. These assets have a high liquidity. However, the firm also has current liabilities and so these have to be taken into account while estimating working capital at the firm's disposal. It is important for a firm to have sufficient working capital to meet all its requirements like paying for raw materials, day-to-day bills, wages etc. A judicious decision in respect of investment in current assets is very important for the company to avoid taking more working capital loan from banks resulting in more interest pay outs.

The amount of investment in current assets depends on the nature of business of the firm. In case of an integrated steel plan, working capital requirement is more. Inventory of finished goods needs to be maintained at a comfortable level to avoid stock out situation at any point of time. However the stock of semi-finished goods can be reduced through ingenuous production planning between processes. This will ease the working capital requirement of the firm.

Working capital can also be high due to high sundry debtors and excess cash of the firm. Sundry debtors level depends on the market condition as ell as collection efforts. In today's steel market, where demand outweighs supply, fresh sundry debtors are also nil for the steel manufacturers. A minimum amount of working capital is required to be held by the firm to meet its day-to-day requirements. This is known as permanent working capital. This is very much required in case of an integrated steel plant like steel Authority of India Ltd. and one of its main producing unit "Rourkela Steel Plant". Estimation of this is governed by working capital policy adopted by Rourkela Steel Plant

The way working capital moves around the business is modeled by the working capital cycle. Between each stage of this working capital cycle there is a time lag. For some businesses this will be very long where it takes them a long time to make and steel the product. Thus these businesses need a substantial amount of working capital to survive.

Net working capital for RSP was on a decline till the year 2003-04. It has increased during 2004-05. Current assets were falling till 2003-04. However, as on 31st March, 2005, current asset is found to have increased over the corresponding period last year. Current liability is found to have fallen as on 31st March, 2005 compared to last year.

Semi-finished and Finished goods stock was the highest as on 31st March, 1998. But there after there has been a steep fall in the stock till 31st March, 2004. This has eased the working capital requirement of the plant considerably. There is also a reduction in Stores and Spares stock over the years, but still the figure is quite high. Raw material stock has also increased considerably as on 31st March 2005 as compared to the previous year. This was due to maintaining a high stock of imported coal to take care of future requirements of the plant. Sundry debtors in RSP books of accounts reflect only the portion of the Defective Iron and Steel products, scrap and byproducts sold by the plant. The major chunk of the sundry debtors, which is from prime products old through Central Marketing Organisation of SAIL does not appear under the heading "Sundry Debtors". The accounting entry for this is done through Inter-unit Current Account (IUCA) code. Since sundry debtors of SAIL appears to be on a declining trend over the years, the same trend can also be assumed true in case of RSP.

Sundry creditor has gone up over the years. The figure is little less in 2004-05 compared to 2003-04. Provision figures are high after 1999. It is the highest as on 31st March, 2004. The reason for this is the pay revision arrear dues of the employees of the plant. However, provision figure as on 31st March, 2005 is much less compared to that of the previous year. This is the reason for a fall in total liabilities figure as on 31st March, 2005 as compared to the previous year.

There is a remarkable improvement in the Semi/Finished stock holding. The stock has declined rapidly during 2002-03 and 2003-04 with improvement in steel market during that period. This has certainly reduced the working capital requirement for the plant during the difficult times. Raw material holding as on 31st March 2005 is more than that of the previous year because of the requirement for stocking imported coal on the face a shortage of the material in the international market. There is reduction in Stores and spares stock during this time. But as on 31st March, 2005 the stock is of 200 days, which is more than six months holding. This needs to be reduced to less than three months holding.

Working capital management of RSP is compared with SAIL, TISCO and the observations are as follows. Raw material holding is the least in case of RSP. It was very high during 1996-97. Since then there has been a continuous decrease in the holding, which is a good sign. Semi-finished and finished goods stock holding is high in case of RSP and SAIL. It was very high during the financial years 1997-98, 1998-99 and 2001-02. No. of days stock holding in RSP was higher than that of SAIL. This was because of poor market condition and may be due to mismatch between sales order and production planning, which resulted in specific grades and sizes of products not having immediate marketability. This affected the working capital position of RSP and SAIL to a greater extent. However the situation started improve form 2002-03 onwards, especially with improvement of steel market. Present no. of days of stock holding is quite comfortable in case of RSP and SAIL, which is closer to that of TISCO too. TISCO on the other hand could manage the stock holding within a comfortable level of around 1 month in all these years. It was little high during 1998-99 when market situation was bad. But with proper planning and sustained efforts in the areas of customer satisfaction, quality improvement etc., stock holding could be maintained at a lower level. Substantial improvement in the inventory holding is observed in case of RSP after 2001-02 due to improvement in quality of products as well as proper production planning and control. This needs to be maintained in future. Number of days holding of Stores/Spares in RSP is more compared to the average figure of SAIL. However, it is less compared to TISCO and there is also signs of improvement over the years. Still there is a lot of scope for improvement in this area. The comfortable level should be 1 month holding, though the ideal number is zero (Just in time). But, since some quantities of spares are required in the stock to take care of break down and emergency situations, zero holding is practically not possible. To reduce the number of days of holding of stores and spares from the present level of 6 months to even 3 months, emphasis on reduction in average processing time of indents, vendor development, proper spares requirement planning may be given. This will reduce generation of non moving stock and the requirement of stocking huge quantity.

Financial Statement Analysis

Analysis of Financial Statements of RSP reveals the strengths and weaknesses of the company. The Profit and Loss Accounts and Balance sheets are analyzed in details and the behaviours of the key factors like Net Profit, Operating Profit, Net worth, reserve and surplus, Capital employed etc. have been captured. Data relating to these factors are tabulated and analyzed.

The pattern appearing in case of RSP is more or less similar to that of its group company SAIL. Depreciation kept on increasing from the year 1995-96 to 1998-99 on account of capitalization of new assets commissioned through modernization in the various production Units of RSP. Major capitalization of modernized units took place in the year 1998-99. Depreciation increased by about 102% during that period compared to the previous year. There after depreciation remained almost steady. This indicates that major capitalization of capital schemes took place in the year 1998-99 and after that capital investment in the various production units has been negligible.

Interest was also on an increasing trend from 1995-96 to 1998-99 an increase of 157% over 1995-96. The increase in 1998-99 over 1997-98 was a whopping 54%. This was on account of more borrowings during this period for funding the on-going capital projects in various production units of RSP. However, thereafter the interest burden gradually declined. Interest reduced by 21% during 1999-00 over 1998-99 on account of waiver of a major chunk of SDF loan utilized in the modernization of the plants, as a part of the Financial Restructuring scheme approved by the Government of India. Interest also reduced between 2000-01 and 2002-03. This was on account of repayment of costly loans with the help of cheaper loans from the market. After 2002-03, there has been a steady decline in the interest between 30 to 40% during 2003-04 and 2004-05 over the previous years. This has happened owing to a better steel market during that time, which resulted in an improved profit and cash position for the company. In these years, the company managed to pay the debt repayment obligation from its own fund. Thus total outstanding borrowings have been reduced drastically during this period too.

The capital employed trend follows the trend in the total borrowings for the company in all to the years except 2004-05. There has been an increase in capital employed till 1998-99. There after there is a gradual decline till 2003-04. During this time total borrowings figures are almost steady. In the year 2004-05 borrowings have reduced, but the capital employed has increased.

The increase in total borrowings and capital employed between 1995-96 and 1998-99 is attributed to more funding for the on going capital schemes in various Departments of RSP through borrowings and increase in net block due to capitalization of new assets. Percentage reduction in the total borrowings is quite high during 1999-00. This was on account of waiver of SDF loan utilized for modernization activities in the production units, as a part of the financial restructuring process for SAIL. There was also about 40% reduction in total borrowing during 2004-05. The reason for this is, better profit for the plant and repayment of loans through own fund. Similarly, the percentage reduction in the capital employed is quite high during 1999-00, which is 20% over the last year. The major reason for this is the reduction in net block due to the waiver of SDF loan utilized for modernization activities.

There is an increase in the capital employed in the year 2004-05 by 3% over previous year against a substantial reduction in total borrowings. The reason for this is, a higher profit and cash balance, which offset the percentage reduction in the borrowings.

PBDIT (Profit before Depreciation, Interest and Tax) has been positive for the company in all other years except 1999-00 and 2001-02. With improvement of steel market from 2002-03 and reduction in interest, PBDIT started increasing from 2002-03 on wards and so also the net profit (PAT). In the year 2004-05, PBDIT increased considerably by 250% over 2003-04 and net profit (PAT) achieved an impressive Rs. 1045 crores.

At the end of the financial year 2004-05, Reserve and Surplus as well as Net worth of the firm are still negative. However there has been an improvement of 26% in Reserve/ Surplus and 29% in the Net worth of the firm during the Financial Year 2004-05 as compared to the previous year. The firm needs to make Net profit at the current rate for few more years to be able to achieve positive Net worth.

Looking at the risk factor of the firm, it can be seen that in spite of having a negative Net worth, there is no threat for the company, since it is a part of a healthy group company, SAIL. The company has shown resilience during the upturn in the steel market and has posted a healthy profit level. It speaks of the internal strength of the company.

Major Weakness of the firm in today's situation is its capacity and capacity utilization. The company can try to achieve 100% capacity utilization through debottlenecking in the logistics and planning processes. A little investment may be required in the areas of technological difficulties to help in removing the bottle-necks in the process. The company will gain further strength after achieving this. It may also try to augment its capacity at least by 100% to secure its viability in the form of an individual integrated steel plant in the future. The investment for capacity expansion needs to be finances mostly from the current and future profits of the company (i.e from internal accruals of SAIL). At the same time, timely project execution and implementation also play a vital role in the success of the firm.

Break-even Point Analysis

Profit is the most important concern of a Business Organization. The profit element depends on the production volume, sales volume, sales price and product mix for a multi product firm. So it is very important to understand Break-even production and sales volume for the Organization. Break-even point is not a fixed point. This depends on the Sales price, Input rates, and other fixed expenditures of the firm. Fixed cost plays a vital role in determining the Break-even point of an organization. It is not really fixed in the organization. This is variable depending the decisions of the management and other situational factors.

The analytical tool used for this is the CVP (Cost, Volume, Profit) analysis. The Break-even point. Analysis brings relationship between sales revenue and cost with respect to the volume of operation. The volume, which brings equilibrium between sales and cost, is called the Break-even Point for the Firm. This is the point at which the firm has no profit and no loss situation.

Sales revenue is the reflection of turnover of a company. It is important to study the cost of the firm too. The company derives the cost from the revenue expenditures made in a specified period. Break-even point for a firm will reach when total sales revenue covers the total variable and fixed cost components. Analysis of break-even point in case of steel sector has been done in details in using formula approach. Break Even Point can be indicated in terms of Number of Units, Percentage Capacity or in terms of sales revenue in Rupee or Dollar.

Per Unit Sales Price of a product covers its own Variable Cost and leaves a remainder, which is known as contribution. This Contribution is supposed to cover the fixed cost per unit of the product to make the product profitable. Going by this concept, it is evident that if per unit contribution is equal to per Unit Fixed Cost of the product, then there is Break-even point. At the Break-even point, profit will be zero. Thus total contribution will be equal to total fixed cost of the firm.

The calculation is based on the data collected and tabulated from Annul Profit and Loss Accounts of M/s Rourkela Steel Plant, M/s Steel Authority of India Ltd., M/s Tata Iron and Steel Company Ltd. Sales related items are tabulated under sales group and net sales revenue is calculated after subtracting Excise duty, Freight and stockyard margins (if any appearing separately) from the Turnover of the firm. Expenditure items are grouped under Variable and Fixed heads. Specific percentages based on a study have been adopted to break items such as Stores and Spares consumption and Employee remuneration and Benefits into Variable and Fixed components.

The analysis shows that net sales revenue as well as net expenditure has increased over the years. After 2001-02, Sales revenue has increased more than proportionate to the expenditure; which has resulted in increased profit for the firm. The Net Expenditure is more than Net sales between 1995-96 and 2003-04. The Firm was making losses from 1995-96 to 2003-04. Loss figures were very high during the financial years 1998-99, 1999-00, 2001-02. Production capacity of the firm has increased after 1997-98. During this time the fixed cost (Depreciation and Interest) burden of the firm has gone up substantially. It is also observed that, after addition of new capacities, capacity utilization has been less than 100% all these years. It slowly improved after 1998-99 after stabilization of the modernization facilities. Capacity utilizations during 2003-04 and 2004-05 have been 92%. The company was making more losses during all these years prior to 2004-05 due to poor capacity utilization, higher fixed cost and lower sales price. Cost of production has been more than Net Sales Price all these years expect in the year 2004-05. After 2003-03, Net sales price increased more than proportionate to the cost of Production. Steel market improved during this time. Capacity utilization also improved substantially. Contribution in all these year has been positive, which saw a steady increase between the years 2001-02 and

2004-05. During this time losses were reduced and the firm registered a high net profit during 2004-05.

Break-even Points between the years 1996-97 and 2003-04 have been more than 100% capacity of the firm. This is the period in which the firm was making losses. Firm registered a very high loss during the financial year 2001-02. The fixed cost of the firm became very high after 1998-99 due to capitalization of all its expansion and modernization projects. At the same time since the capacity utilization was less than 100% and due to lower sales price of steel products, the firm suffered successive losses till the year 2003-04. During this time, the margin of operation was also negative. However, the Break Even Point during the financial year 2004-05 has seen a marked improvement over the earlier years. This has been 51% during this time. A strong steel demand has pushed up global steel prices, which improved the profitability of the company and at the same time helped in reducing the interest burden drastically. All these account for reduction in the B.E.P. to 51% level. Also the margin of operation during this time has been 694759 tons. But, Steel demand and steel prices may not remain at this level in future. With new steel units coming on stream soon and China changing its status from net importer to exporter of steel products, there will be a pressure on the steel prices in the near future. After that the prices will come down slowly and will stabilize at a certain level.

The raw material prices may increase in the short-term period. How ever in all profitability, the slide in Sales price will be more than the increase in the raw material prices. On the front of raw materials, the prices of coal, boiler coal and the Ferro alloys mostly affect the profitability of the firm.

Sensitivity analysis gives an indication about the revised B.E.P levels for operations of the firm to maintain its profit at different levels of sales price and input prices. Incase the sales price falls by 20% and Raw material cost increases by 10% then the Break even point will get shifted from the present level of 51% to 87%. However, if the sales price falls by 20% and Raw materials cost also increases by 20%, the Break-even point will shift from the represent level of 51% to 100%. Thus it is evident that the firm needs to prepare itself to operate at 100% capacity in the future to maintain profit. Sales price may stabilize at a lower level in the future and the raw materials expenditure may increase compared to 2004-05 due to increase in the imported coal prices, Ferro alloys prices etc. However the company is insulated from the increase in the input price of Iron ore raw material due to sourcing of the material from the captive mines of SAIL. Thus resilience in the profitability strength is quite high for the company.

Cash flow Analysis

It is mandatory for the companies filing reports with the SEBI (Securities and Exchange Board of India) to include a cash flow statement in their quarterly and annual reports. This is as per Accounting Standard-3 published by ICAI (Institute of Chartered Accountants of India). The cash-flow statement does not consider the non-cash items such as depreciation and tells how much actual money the company has generated and spent during a particular time frame. It is distinct from the Profit and Loss Account and balance sheet because it does not include the amount of future incoming and outgoing cash that has been recorded on credit. Therefore, cash is not the same as net income. Cash flow shows how the company has performed in managing inflows and outflows of cash. It also gives a clear picture of the company's ability to pay bills, creditors, and finance growth. Cash flow is determined by looking at three components by which cash enters and leaves a company: operations, investing and financing.

The source of cash in RSP is from allotment of fund by SAIL corporate office. As this makes RSP dependent so far as the sources of fund are concerned, therefore, cash management at RSP is done under some constraints. In addition, a small amount of cash is also generated in RSP through secondary products sales. We know that when there are limited sources of funds, an efficient management should take steps in utilizing the funds properly.

It is observed that Cash flow from operating activities for RSP has been increasing over the years except during the years 2000-01 and 2001-02. It has witnessed a major upward jump of about 287% during the financial year 2003-04. Cash flows form operating activities were negative during the years 1996-97, 1997-98 and 2001-02. The reasons for increase in cash flows during 2003-04 were substantial reduction in the Loss, Decrease in inventory levels and increase in provisions, which has an effected on the Net Profit. During this year, the steel market revived after a long spell of slow down. Cash flow from operating activities is the highest during the year 2004-05 due to very high profit for the Firm. During the financial year 2000-01, although there was a reduction in net loss as compared to the previous year, reduction in inventory was very less, which has affected the cash flow. The cash flows during the financial years 1996-97 and 1997-98 were negative due to losses suffered by the company and increase in inventory levels by a substantial percentage. It was also negative in the years 2001-02 due to a substantial increase in the net loss of the firm during that period.

Cash flows from investing activities have been positive during 1999-00, 2000-01, 2001-02 and 2003-04. In all other years, it was negative, i.e. there were cash outflows during these periods. There was a steep increase in cash flow during 1999-00 and a steep fall during 2000-01. Due to financial restructuring approved by the Government of India and effected during the financial year 1999-00, there was reduction in the asset value. The reduction in the asset value during that year was Rs. 889 crores. Due to this reason, and cash outflow on account of addition of assets compared to the last year being too less, the net cash flow was positive in that year. During the financial years 2000-01, net cash flow was positive mainly due to sale of Power plant into a Joint Venture company. Major additions of assets have taken place between the financial years 1996-97 and 1998-99. Addition of assets is also high during 2004-05 due to high work in progress figure.

Cash flows from financing activities were positive during 1996-97, 1997-98, 1998-99 and 2001-02. In all other years it is negative. Net cash outflow is very high in the year 1999-00. The variation in cash flows over the years is mostly due to the changes in the borrowings and IUCA balances of the firm. RSP is one of the main plant units of SAIL. As per the Accounting policies of SAIL, the transactions of the plant units with other units and central units like Head Office, Central Marketing Organisations, Transport and Shipping Unit, Central Coal Supply Organisation, Raw Material Division etc. are done through Inter Unit Current Accounts (IUCA) appearing in the Balance Sheet both in the Asset and Liability sides. Majority of the loan amounts are transferred by the Head office (SAIL) to RSP through IUCA. Sundry debtors balances also appear in the IUCA. It is not easy to segregate these items directly. Reduction in the borrowings and IUCA was the highest during 1999-00. This was mainly due to the waiver of a major portion of SDF loan as a part of the financial-restructuring scheme approved by Government of India for SAIL. Again borrowings increased by a bigger amount during the year 2001-02 due to huge loss suffered by the company. Considerable reduction in borrowings have taken place during the financial years 2003-04 and 2004-05 mainly due to an improved profit and cash situation of the firm.

It is observed that the net cash flow and the closing balance appear to move in the same direction. These are negligible every year due to the nature of cash transactions done at the plant Unit levels of SAIL. Major chunk of closing balance of Cash is maintained in the Corporate Office (SAIL) books.

It can be seen from the comparative graphs that, the cash flows in case of RSP and SAIL have not been smooth like that of TISCO. Investment plans are quite smooth and gradual in case of TISCO, but it is not so incase of SAIL and RSP. Smooth investment plans don't affect cash flows from operating activities severely. This is one of the main reasons behind huge fluctuations in profit and loss figures of SAIL and RSP. However, in the last few years, the efforts behind reduction in borrowings and inventory levels have reduced the interest and finance charges considerably in case of SAIL and RSP. RSP and SAIL need to achieve more than 100% capacity utilization so as to increase cash flows from operating activities in future. RSP also needs to curtail its fixed cost component further to keep its cash flows from operations and PAT sustainable in future.

Ratio Analysis

Ratio analysis is a powerful tool of financial analysis. It is the method of calculating and analyzing the financial strengths and weaknesses of a company from its financial statements, i.e. Balance-sheet and Profit and Loss account. The historical trends of these ratios indicate a company's financial condition, its operations and attractiveness for investment. Ratio Analysis enables the business owner/ manager to spot trends in a business and to compare its performance and condition with the average performance of similar businesses in the same industry.

The financial ratios can be grouped under the following categories which tell us about different facets of a company's finances and operations. Liquidity Ratios give a picture of a company's short-term financial situation or solvency. These show the firm's ability to meet current obligations. Leverage Ratios show the extent that debt is used in a company's capital structure. These show the mix of debt and equity, activity/ Operational Ratios show efficiency of a company in its operations and use of assets. These use turnover measures to calculate the ratios. Profitability ratios measure overall performance and efficiency of the firm. These use margin and show the return on sales and capital employed.

Liquidity Ratios: These ratios indicate the position of the firm to meet the short-term obligations. These ratios include the Current Ratio, Quick Ratio, and Working Capital.

Leverage Ratio: This indicates the composition of capital structure in the business and the risk factor associated with it. Capital structure includes owner's capital, reserve and surpluses, creditors money like short-term borrowings/long-term borrowings/public and corporate deposits through debt instruments. These ratios include Debt ratio, Debt-Equity ratio, Debt/Worth Ratio. These ratios are also known as "Leverage ratios", "Gearing ratios". These show the short-term and long-term solvency of the firm. Generally, the higher is this ratio, the more risky a creditor will perceive its exposure in the business, making it correspondingly harder to obtain credit.

Among all of these, the most popular ratio is Debt-Equity ratio. It is quite simple, easy to understand and interpret. The maximum limit of Debt-Equity ratio generally accepted is 2:1. However, it varies from sector to sector. A sector where more amount of credit sales takes place, the norm will be higher and for a sector having almost nil credit sales like services sector, the standard will be quite low. A comfortable ratio will be less than 1:1. Lower Debt-Equity ratio gives financial flexibility for the management to take dynamic decisions like business expansion, diversification etc.

Activity Ratio: This includes the ratios like Inventory Turnover Raito, Accounts Receivable Turnover Ratio, Return on Assets Ratio.

Profitability Ratio: Profitability ratios are calculated in relation to Sales Turnover, Investment. Some of the profitability ratios are Gross Margin Ratio, Net Profit Margin Ratio, Return on Investment (ROI) Ratio. While the Gross margin ratio shows the operational efficiency of the company, the net margin ratio shows the total performance, if both Gross margin as well as net margin ratio is lower, then it indicates serious problems in the operations of the company and the management needs to take corrective measures to come out of this situation in the short-term.

Important Financial ratios are analyzed for RAP, SAIL and TISCO and a comparison is made. Even if analysis is made for most of the possible ratios in case of RSP, these cannot be read in isolation. RSP being an integral part of SAIL, it is directly influenced by the performance of its parent company. In fact the interpretation of various ratios of SAIL is useful to assess financial health of RSP too. Similarly, if RSP's financial ratios are improved, those of SAIL will also improve.

It is observed that RSP maintained very comfortable current ratio of more than 2:1 between the financial years 1995-96 and 2001-02, which is considered comfortable for smooth operations of the business. The quick ratio of RSP is not very indicative of the real situation. This is because of the fact that cash balance of RSP is transferred to the

Corporate Office (SAIL) at the end of each day and necessary accounting entries are passed through IUCA (Inter-unit Current Account) Codes. Thus this ratio needs to be interpreted along with that of SAIL.

Going by this it can be concluded that the acid test ratios from 1995-96 to 1998-99 and from 2003-04 to 2004-05 were quite comfortable for the business operations of the firm.

Debt-Equity ratio was worse from 1996-97 on wards till now. From the year 1998-99 till date the net worth of the firm is negative and so also the ratio. Even though the firm made huge profit of Rs. 1045 crores during the financial year 2004-05, the accumulated losses are not yet fully wiped out. The firm needs to maintain profit every year to improve its ratio in the coming years. However, since RSP is an integral part of SAIL, the risk perceived on the business is linked to the ratio of SAIL, which indicates that it was bad from 1998-99 to 2002-03 and improved fast after 2002-03.

So far as the activity ratio of the firm is concerned, it is observed that there is a sign of improvement from the year 2002-03 onwards. During the financial years 2003-04 and 2004-05, the ratio crossed 7 with proper inventory management and drastic improvement in sales turnover of the firm, which is quite a healthy number for the firm.

Gross margin has been positive in all other years except in 1999-00 and 2001-02. Net margin has been negative from the year 1995-96 to 2003-04. Huge burden of Depreciation and interest as well as a poor steel market created this situation for the firm. However, the sustained efforts of the firm in cost reduction drive and an improved steel market have brought it out of this crisis situation after 2002-03 and made it emerge stronger.

Return on Investment figures were negative from 1995-96 to 2003-04, due to the losses suffered by the firm during that period. However, the ratios improved remarkably during the years 2003-04 and became 27% during the year 2004-05. The firm needs to maintain a good return on investment from this point onwards.

A comparative analysis shows that the current ratio of RSP is higher than those of SAIL and TISCO. While TISCO has maintained a low ratio, the ratio of SAIL is quite comfortable from business point of view. RSP's ratio is generally on the higher side. It needs to improve working capital management to bring down this ratio. Debt-Equity ratio of TISCO has been quite comfortable over the years. In case of SAIL, the ratio kept on increasing the till year 2002-30 to a very unmanageable level, after which it started improving remarkably. As on 31st March 2005, the ratio for SAIL was 0.58, which is very comfortable for the firm to take strategic decisions in the future. Since, RSP is one of the main Units of SAIL, the leverage ratio of SAIL applies on RSP also for taking any major decision for the plant unit, which requires Board approval. However going by the ratio of RSP alone, it had negative ratios after 1998-99 due to losses suffered by it. However in the recent times, since the company started making profit, the ratio has started improving. The inventory turnover ratios of RSP and SAIL moved almost in the same lime. However, during the year 2004-05, the ratio for RSP has been more than that of its parent company SAIL. This is a very good sign for RSP. The inventory turnover ratio for SP during the year 2004-05 is a landmark, which needs to be crossed by itself in the subsequent years. The company needs to integrate its production activities to the order booking so as to avoid generation of non-moving stock in finished products. The rise and fall of Return on Investment for SAIL, RSP and TISCO have followed the same pattern, which is seen from the above graph. It was the lowest during the years 2001-02, when the steel market was in a very bad shape. RSP and SAIL had negative return on investment for some time. During the financial year 2004-05, these firms have witnessed very high ratios, which shows their internal strength.

Suggestions for Rourkela Steel Plant (RSP)

Inventory management plays a vital role in limiting the working capital requirement by the company to a minimum level. In the inventory holding, RSP can set an optimistic target for itself. An optimistic target could be set as follows:

Item	Target (No. of Days)	Present Position (No. of Days)
Raw Material	15	34
Semi/Finished	15	25
Stores/Spares	30	200

Rourkela Steel Plant has managed to reduce the holding period considerably over the years. There was a lot of improvement in the input raw material inventory holding in the earlier years. However due to imported coal supply problem during the financial year 2004-05, the company maintained a high inventory at the end of the financial year to meet the exigencies in future. Thus Input raw material stock as on 31st March 2005 has been high. In the normal circumstances the level may be kept close to the target. The parent Company SAIL may decide to hold major stake in the coalfields abroad to ensure uninterrupted supply through out the year with comfortable transfer pricing.

Semi-Finished inventory value is high for the company. This needs to be brought under control. Maintaining a high inventory runs the risk of

1) Blockage of working capital.
2) Deterioration of stock and consequent decline in market realization for the product.

Thus top and bottom line of the company get affected severely on account of both the reasons cited above.

Following steps can be adopted to achieve this objective:

1) Improvement in quality and packaging of the product.
2) Meeting the specification required by the customers.
3) Managing key accounts (customers) properly.
4) Proper coordination between marketing, PPC (Production Planning Department) and the Mills.
5) Extensive computerization of material flow and planning, so as to track each product in its value chain.

6) Proper dispatch/loading scheduling
7) Introduction of ERP (Enterprise Resource Planning) in the organization, which will work nicely in bridging the information gap among customers, marketing and production units.

Stores and Spares stock holding of the company is very high, which is more than 6 months consumption. There is a need for considerable improvement in this area.

Emphasis on the following steps will ease the situation:

1) Reduction of lead-time between indenting and receipt of the material in the stores. This is possible if the user departments do proper planning before indenting and reduce proper work during the indent processing phases.
2) Adoption of Supply Chain Management in the company. Key vendors are to be identified; long-term relationship is to be developed with them. Efforts need to be made to receive quality spares in short notice.
3) More importantly, Preventive maintenance and house keeping activities need to be further strengthened through out the production facilities so as to achieve zero breakdowns in the shops. This will not only reduce the requirement of spare parts by the shops but also give quality time to concentrate on proper planning for procurement of materials for future preventive maintenance jobs.

The net worth of the company as on 31st March 2005 is negative, in spite of having a huge profit of Rs. 1045 crores during the financial year 2004-05. RSP needs to make substantial profit in the coming years to become a positive net worth company. However, in spite of having a negative net worth, the company doesn't have any risk, because of being a part of a healthy group company, SAIL, which is a virtually zero debt company (net of borrowings and Cash in hand/bank). But to correct its fundamentals and balance sheet, RSP needs to take the following steps:

* Achievement of 100% capacity utilization in crude steel.
* Zero dependence on Inter Plant transfer of semi finished steel materials.
* Improvement of quality of steel products in the down stream mills.
* Proper advertisement and creating dealer network for its special products.
* Reduction in manpower so as to reduce the fixed cost in the long-run.

To achieve 100% capacity utilization as well as quality standards, RSP may require little investment in coming 2 to 3 years time to meet the technical requirements in the shops, mills and related areas. These are the short-term measures in the next 2 to 3 years for viability of the firm. The firm should be able to make more profit year after year during this time.

However to make the firm vibrant and progressive in the long run, RSP may consider augmentation of capacity from the present level. The capacity of the plant can be doubled from the existing 2.00 million tons of Hot metal to 4.00 Million tons. The investment for this should be gradual; partly from the accumulated profits and partly from fresh borrowings. Care needs to be taken to maintain debt to equity ratio under control at any point of time. At the same time project completion within due time and cost is of paramount importance for the profitability of the company in future after capitalization of new facilities.

Smooth investment plans don't affect cash flows from operating activities severely. The RSP needs to achieve more than 100% capacity utilization so as to increase cash flow from operating activities. It also needs to curtail its fixed cost component further to keep its cash flows from operations and PAT sustainable.

The RSP had negative return on investment for many years. However, during the financial year 2004-05, it achieved a very high positive figure, which shows its internal strength in a buoyant market.

Break-even point analysis shows a clear direction to the management to steer the company towards a richer future. Some of the possible options in the near future for RSP are analyzed and tabulated below.

	No change in Sales Price and 25% increase in Raw material cost	10% Reduction in Sales Price and 25% increase in Raw material cost	10% Reduction in Sales Price and 20% increase in Raw material cost
Unit Net Sales price	25526	22565	22565
Unit Cost	20927	20927	20514
- Variable Cost	12776	12776	12364
Unit Contribution	12749	9789	10202
B.E.P			
-Percentage	59%	77%	74%
-Volume	986896	1285399	1233250
Available Volume	684104	385601	437750
Estimated Profit (Rs. Crores) at 100% Capacity Utilisation	872	377	447
Estimated Return on Investment	22%	9.4%	11%

The fixed cost (expenditure) of the plant will almost remain steady in near future till the year in which new major capital schemes get commissioned. It may further fall on account of reduction in interest if the company makes profit every year till such time.

Keeping in view, the increase in the input prices of metallurgical coal, boiler coal and Ferro alloys, it is expected that the total expenditure on raw materials may go up by 20 to 25% in the coming years as compared to 2004-05 at the same level of production. The average sales price may slide by 10% to 20% as compared to that of 2004-05.

Considering these assumptions and keeping 2004-05 as the base, it can be seen from the above table that the company will be able to make around Rs. 400 crores profit at 100% capacity utilisation. However, if there is no drop in Sales price the company has a potential to register around Rs. 872 crores at 100% capacity utilization.

This shows that RSP's bottom line is highly sensitive on the sales price rather than on the Raw materials prices. It is important to operate the plant at 100% capacity utilisation.

The capacity utilisation trend for RSP is tabulated below:

	1995-96	1996-97	1997-98	1998-99	1999-00
Capacity Utilisation	90%	91%	92%	65%	68%

	2000-01	2001-02	2002-03	2003-04	2004-05
Capacity Utilisation	76%	80%	89%	92%	92%

RSP needs to achieve 100% capacity utilisation so as maximize profits. During the financial year 2004-05, the capacity utilisation was 92% and the plant registered the highest ever profit of Rs. 1045 crores. If the company had achieved 100% capacity utilisation during that year, the profit would have increased by Rs. 170 crores in the buoyant steel market. This shows that 8% increase in production would have resulted in 15% jump in profit during that year.

The firm may take quick decisions in terms of increase in capacity and capacity utilization so as to create more wealth in the future and protect itself against competition from the new players.

Practical Utility of the Study

The present study, *Financial Performance of Steel Sectors*, is a research work, which focuses on the changes taking place in the steel sector world over in the recent times, with a detailed analysis on the performance of Rourkela Steel Plant, one of the first few integrated steel plants to have been set up in country. Rourkela Steel Plant (RSP) has played an important role in the infrastructure development of the nation in the past.

The study tries to position RSP in to day's competitive steel market and goes ahead further to discuss about the areas of preparedness required to face the onslaught of competition ahead. This piece of work is an eye opener for RSP and SAIL, which can readily be referred to by the Management of Rourkela Steel Plant and Steel Authority of India ltd. to implement the strategies for future.

A practical piece of work, this thesis deals with the macro level changes shaping up in the steel arena today and at the same time has discussed about the micro-level activities of RSP in details with respect to business, technology and finance. This research work is a fact-finding tool using historical data from 1995-96 to 2004-05 to find out the trajectory of growth of the business organisation in the present and the past and tries to formulate the changes required from now onwards, based on a sound logic, to keep itself vibrant in the future. Owes of the past for RSP and its parent company SAIL has been dealt with in different sub chapters and future strategies for the company have been brought out keeping in view the lessons from this. The great turn around of RSP and SAIL has been analysed from time to time in various sub chapters in this piece of work.

The study is of immense help to the Rourkela Steel Plant, as it can know its strengths and weaknesses besides knowing the opportunities and threats in the fast-changing steel market having a linkage to the turbulent international steel market too. As such RSP's management may take cue from the research work and bring changes in marketing, Human resources, investment and finance policies and practices so as to improve its business performance in future.

The study gives a comprehensive idea about the national and international steel dynamics today, performance of RSP, SAIL and TISCO the major integrated steel plants in the country and the new and upcoming integrated steel plants in the country.

This will be quite useful for the managements of the present day steel plants to draw competitive strategies for themselves; for the researchers in this filed to get an initial start up idea to drive their work further. The finding may be also used by the Government and steel policy formulators in the country to see the results of steel policy changes in the recent times and to frame appropriate and relevant policies for future.

SCOPE FOR FURTHER EXTENSION OF THE STUDY

The study is based on the changing steel scenario to day and expected changes to shape up in future. Further studies in future with ever changing steel dynamics can be undertaken with this research work as the starting point.

Although microanalysis has been done for RSP on financial performance, there is a scope for further detailing in the areas of technology up gradation, investment decisions, marketing strategies and human resources strategies for the company. Further studies on steel sector may be taken up using the present piece of research work.

Bibliography

Book References

1. Anthony, P. D'Costa, *The global restructuring of Steel Industry: Innovations, Institutions and Industrial Changes*, Routledge (UK), Taylor and Francis Group, 11 New Fetterlane, London, 1999.
2. "Asia: Global steel's engine of growth", *"ron and Steel Review*, May, 2004
3. Chakraborty, S., Ray, A.K., Ray, S.K., "Concepts of Emerging Steel Technologies", *Steel Scenario – A journal on Steel and Economy*, Vol. 13, Jan-Mar 2004.
4. Cochran, E.B., *Planning Production Costs: Using the improvement Curve*, Chandler Publishing Coy, Sanfransisco, California, 1968.
5. Das, Debendra Kumar, *Economic Development Opportunities Through Liberalisation*, UGC, 1998.
6. Dutta S, Zamindar D, Kumar P and Banerjee U.K, "R and D efforts in improving the product quality of an old mill for its survival", *Iron and Steel Review*, 45(6), 2001, Page-45.
7. Erich, A. Helfert, *Financial analysis tools and techniques: A Guide for Managers*, McGraw-Hill Publications, Sep, 2001.
8. Garth, L., Magnum, Sae, Young Kim, Stephen, B. Tallman, *Transactional Marriages in Steel Industry: Experience and lesson for global business*, Quorum books, 88 Post Road west, West Port, CT 06881, 1996.

9. Garth, L., Magnum, R., Scott, McNabb, *The rise, fall and replacement of Industry wide bargaining in the basic steel Industry*, M.E. Sharpe Inc., 80, Business Park Drive, Armonk, New York-10504.

10. Gupta, S.K., "The relevance of different technologies adopted by flat product producers in the country-balance between investment and cost of production", *Iron and Steel Review*, December, 2003.

11. James, O Gill, Moira, Chetton, *Financial analysis-the next steps*, Thomson Crisp learning, Crisp Publications Inc., 2001

12. Krishna Gopal M, Santra A.K, Khan S.C. and Karan B.M, "Steel demand forecasts: India 1999-2000", *Steel Times International*, 23(4), 1999, p. 14.

13. K. Krishna Moorthy, *Engineering Change-India's Iron and Steel*, Tech Books, India, 1985.

14. Muthuraman, B. and Sen Anand, "The future of Flat products in India", *Iron and Steel Review*, Vol. 37, Sep, 1993.

15. Naib, Sudhir, *Disinvestment in India: Policies, Procedures, Practices*, Sage Publications India Ltd., New Delhi.

16. Parida[26], Ph. D thesis on Working Capital Management in RSP, 1992.

17. Patnaik, N.K., Patnaik R.N, Mishra B.K, "Steel making through Sponge iron route-Problems and Prospects", *Steel Scenario- A journal on steel and economy*, Vol. 13, Jan-March 2004.

18. Prasad K.K, Mediratta S.R, "Forecasting demand for Steel", *Steel Technical Report*, 1997, p. 16.

19. Samantaray B[27], Ph. D thesis on Incentive structure in RSP, 1990.

20. "SAIL - A successful Turn around story among Indian PSUs", *Kaleidoscope*—Standing Conference of Public Enterprises, March 2004, Vol. 23.

21. "Sailing into the future- an overview of Corporate Plan 2012", *SAIL News*, Vol. 31, Apr-May, 2003.

22. Sharon, M. Oster, *Modern competitive Analysis*, Oxford University Press USA, 1999.

23. Sinha, S.N, Kundu, A.L., Muthuswamy C., "Iron and Steel Industry in India: Past, Present and future", *Iron and Steel Review*, Vol. 37, Sep, 1993.

24. Roy, T.K., "Steel – a die-hard material: Yesterday, today and tomorrow", *JPC Bulletin*, December, 2003.

25. Stovell Sam, "The spring in Steel", *Business Week magazine*, August 2005.

26. Surma, John P., "Is Steel back on the Financial committees' radar screen", *World Steel Journal—Steel at the cross roads*, IISI, Vol. 38.

27. Usman M., *Statistics for Iron and Steel Industry in India*, SAIL, 14th Edition, 2004.

28. Varshney R.P., "Cost economics of Sponge Iron Plants and EAFs", *Steel Scenario—A journal on Steel and economy*, Vol. 13, Jan-March 2004.

29. Vikraman Shaji, "Steel sector Bail out: taking a leaf out of Uncle Sam's book", *Business Line*, 25th Feb, 2002.

30. Vipin Gupta, *Transformative Organisation – a global perspective*, Grand Valley State University and University of Pennsylvania

31. Vijay Vergis, R.K. and Bhattacharya, S.K., "Technology Management in Steel Sector", *The Management Accountant*, 1996, 31(5), p. 335.

32. Yi Tian Wang, "Riding China's growth curve", *Iron and Steel review*, April, 2004.

33. Anthony, P. D'Costa, *The global restructuring of Steel Industry: Innovations, Institutions and Industrial Changes*, Routledge (UK), Taylor and Francis Group, 11 New Fetterlane, London, 1999.

34. Brealey and Myers, *Fundamentals of Corporate Finance*, McGraw-Hill Publications.

35. Brigham, F. Eugene and Gapaneski, C. Louis, *Financial Management - Theory and Practice*, Dryden Press.

36. Chandra, P., *Financial Management- Theory and Practice*, Tata McGraw-Hill.

37. Jain, S.P., and Narang K.L., *Advanced Cost and Management Accounting*, Kalyani Publishers, 2001.

38. Pandey, I.M., *Financial Management*, Vikash Publishing House Pvt. Ltd.

39. Peterson, P Pamela, *Financial Management and Anlaysis*, McGraw-Hill Publications.

40. Sharma R.K. and Gupta Shashi K., *Management Accounting - principles and practice*, eighth edition, Kalyani Publishers, New Delhi, 2001

41. Vanhorne C. James, *Financial Management and Policy*, Prentice-Hall of India

Journals and Periodicals

1. "Asia: Global steel's engine of growth"30, *Iron and Steel review*, May, 2004

2. Chakraborty S, Ray A.K, Ray S.K, "Concepts of Emerging Steel Technologies", *Steel Scenario - A Journal on Steel and Economy*, Vol. 13, Jan-March 2004.

3. Dutta, S., Zamindar, D., Kumar, P. and Banerjee, U.K., "R and D efforts in improving the product quality of an old mill for its survival", *Iron and Steel Review*, 45(6), 2001, p. 45.

4. Gupta, S.K., "The relevance of different technologies adopted by flat product producers in the country-balance between investment and cost of production", *Iron and Steel Review*, December 2003

5. Krishna Gopal, M., Santra, A.K., Khan, S.C. and Karan B.M, "Steel demand forecasts: India 1999-2000", *Steel Times International*, 23(4), 1999, Page-14.

6. Patnaik, N.K., Patnaik, R.N., Mishra, B.K., "Steel making through Sponge iron route-Problems and Prospects", *Steel Scenario - A Journal on Steel and Economy*, Vol. 13, Jan-March 2004.

7. Sinha, S.N., Kundu, A.L., Muthuswamy C., "Iron and Steel Industry in India: Past, Present and future", *Iron and Steel Review*, Vol. 37, Sep, 1993.

8. Stovell, Sam, "The spring in Steel", *Business Week magazine*, August 2005.

9. Surma John, P., "Is Steel back on the Financial committees' radar screen", *World Steel Journal - Steel at the cross roads*, IISI-Vol.38.

10. Muthuraman, B., and Sen, Anand, "The future of Flat products in India", *Iron and Steel Review*, Vol. 37, Sep, 1993.

11. Prasad, K.K., Mediratta S.R, "Forecasting demand for Steel", *Steel Technical Report*, 1997, p. 16.

12. Roy, T.K., "Steel – a die-hard material: Yesterday, today and tomorrow", *JPC Bulletin*, December, 2003

13. "SAIL – A successful Turn around story among Indian PSUs", Kaleidoscope – Standing conference of Public Enterprises, March 2004, Vol. 23.

14. "Sailing into the future – an overview of Corporate Plan 2012", *SAIL News*, Vol. 31, Apr-May, 2003.

15. Usman, M., "Statistics for Iron and Steel Industry in India", SAIL, 14th Edition, 2004.

16. Gupta, Vipin, "Transformative Organisation – a global perspective", Grand Valley State University and University of Pennsylvania

17. Varshney, R.P., "Cost economics of Sponge Iron Plants and EAFs", *Steel Scenario – A journal on Steel and economy*, Vol. 13, Jan-March 2004.

18. Vijay Vergis R.K. and Bhattacharya S.K, "Technology Management in Steel Sector", *The Management Accountant*, 1996, 31(5), p. 335

19. Vikraman Shaji, "Steel sector Bail out: taking a leaf out of Uncle Sam's book", *Business Line*, 25th Feb, 2002

20. Yi Tian Wang, "Riding China's growth curve", *Iron and Steel Review*, April, 2004

Other Reports

1. Annual Accounts of M/s Steel Authority of India Ltd.
2. Annual Accounts of M/s Steel Authority of India Ltd., Rourkela
3. Annual Accounts of M/s Tata Iron and Steel Company Ltd. (TISCO)
4. Segment reporting of SAIL
5. Press releases on Steel Sector
6. Web sites of SAIL, TISCO
7. "*Iron and Steel Review*" journals
8. "Steel Metals and Minerals" journals
9. Joint Parliamentary Committee (JPC) Journals and reports

Index

❑❑❑